THE DIVORCE DECISIONS
WORKBOOK

THE DIVORCE DECISIONS WORKBOOK
A Planning and Action Guide

Margorie Louise Engel

Diana Delhi Gould

McGraw-Hill, Inc.
New York   St. Louis   San Francisco   Auckland   Bogotá
Caracas   Lisbon   London   Madrid   Mexico   Milan
Montreal   New Delhi   Paris   San Juan   São Paulo
Singapore   Sydney   Tokyo   Toronto

This publication is designed to provide accurate and authoritative information in regard to the subject matter covered. It is sold with the understanding that neither the publisher nor the authors are engaged in rendering legal advice. If legal advice is required, the services of a competent professional should be sought.
— *From the Declaration of Principles jointly adopted by a Committee of the American Bar Association and a Committee of Publishers and Associations*

1 2 3 4 5 6 7 8 9 0   HAL/HAL   9 7 6 5 4 3 2 1

ISBN   0-07-019572-2   {HC}
ISBN   0-07-019571-4   {PBK}

The sponsoring editor for this book was James H. Bessent, Jr., the editing supervisor was Jim Halston, and the production supervisor was Donald Schmidt. It was composed in Baskerville by McGraw-Hill's Professional Book Group composition unit.

Printed and bound by Halliday Litho.

Dedicated to
STEVE AND PAM
who "hung in there" while we were writing this book.

Contents

List of FORM-ulas

These FORM-ulas appear as Appendix D, which precedes the index, in the numbered sequence listed here.

FORM-ula 1: MARRIAGE ASSESSMENT
FORM-ula 2: OBSERVING CHILDREN'S DIVORCE BEHAVIOR
FORM-ula 3: DIVORCE BUSINESS SUPPLIES
FORM-ula 4: PROFILE SELF AND SPOUSE
FORM-ula 5: MYSELF
FORM-ula 6: PROFILE CHILDREN
FORM-ula 7: CHILD IDENTIFICATION
FORM-ula 8: EXTENDED FAMILY
FORM-ula 9: CHRONOLOGICAL MARITAL HISTORY
FORM-ula 10: CHILD CARE
FORM-ula 11: EMOTIONAL ABUSE
FORM-ula 12: CURRENT PERSPECTIVES
FORM-ula 13: GROCERY SHOPPING
FORM-ula 14: HOUSEHOLD CHORES
FORM-ula 15: EMERGENCY TELEPHONE NUMBERS
FORM-ula 16: RESOURCE TELEPHONE NUMBERS
FORM-ula 17: CHILDREN'S WHEREABOUTS
FORM-ula 18: HOUSEHOLD SUPPLIES
FORM-ula 19: A FUNCTIONAL AUTOMOBILE
FORM-ula 20: CHILD CARE OUTSIDE OF THE HOME
FORM-ula 21: VISITATION SCHEDULE AND RECORDS
FORM-ula 22: EXPENSES
FORM-ula 23: INCOME
FORM-ula 24: CREDIT CARD INVENTORY
FORM-ula 25: REQUESTING AN INDIVIDUAL CREDIT REPORT
FORM-ula 26: PERSONAL PAPERS
FORM-ula 27: HOUSEHOLD INVENTORY AND APPRAISAL
FORM-ula 28: MISSING ITEMS
FORM-ula 29: PERSONAL BANKING
FORM-ula 30: MONEY LOANED TO OTHERS
FORM-ula 31: MONEY BORROWED FROM OTHERS
FORM-ula 32: INVESTMENTS
FORM-ula 33: TITLES AND DEEDS
FORM-ula 34: REAL ESTATE CAPITAL IMPROVEMENTS
FORM-ula 35: PERSONAL HEALTH
FORM-ula 36: MEDICAL INSURANCE
FORM-ula 37: LIFE INSURANCE

Preface

Today, management of the personal world requires increasing business knowledge. Perhaps nowhere is this more important than in the area of divorce—a highly private matter with, at the same time, profound economic implications.

The Divorce Decisions Workbook is the first book that looks at both sides of a divorce in a manner that makes the information readily understandable and the process manageable to the divorcing couple and their family. By the same token, it will facilitate the work of attorneys, judges, court personnel, accountants, and therapists who are professionally involved in the divorce process.

Through my work in business counseling, I recognized that there was no single and complete information resource that offered understanding and order for handling the personal business issues in a divorce. In addition to business information, I developed checklists, personal and financial information forms, and reference and resource lists for my clients. It became increasingly obvious that my research, information, and tested experience should be available to a broader audience. Hence, the decision to write this book was made.

I approached Diana Gould about collaborating on the writing of the text. Diana brings to this task her creativity and professional experience as a career counselor. She believes in the value of the book concept because she has seen many clients whose work life has been disrupted, or unexpectedly created, by an inequitable divorce. Diana also provided some necessary distance from the details and technical language of the financial and legal material which allowed us to present the information in an easily readable manner.

We, the authors, are convinced that this book will be an indispensable reference guide for individuals and professionals working with the personal business issues of a divorce.

For further information on the courses, seminars, and workshops that we present, please contact:

Hamilton-Forbes Associates
Exchange Place, 33rd floor
Boston, MA 02109
(617) 248-5013

ACKNOWLEDGMENTS

A resource book on a subject that includes a number of disciplines benefits, of course, from the expertise, information, opinions, advice, and encouragement from many people. Special help came from the following people.

Legal: Elaine Amendola, Esq. (Zeldes, Needle and Cooper, Bridgeport, CT); Sam Pasternack, Esq. (Choate, Hall, and Stewart, Boston, MA); The Honorable Robert Hansen, Retired (Milwaukee, WI); Joseph Dumond, Esq. (Assistant Attorney General, CT); Gil Stallings, Esq.; Lawrence Engel, Esq. (Wiley, Engel, and Packard, Baltimore, MD).

Business: Stanley Carp, CPA (Nishball, Screbnik, Zaluda, Carp and Niedermeier, Bridgeport, CT); C. D. Peterson (business book author who led us to McGraw-Hill); Cynthia Kelly (TRW Information Services, CA); Pamela G. Massey (New York City); Stephen Boyle (Fiduciary and Investment Services, Choate Hall and Stewart, Boston, MA); Daria Lewis, Julia Ashmun, and Ted Woods (computer wizards, CT and NH).

Practical: Marcia Liebowitz, Director (Children's Divorce Center, CT); L. John Isselhardt (Newfane, VT); Catherine Ross (Alcoholism and Drug Dependency Council, Westport, CT); Elizabeth Waldron (MD); Jennifer Waldron (CT); Silvana da Silva and Karl Sauvant (NY); Jo Kmetzo (CT); Debbra and Thomas Michaels (NJ); Margorie and William Engel (MD); Donna Starr (KY); Dora Gunnell (CT); the staff in the offices of Christopher J. Dodd, Christopher Shays and Barbara Kennelly, Members of Congress (CT); the authors of the books in our Reference List, and the individuals to contact by telephone for the organizations in our Resource List.

To each of them, thank you very much.

Margorie Engel
Diana Gould

ABOUT THE AUTHORS

Margorie L. Engel is president of Hamilton-Forbes Associates, a private business counseling firm specializing in the practical and financial implications of divorce. She is a speaker, writer, and instructor on this and other entrepreneurial topics. Engel has served on numerous advisory boards for family and legislative issues at both the state and national levels. She lives and works in Boston.

Diana D. Gould is founder of Daily Bread, Inc., a not-for-profit center for career counseling. A director of training workshops and frequent speaker and panelist on divorce-related topics, Gould specializes in the connection between career development and personal recovery issues such as major illness, unemployment, divorce, and drug/alcohol abuse. She is located in Westport, CT.

THE DIVORCE DECISIONS
WORKBOOK

INTRODUCTION

"For better, for worse, 'til death do us part." Once upon a time, those words were the rough equivalent of a lifetime warranty. Nowadays, too many marriages are over before the bottle of Tabasco is empty.

Divorce, dissolution, legal separation, however it is expressed, this can be a crummy, rotten period in your life. Much of what you took for granted is disappearing. Rapidly fading are the familiar network of friends, financial stability, conveniences, and family and social activities.

There is probably no such thing as a "mature" person going through a divorce. The best you can hope for is to be informed and to behave with some kind of dignity. Deep down, you know that you will survive.

Beginning to learn how to survive is a matter of timing. You acquire knowledge when you are ready to receive it. There is a certain kind of pride that comes from handling problems and change.

If you think education is expensive, try ignorance. All you really know, if you are being realistic, is how much you don't know. In getting a divorce, what you don't know *can* hurt you! Experience is what you get when you are expecting something better.

You may want to think and act logically but really don't know how to go about it. If you want the right answers, you must ask the right questions.

1. What information do I already have that will help me?

2. What information must I acquire?

3. Where can I find the information I need?

4. What do I do with the information once I get it?

5. When am I prepared to make decisions?

In the workbook of life, the answers are not in the back. They come from taking the responsibility and time to get adequate information. Only then can you make informed decisions. The reality is that divorce is a *business deal*—an extended contract negotiation. You may not like it, the very idea may offend you, but it is the God's honest truth.

The business of divorce involves organizing all of the things you must do. The biggest decisions have a way of coming when you are least ready to cope with them. If you find that your decisions are simply a capitulation caused by brain drain, let the information that you organize using this book become your guide.

The most difficult work of divorce does not take place at your desk or in your attorney's office; instead, it occurs in your mind, through the processes of disconnecting, rearranging and rebuilding your thoughts and feelings. By taking a one-day-at-a-time and a step-by-step approach, you will succeed in the business of divorce. A side benefit is finding that you are also making some of the changes necessary to proceed more smoothly with the rest of your life.

Use *The Divorce Decisions Workbook* as your silent business partner. It is a comprehensive reference book for people who need to know about the business of divorce. The book is less about how to solve difficult divorce problems than it is about how to avoid them. It is the ultimate "how to" book with an

1

unprecedented collection of practical information on what divorce is like and what you need to do. It also shows you how and when to do it.

For easy reference, *The Divorce Decisions Workbook* is divided into eight sections:

- Understanding the Divorce Process
- Getting Personally Organized
- Pulling Yourself and Your Family Together
- Financial Value of the Marriage
- Learning About Divorce Law
- "Big Picture" Planning
- Getting Your Legal Decree and a "Successful" Divorce
- After Words

The book contains factual information, procedures to follow, functional FORM-ulas™ for compiling divorce information, and reference resources listed by topic.

We have included our research and observations on many of the emotional issues encountered during a divorce. You may consider this information less important than the financial and legal portions. However, we encourage you to view the overall effects of divorce in making each of your decisions.

In no way is *The Divorce Decisions Workbook* a do-it-yourself book! We provide information, not legal advice. The book is designed to be used with an attorney, a therapist, and an accountant or financial advisor. It is important to recognize when you need help and what kind of help you need. We support and emphasize this fact throughout the book. Your professional advisors can do more to facilitate your divorce if you are knowledgeable about the business issues involved. Divorce laws are mandated by the individual states and vary considerably. Therefore, they must be properly interpreted by an attorney in the light of your own unique circumstances.

In a divorce, there are certain elements over which you will have little or no control. It is important to recognize which parts of your divorce fall into this category. You can waste a lot of time and energy trying to work against, rather than with, the system.

To function during a divorce, you are forced to assimilate a body of knowledge that is expanding by the minute. There is bound to be an ever-widening gap between what you understand and what you think you should understand. We call the usual emotional response to this divergence *information anxiety*.

The glut of divorce material on the market obscures the distinction between what is purely informational and what is truly usable. Many of the "war stories" you have heard or read about may be emotionally applicable to your situation but not necessarily helpful to the business of your divorce. Use *The Divorce Decisions Workbook* as a manageable source of personal information that is timely, concise, and complete.

The main purpose of *The Divorce Decisions Workbook* is to help you make informed and intelligent choices. If there is anything in this book that gives you the impetus and courage to renegotiate a healthy marriage relationship instead of negotiating a separation agreement, we will be very happy for you. If that is not possible, we hope that *The Divorce Decisions Workbook* will help you to achieve a satisfactory separation agreement—one you can live with after divorce.

Section *I*
UNDERSTANDING THE DIVORCE PROCESS: WHAT DIVORCE IS LIKE

Experience is something you don't get until just after you need it!

Entry into the game of "Divorce Court" may or may not be of your own choosing but, like it or not, here you are and you need information.

A divorce decree is a piece of paper. It is not a resolution of problems.

THREE DISTINCT PARTS

Divorces have three distinct parts: the *feel* of divorce, the *practical,* or real, aspects of divorce, and the *legal* issues of divorce.

The Feel of Divorce

The *feel* of divorce includes all of the things that go on in your mind, body, and spirit. Feelings can range from nightmarish to liberating.

■ At some point you will probably feel like a "basket case."

■ Your physical endurance will be stretched to the limit.

■ Spiritual values can be severely shaken.

The Practical (Real) Divorce

In the *practical* (real) divorce you face a separation from both your spouse *and* the person you were as a marriage partner. Things will never be the same again.

The practical divorce is about ending your former way of life and beginning a new way of life. It is about seeking a brand new center of balance for yourself that can then radiate out to those affected by your ultimate decisions. You may think that divorce represents your salvation, but how you handle the process will determine the way that your children, extended family, friends, and community associates react to the changes. From a practical standpoint, you seem to be starting adulthood all over again, only this time you are carrying a lot of accumulated emotional baggage.

The Legal Divorce

The *legal* side of divorce is considerably more cut-and-dried. The system has its own methods of operating that vary from state to state. You cannot control the events or the basic issues upon which the court will make its judgment rulings.

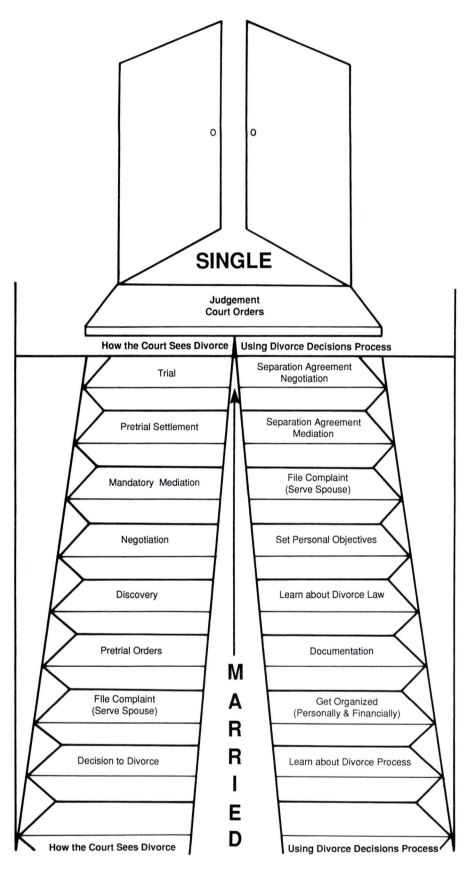

SINGLE

Judgement
Court Orders

How the Court Sees Divorce | Using Divorce Decisions Process

How the Court Sees Divorce	Using Divorce Decisions Process
Trial	Separation Agreement Negotiation
Pretrial Settlement	Separation Agreement Mediation
Mandatory Mediation	File Complaint (Serve Spouse)
Negotiation	Set Personal Objectives
Discovery	Learn about Divorce Law
Pretrial Orders	Documentation
File Complaint (Serve Spouse)	Get Organized (Personally & Financially)
Decision to Divorce	Learn about Divorce Process

MARRIED

How the Court Sees Divorce | Using Divorce Decisions Process

STEPS TO DIVORCE

HOW THE COURTS SEE DIVORCE

The courts see divorce issues as:

- Keeping the peace.
- The division of assets and liabilities.
- Spousal support.
- Responsibility to children (custody and support).

Within the framework of the law, the court does give you and your spouse the opportunity to structure a divorce agreement to meet your family's unique circumstances. When the court finds the agreement reasonable, it will usually be approved.

Repeat: You and your spouse have the opportunity to structure your separation agreement to meet the particular circumstances of your family. If one or both parties to the divorce take advantage of this opportunity, it is possible to:

- Structure a satisfactory end to the marriage.
- Provide a workable beginning to a new life.

HOW *THE DIVORCE DECISIONS WORKBOOK* SEES DIVORCE

Most people heading toward divorce go immediately into the legal pipeline without understanding or having prepared for the inevitable process they have begun. We are convinced that thorough preparation personally, financially and legally makes an enormous difference in the outcome.

Whether or not you prepare in advance, the legal procedures are the same. If you follow the process we suggest, you will be well-versed in every phase of the divorce process. You may even be able to move more rapidly through the legal system.

INTRODUCING THE DIVORCE DECISIONS FORM-ulas™

From now until the divorce decree is granted, the legal system will inundate you with questions requiring detailed and accurate answers. Sometimes, you will be expected to provide timely responses when you can barely remember your own name.

Virtually all of this information is incorporated into the *The Divorce Decisions Workbook* FORM-ulas (see Appendix D, starting on page 167). Filling them out may seem like an enormous burden when you are already too busy. Actually, what you are doing is developing and filing your own portfolio of reference material so that you will be prepared in advance for whatever part of the divorce process lies ahead. A very important side benefit of this effort is the accumulation of material and information that will help launch you into your new life.

Note For additional blank copies of the FORM-ulas please contact:

Hamilton-Forbes Associates
Exchange Place, 33rd Floor
Boston, MA 02109
(617) 248-5013

Chapter 1
THE FEEL OF DIVORCE

Although no two divorces are alike, there are general principles and standards that apply to all of them. It is essential that you are aware of the process and its likely effects. *Correct information can prevent you from victimizing yourself.* You are not under a life sentence to be unprepared for what lies ahead. Your consent to transactions should come from informed decisions. Before addressing information, however, we will first turn to the "feel" of a divorce. In order for you to understand the feelings in a divorce, we are going to examine its emotional, physical and spiritual consequences.

EMOTIONAL CONSEQUENCES

People who have given up don't usually get divorced. Those who are divorcing often feel that life has something more to offer them than what they currently have. We humans do not take personal attachments lightly. We never did. Just because divorce is more prevalent and more socially acceptable than in the past, don't think for one minute that it is easier on the emotions.

Divorce sets in motion a seemingly endless wave of emotions, especially worries and feelings of loss from which family members must recover.

There is a tendency to become overinvolved in an obsessive analysis of "what went wrong?" Seesawing between anger toward your spouse and self-blame causes fluctuations in behavior that interfere with concentration, sleep, and the proper care of oneself and children. Eventually you will have to get rid of these emotional alibis.

Your head may say living apart is logical, but your heart can have enormous reservations. Even though the basic components of love have probably faded in a troubled marriage, attachment persists and becomes the hang-up of wanting to be together again.

Feelings About Your Spouse

The following list presents feelings commonly felt by one spouse toward another during divorce.

- Doubts and second thoughts.
- The illusion that the situation is not real, often expressed as "this can't be happening to me."
- Every negative event and feeling is blamed on the missing spouse: "My life is a mess, thanks to you!"
- The desire to move things along (sometimes too hastily) just to get that spouse "out of my life!"
- A hasty willingness to forgive and forget without giving proper thought of the future.
- Excessive meanness and resentment.

- The frustrating feeling that the situation seems virtually impossible.

Regardless of whether your marriage was that good or that bad, the recurrence of family memories and images is wholly predictable. Letting go of a married identity is a push-pull process that remains everpresent in one's thoughts and feelings.

Feelings About Your Situation

You may experience a variety of "ups" and "downs" throughout the divorce. Here are some to expect:

Downs

- Out-of-control, failure, interrupted, rage, terror, denial, sadness, incredible pain, anxiety, bitterness, hell-of-a-mess, doom-and-gloom, island without a bridge, major surgery without anesthetic

Ups

- Nostalgia, resolution, relief, curiosity, adventurousness, righteous indignation — "I'll show you!", gratitude, release

Often the feelings are intensely uncomfortable and sometimes they are socially unacceptable and self-destructive.
"I'll never marry again" is the predominant recurring thought and the major statement for self-protection at this time.

Typical Divorce Behaviors

You will probably become intimately familiar with some of the following forms of behavior:

- A bewildering inability to remember anything. The "forget factor" is the emotional and psychological trauma that prevents clear thinking and in which the mind feels numb.
- Wide swings of emotions: from anxiety and panic to clarity and calm; anger and rage to elation; depression to cockeyed optimism.
- The sense that no diversion will work for more than a few minutes at a time.
- A readiness to jump from the frying pan into the fire.
- A feeling of going down the proverbial "tubes."

PHYSICAL CONSEQUENCES

Both medical doctors and therapists tell us that the changes you face during a divorce won't just bother your mind, they will probably also affect your body. In fact, so many things can happen to you physically that you might think you are becoming a hypochondriac. Below is a checklist of the general divorce complaints:

Common Complaints

- Loss of concentration.
- Nausea.
- Insomnia or excessive sleep.
- Fatigue.
- Nightmares.
- Tension.
- Weight loss or gain.
- Nervousness.
- Headaches.

Frequent Physical Reactions

- Increased use of health-care systems.
- Tendency to illness and accidents.
- Lowered immune system efficiency.
- Erratic eating habits.
- Neglect of appearance.
- Carelessness toward hygiene.

During the period of divorce, you are also more susceptible to all kinds of addictions (alcohol, drugs, eating, sex, and so forth). This is a time to observe your behavior and take better-than-usual care of yourself. These issues will be discussed in detail in Chapter 8.

SPIRITUAL CONSEQUENCES

If you have lived with the beliefs that marriage is for life and that your spouse should be your most trustworthy friend, then divorce can shake the foundations ofyour religious faith. You may well feel that God seems unconcerned about your pain now.

Your Personal Philosophy

The period of divorce is probably one of the most important times in your life to find a spiritual center of gravity. It helps a lot to have a personal philosophy and a strong perception of who you are and what is important to you. Without these, every whim or idea that gives you gratification will send you scurrying off in a different direction, adding more confusion and disorganization to an already difficult situation.

Religious Ramifications

Divorce also has religious ramifications regarding annulment, the raising of children, and remarriage. It may lead you to feel that moral values have fallen apart, or that there is no place left for you to put your energies. Ties have been severed. Trust has been broken.

This is the time when core beliefs are shaken. Eventually they will either stand you in good stead or you will be compelled to reexamine them. This is a time, if you will, when "Let go and let God" may be the only applicable motto.

Chapter 2
THE PRACTICAL DIVORCE

In reality, a divorce simply exchanges one set of problems for another.

Marriage stands for familiar patterns and systems. Heretofore, you have had a niche in life, although not necessarily the best or most comfortable one. Perhaps you have had identity, social status, financial stability, a family unit, friends, relatives, home, community associations, habits, or pleasant holidays, all of which reflect assumptions and expectations based upon the ground rules of "being married."

WHAT ARE YOU GETTING YOURSELF INTO?

Now, you are faced with changing most of your life. In divorce, there are new ground rules and systems to learn. These include living arrangements, work, and relationships with family, friends and community members. There will be radical changes in the relationship with your children.

Change also includes the distribution of goods. For instance, who gets what furniture? Where will the family pet live? Who goes where with whom for holidays and family religious observances? What will happen to your assets and liabilities?

Up to now, you have taken certain services in marriage as a matter of course. Divorce will change the division of such common daily labors as:

- Housekeeping versus repairing broken objects.
- Cooking versus paying for groceries.
- Laundering and sewing versus plumbing and electrical work.
- Budgeting and keeping the books versus planning insurance and savings.
- Planning activities versus running errands.
- Arranging social activities versus acting as chauffeur.

There will also be changes in the work associated with parenting. Some couples do stay together for the sake of the children because divorce can be emotionally devastating as well as financially brutal. However, remaining in a very difficult marriage can be emotionally and psychologically disastrous to everyone, especially the children. It's the old story of being stuck between a rock and a hard place.

COPING ALONE

Coping alone can best be likened to becoming a generalist instead of a specialist...M/F Single instead of Mr. and Mrs. Happy Couple.

It does not mean that you have to do everything alone. It simply means that you have full responsibility for a wide variety of situations.

Seeking Help and Guidance

In the first few months of your separation, the need to seek help and guidance is almost a given. There is no shame or weakness in wanting advice and support. Vulnerability and instability are quite normal under the circumstances.

When you are exploring unfamiliar territory, you must ask questions. If you are unaccustomed to handling the household finances, this may mean getting the advice of an accountant, stockbroker, or knowledgeable friend. If you are unaccustomed to handling daily domestic routines, this may mean getting advice regarding chores, services to hire, and the best places to buy basic household items.

In the interest of saving time and energy, you will want to devise new methods and shortcuts for yourself that will give you much-needed "space" in which to rest and think. You'll find specific suggestions for doing these things in Section 3, "PULLING YOURSELF AND YOUR FAMILY TOGETHER."

If being alone represents a significant change in your life, it is generally suggested that you postpone selling or moving from your home until your divorce process is well under way. This is especially true if there are children in the household. In spite of possible appearances to the contrary, children are generally very shaken by a marital split. They need the security of familiar surroundings and friends to help them. So do you. For a detailed discussion on moving out or remaining in your current home, see the section on shelter in Chapter 9.

During the first year of separation, your opportunity for the best possible separation agreement will come from a willingness to talk a great deal with your spouse. You have got to get through such emotional blocks as the tendency to be overly antagonistic or pliantly agreeable. You have serious business to negotiate.

MAKING THE DECISION

The first shoe to fall is the decision to divorce. Nobody works harder to put the pieces of life back together again than a divorcing person. It takes far less energy to work at improving your marriage than to get a divorce. This is the time to take a very practical look at the motives involved in your divorce.

Once you have made up your mind or the decision has been made for you that divorce is inevitable, you need to address the situation as a problem to be solved. It is time to stop trying to fix things that you cannot fix. When there is no alternative, you must learn how to adapt.

HEALTHY SURVIVORS

How do some people manage to make the best of difficult situations? There is every indication that those who are the true and healthy survivors of divorce are the ones with the strongest desire to be practical about the irreversible aspects of the process. They deal with their emotions by using a network of professional and personal support.

Our research shows that people who have suffered terrible losses, including divorce, seem to end up in one of three groups:

- Those who are broken by the experience and never really get on with their lives.
- Those who struggle with their grief, eventually accept their loss, and move forward.
- Those who not only rebuild their lives but emerge stronger, wiser, and more determined than ever to live up to their fullest capacities.

Recognizing the Healthy Survivors

In the beginning of a divorce process, the healthy survivors often appear to function in about the same way as those in the first two groups. Their pain is the same and they, too, become mired in grief for periods of time. The difference is that healthy survivors learn how to:

- Completely say good-bye to the marriage.
- Avoid domination or control by the other spouse.
- Deal with the pain in small doses, taking their experiences one day at a time.
- See beyond the divorce period.
- Accept reality whether or not they were "entitled" to a better deal.

How do you develop the self-confidence to handle the problems and tough questions that come up? Frankly, in the beginning, you do it by acting as though you have the important things under control. Little by little your confidence will begin to grow.

Very few people can go it alone. It is important to remember that this workbook connects you to a process of support and helps you to find the way back into a sane and solid existence.

REASSESSING YOUR MARRIAGE

To understand what is happening and how you feel about your divorce, you will want to compare the components of your marriage with the list we compiled of generally recognized standards for a healthy marriage. Use **FORM-ula 1: Marriage Assessment** as a guide. It is a checklist for three areas of marriage: healthy relationships, common causes of marital breakdowns, and sneaky reasons for staying married. In addition to checking relevant items, make personal notes on this FORM-ula. They will be useful to you later on during the divorce proceedings.

As you make your evaluation, remember that in healthy relationships, couples don't expect their marriage to be completely smooth. They don't assume that all difficulties and conflicts will resolve themselves. They know there may be financial problems, emotional hassles, and ill health.

In addition to the behaviors listed, remember to consider feelings. In a marriage that feels good, the partnership is strengthened by closeness and the encouragement for each other to change and grow. There is little or no feeling of giving up anything for each other or of giving in to each other. There are only feelings of giving to one another.

GETTING ON WITH IT

Even though the recognized causes of divorce can be listed, the situation is rarely cut-and-dried. The obvious isn't necessarily the case. On the surface, it may appear that there is one "guilty" and one "innocent" mate. Therapists frequently find that the so-called innocent spouse, deliberately or not, actively contributes to the end of the marriage through negative, provocative, or withholding behavior.

While one of the common causes of marital breakdown (listed in **FORM-ula 1: Marriage Assessment**) is likely to be a trigger for the ultimate separation, a long series of disagreements and disappointments (spoken or unspoken) have inevitably stored the ammunition. By the time you seriously consider divorce, the desire to create a satisfactory marriage with your current spouse is gone.

Family and friends sense tension and frustration, often without comment or discussion. Children don't miss much, either. They may be just as glad when separation finally occurs because it might mean that at least one parent is going to try to provide a more nurturing environment for them.

Midlife or later divorces may be a great relief to the partner who is ready to get on with life.

Wrong Reasons for Going Back

There will be moments when you feel particularly vulnerable and that the best solution is to go back to the familiar (thinking that the devil you know may be better than the devil you don't know). This feeling is natural. Some of those potentially vulnerable times are:

- Holidays.
- When you are sick or have had an accident.
- When your child is sick or has had an accident.
- When you break up with someone new.
- When you lose your job or are having trouble getting one.
- When your parents are critically ill.
- When you have very young children.

Potential Benefits of a Divorce

Maybe you can manage to stay in your present situation by centering all of your attention on your work, children, or hobby. Will this be enough? If not, take a look at some of the potential benefits of divorce, including:

- A much-needed catalyst for change in lifestyle, job, values, social structure, or living environment.
- Knowledge that traditional roles don't have to continue. (You can tap the well-springs of your own deepest needs and desires.)
- For parents, a much better relationship with their children. (This is particularly true in the case of the supporting parent who has played the role of provider, leaving the role of caretaker to the other parent.)
- The recognition and change of destructive patterns of behavior so that new relationships can benefit.
- The opportunity for personal growth and freedom, especially if you have been living in the shadow of a more powerful and controlling spouse.

A new perspective can bring with it a resurgence of energy, hope, and self-esteem that may have been buried for a very long time. In fact, many divorcing couples tell us that their greatest regret is that they waited so long to make the decision.

DEFINING A SUCCESSFUL DIVORCE

We have found that the most stable settlements occur when both spouses take an active role in negotiations. The healthiest way towards later success is to begin with a mutual decision to divorce. This means that both of you realize and accept divorce as the best direction under the circumstances and, if there are children, that you will be mutually active in co-parenting.

In summary, a successful divorce means:

- Completing the physical and emotional processes of separation.

- Establishing a balanced view of each other and the marriage.

- Finding an appropriate new direction for your life.

- Feeling good about your relationship with your children.

Chapter 3
THE LEGAL DIVORCE

There are laws in each state that govern marriage, separation, annulment, and divorce. The legislature of each state decides how a marriage can be dissolved. A divorce occurs as a formal court procedure.

From a legal perspective, marriage is a civil contract between two people. Almost any adult has the legal capacity to get married. The obligations of this legal act cannot be transferred or assigned. The marriage license and certificate affirm this act and give the courts the sole legal means to dissolve it.

Couples cannot end a legally valid common-law marriage by simply moving apart. They must obtain a divorce decree from a court. States that don't recognize common-law marriage for their own residents must recognize marriages that are legally formed in other states.

This section relates the legal implications of dissolving a marriage. The process is impersonal. You must function within a prescribed set of rules and regulations. There is a new language to be understood and used.

LEGAL ISSUES

Up to now, your divorce has had a single dimension: *personal*. Filing official papers for divorce adds a second dimension: *legal*.

Remember, the court sees divorce based upon:

- Keeping the peace.
- Division of assets and liabilities.
- Spousal support.
- Responsibility to children (custody and support).

Under the existing system, the primary concern of the court is to keep nonearning individuals off of public assistance.

Keeping the Peace...A Separate One

Issues of property, support, and custody revolve around the success or failure of keeping the peace. This means that there must be freedom from physical harm or mental abuse. Because maintaining the peace is so important, the courts are prepared to offer some remedies.

Injunction

If peaceful interaction is not possible during the divorce process, either party may request the court to issue a temporary injunction, directly or through an attorney. (Incidentally, this step does not require advance notice to the other spouse.) Such an injunction could:

- Keep your spouse from transferring funds, loading you with debt, or concealing or disposing property.

- Keep your spouse out of your home when there is court-accepted evidence of physical or emotional harm.

- Prevent your spouse from molesting or disturbing the peace of the family.

An injunction can be used as part of family law during the divorce process. If these same kinds of problems surface after the divorce decree, civil law becomes the recourse.

While the initial period of divorce can be volatile, statistics indicate that about 50 percent of divorced couples achieve amicable postdivorce relationships.

If there are no children, it won't be necessary to have continuing contact. If you have children, continuous contact is inevitable. In order to continue participating in your children's lives, you may both choose to stay in the same community and even attend the same religious institution. You will both want to go to the events and family gatherings that are important to your children. Establishing a peaceful coexistence is a gift of love to your children. Both women and men are pressing for new ways to humanize divorce by providing options that will allow both parents to maintain viable relationships with their children after the marriage has ended.

Division of Assets and Liabilities

On the asset side of the divorce ledger, all fifty states have slightly different ways to decide who gets what in a divorce. Property will be valued during the drawing up of the settlement agreement or at the time of trial. On the liability side of the ledger, both spouses are equally liable for debts incurred during the marriage. The states' positions are categorized as:

- Equitable distribution.
- Marital, or community, property.
- Common law.

Equitable Distribution

Equitable distribution is used by the majority of states. This means that each spouse is recognized as a partner to the marriage and the assets the partnership produced. If you and your spouse don't negotiate an acceptable agreement, the judges distribute marital property *equitably* (not necessarily equally) based upon the following considerations:

- Duration of marriage.
- Each partner's contribution towards the acquisition, preservation, and appreciation of marital property.
- Both parties' preseparation standard of living.
- Past, present, and prospective earnings of each partner.
- Vocational skills of each partner.
- Respective age and health of each partner.
- Contributions of the homemaking spouse.
- Relative necessity of the custodial parent to work or remain at home with the children.

Marital, or Community, Property

Marital, or community, property is all property acquired during marriage, except for property purchased with the proceeds of separate property or excluded by valid agreement. *Separate property* is any property owned before marriage (earned, acquired by gift or inheritance), or earned after a formalized separation. If an asset is bought with both marital and separate property funds, it may be considered part separate and part community property. The process for distribution is:

- Description of property as either marital or separate property.
- Valuation of marital property.
- Division of marital property between the spouses.

Note 1 While we are writing this book, Arizona, California, Idaho, Louisiana, Nebraska, New Mexico, Texas, and Washington are considered community property states. Wisconsin is classified as a modified community property state.

Note 2 Neither equitable distribution nor community property states officially consider fault as a factor in the settlement of property distribution. A discussion of fault and no-fault is presented later in this chapter.

Common-Law Division of Property

The *common-law division of property* exists on the books in only a few states. In actual practice, Mississippi is the only one of these states that is not using the equitable distribution concept. By strict interpretation, the courts of common-law states have no power to award equitably. They must distribute property solely on the basis of who holds the legal title of ownership. They place no value on homemaking services, companionship, professional degrees, or pensions in making decisions about property awards.

Spousal Support

The court can and does order either partner to pay for the support of the other, in any amount and for any time period that the court finds reasonable. The laws that govern the amount and time period seem to change with regularity.

Amount and Duration

In deciding the amount and duration of a support obligation, the court looks at the following factors:

- Earning capacity of each partner.
- Needs of each partner.
- Obligations and assets, including separate property of each partner.
- Living standard of each partner.
- Duration of the marriage.
- Age and health of each partner.
- Time required by supported partner to acquire education, training, and employment.
- Needs of the dependent children.

Either spouse can waive support for their own benefit or agree upon a fixed amount of support regardless of present or future financial changes.

Note Parents do not have the right to make such agreements on behalf of their children!

Unless a partner waives this right to support, the court has the right to authorize a change in the amount of spousal support whenever there is a significant change in either partner's financial resources. Remember, it is the court's responsibility to keep ex-spouses financially independent and off public assistance.

Responsibility to Children

The two major issues regarding children are custody and support. The court concerns itself with where the children of divorced parents will live, who will raise them, and how the expense of raising them will be managed.

Custody

Custody regulates parental rights with respect to rearing children upon the dissolution of a marriage.

In spite of a supposedly more broad-minded society (accepting alternative life styles with consciousness-raising and free-to-be-me concepts) our legal system still assumes there are proper family roles for men and women.

When a family needs to be legally taken apart and reassembled, the complexities can be all but insurmountable. The current preference of the law seems to be for joint legal custody in which the parents share rights and responsibilities. Custody includes issues of health, education, general welfare, and religion.

Support

Unless there are unusual circumstances (physical disability of either parent or child, for instance), both parents are obligated to support their children. The court can determine the amount that the non-custodial parent will pay for child support relative to the resources of each parent.

The court has the power to make the final determination on both custody and support until a child reaches the age of emancipation, usually at age 18. You will find a detailed discussion about custody and child support in Chapter 21.

BECOMING DIVORCED

When you file the papers to begin your legal divorce, you are making an official statement to your spouse and to the world at large that your decision has been made. The minimum length of the legal divorce process varies between 3 and 18 months. The actual length of time varies according to the local rules, the number of issues, and the extent of debate.

In some states, it is possible to get a divorce without a final separation agreement. With or without the completion of the "contract," you end up with a piece of paper with court orders written on it. States vary in their requirements for a divorce action to be officially closed.

The court may have continuing jurisdiction over the marriage (even after it has been dissolved) to rectify a fraud, amend support directives or custody and visitation rights, and to keep the peace.

Divorce Is Not a Problem-Solver

You may believe that a legal divorce will solve many or all of your problems. It won't, even though it may appear to be the short term answer. It is extremely important for you to understand this fact so that you don't expect too much. Separation and divorce can be a frustrating and disappointing experience if you are not simultaneously pursuing the solutions to other personal problems.

OPTIONS OTHER THAN DIVORCE

If divorce is not appropriate and you don't want to continue living together, there are two useful alternatives. Consider either a legal separation or an annulment.

Legal Separation Decree

The purpose of a *legal separation decree* is to live separately while remaining married. This is sometimes preferred for economic, religious, or moral reasons. The process of obtaining a decree of legal separation is almost identical to the divorce process. Usually the agreement must be in writing and presented to the court. Judges will accept the agreement unless the terms are seen as unfair or not in the best interests of the children.

Note A legal separation does not dissolve a marriage. That can only be done by obtaining a divorce or an annulment.

Advantages of Obtaining a Legal Separation

The following list presents several advantages to securing a legal separation instead of other types of separation.

- It allows both parties time to resolve their marital difficulties (a cooling off period leading to possible reconciliation).
- Since courts have an interest in preserving marriage, they are more willing to grant a judgment of separation than a divorce.
- It prepares both parties for the possible trauma of divorce.
- It is easier to prove grounds for separation than for divorce in those states that still require proof.
- Legal and financial obligations including inheritance, pension rights, and death benefits are still maintained.

Disadvantages of Obtaining a Legal Separation

The following list presents disadvantages to legal separation.

- It may be merely postponing the inevitable.
- Parties may incur double expenses: costs for the separation and for the divorce.
- It may leave the nonworking spouse with fewer means of support and no property distribution benefits.
- Legal obligations including inheritance, pension rights, and death benefits are still maintained.
- Neither party can remarry or disinherit the other spouse.

Annulment

Annulment is another way of saying that, in the eyes of the law, this marriage never happened. Sometimes an annulment doesn't carry the so-called stigma of divorce.

It is generally assumed that at the time of marriage, both partners were legally capable of entering into a valid contract. This means:

- Both partners were capable of having sexual intercourse.
- Neither partner was a minor.
- No important information was deliberately concealed.

Most annulments are obtained on the grounds of fraud in one or more of these categories.

A religious annulment is not the same as a legal annulment. Some religions have particular restrictions following the breakup of a marriage that are entirely separate from the legal process. If you want a religious annulment, be aware that your legal annulment or divorce must be completed before filing the petition.

OUR JUSTICE SYSTEM, *OR*, YOU CAN'T FIGHT THE SYSTEM!

What is the first thing you think of when the word *divorce* is mentioned in a legal context? Very often, it is *no-fault*. What does this term really mean?

No-Fault

Many people mistakenly think that no-fault implies post-divorce economic equality between the spouses. It doesn't. Another common misconception is that the no-fault divorce concept was created by feminists. It wasn't. Actually, it was the result of legal professionals trying to reduce the level of blame-laying and "legal" gamesmanship used to force divorce settlements.

Advantage of the No-Fault Divorce

The advantage of the no-fault divorce is that victory does not go to the spouse with the most spectacular list of complaints. (In the past, gathering or fabricating evidence seemed like a messy business but it sure made for dramatic court sessions!) No-fault recognizes that both parties have contributed to the death of the marriage. It allows for the possibility of a more equitable agreement based upon the realities of what is necessary to divide a marriage into two parts. However, it hasn't really cleaned up divorce proceedings because clients and attorneys have become greedier.

Disadvantage of the No-Fault Divorce

A negative side to no-fault divorce is that without any legal recognition of blame, the injured or rejected partner is left with little financial or emotional recourse. This, in turn, fosters hostility and retaliation, sometimes using settlement negotiations or custody and visitation arrangements as pawns in the game. If there are children, this can become a devastating power struggle.

In states that accept marital misconduct as grounds for divorce, the most commonly cited are:

- Adultery.
- Constructive abandonment (refusing to recognize the marriage or to act married).
- Cruelty.
- Desertion.
- Physical incapacity.
- Habitual use of drugs or intoxicants.

The Adversarial System

Our basic justice system is known as the *adversarial system*. It has its origins in medieval days when trial by combat meant that the survivor was right! It is recognized, both by professionals and those "caught" in the system, that it is a poor forum for the settling of marital disputes. It tends to increase conflicts and does little or nothing to resolve important life issues.

Divorce Attorneys

Attorneys, by training and professional standards, are expected to handle divorce strictly in keeping with the American Bar Association's (ABA) *Model Rules of Professional Conduct* (1983). An attorney's primary responsibility is to represent the client. The welfare and interests of the other spouse or children are not the attorney's professional concern since the assumption of the law is that they will be equally represented by opposing legal counsel. This means that attorneys often have a one-sided view of the case.

Realistically, in any community, divorce attorneys are likely to know each other and work together for most of their professional lives. The resulting bond between opposing counsel in a divorce can often be stronger than the relationship between attorney and client. Attorneys have their future practice to think about. Whether this personal concern is right or wrong has no bearing; it is reality. Suggestions for the best way to select an attorney to represent you are given in Chapter 25.

The procedures of the legal system often increase the conflicts in divorce. The legal system emphasizes manipulation and aggressive or defensive strategy. Law students learn how to take either side of a case and argue it—to get the most out of any situation.

Many law schools do not require courses in counseling, family dynamics, or communication skills and offer very little instruction on family negotiations. There is an on-going professional debate about just how far into a counseling mode an attorney should go.

Two Courtroom Scenarios

The divorcing couple enters a courtroom under one of two scenarios:

- They will present a completed separation agreement to the judge for approval as the final step in obtaining their divorce decree.
- They are abdicating personal decision-making and hope the judgment of the court will resolve all remaining disputes more to their liking.

Before you and your spouse decide to give the court such decision-making powers, you need to know that the court is guided by formulas. In spite of no-fault, the adversarial laws governing divorce historically cast the judge's role as one of determining which party is innocent and which party is guilty. This puts both attorneys in the position of struggling to obtain maximum benefits by attempting to show their own client in the best possible light. This is where fault creeps in.

Note There is a legal concept known as the *Clean Hands Doctrine*. It means that a person who has acted wrongly (morally or legally) generally won't be helped by the court system when complaining about the other spouse's actions.

Judges

In addition to using experience, procedures, and legal precedence, individual judges insert their own biases (consciously or not) into their readings of family law. Unfortunately, all judges do not have the wisdom, time, or inclination to be responsive to each separate case with regard to the unique needs of the two divorcing individuals.

In reality, the outcome of most legal divorce action is highly predictable once the available facts are established. An experienced attorney, who knows the law and the local judges, can usually make a pretty accurate educated guess as to what the outcome will be.

Note The system runs on the presumption that presenting the opposing interests of two parties before a judge, governed by rules of law, will result in the best possible solution.

THE ADVERSARIAL DIVORCE

When marriage partners consider each other as enemies, they are not working together toward the common objectives of the divorce. They are functioning in an adversarial divorce relationship in an already adversarial justice system. However, an adversarial relationship with your spouse does not necessarily imply that your divorce case will go to trial. It simply indicates that you have many unresolved issues requiring extensive negotiation. Records confirm that most of the cases (even the initially chaotic and bitter ones) reach an agreement, although sometimes in the doorway of the trial courtroom!

Advantages of an Adversarial Divorce

Contrary to what one might first think, there are some advantages to an adversarial divorce; these include:

- Using the fight as an outlet for the pain.
- The psychological vindication and economic rewards that come from "winning."
- Using additional anger with spouse to help sever lingering ties.
- Sensing from a case that has gone to trial that the marriage is emphatically over.

Disadvantages of an Adversarial Divorce

The disadvantages of an adversarial divorce include:

- In the heat of battle, the couple loses sight of long-term interests.
- The "loser's" morale is crushed; the "winner's" self-esteem is diminished by unsavory tactics used to win.
- The cost of extended litigation will make the financial situation worse for both parties.
- Adults who decide to go to court will inflict additional hurt and hardship on themselves and on their children.
- If the case goes to trial, judgments imposed by the court are less likely to be honored because they were not voluntary.

Popular Threats

Traditionally, the two most popular female threats in an adversarial divorce are:

- "I'll take you to the cleaners!"
- "I'll get the children, and you'll never see them!"

The two most popular male threats in an adversarial divorce have traditionally been:

- "You'll get no money!"
- "I'll take the children!"

Remember that within the framework of the adversarial system, it is possible to resolve many, if not all, of the issues. The court only makes legal judgments on what is unresolved.

If left totally to the court, all of the valued possessions of the marriage will be divided by the judge. The judge can also make all decisions regarding custody and visitation for minor children. Is this the way you want to end your marriage?

From a functional standpoint, divorces fall into two categories:

- Uncontested divorce
- Contested divorce

An Uncontested Divorce

An *uncontested* divorce case is any suit for divorce (including legal separation or annulment) in which the final judgment is entered without the need for a trial. This doesn't mean that the issues between spouses have been resolved quickly or easily. It means that there has been successful negotiation about support, custody, and the division of assets and liabilities which can then be presented to the court. This agreement will not need any determination by the judge as to who should get what or do what. It does, however, require a judicial proceeding under the laws of your state before you are issued a legal divorce decree.

A Contested Divorce

A *contested* divorce is one that will go to a trial before a judge. The case is contested because one or more important issues relating to the divorce, the most usual being custody or property, have not been resolved.

Reasons for a Contested Divorce

The following list presents typical reasons for contesting a divorce.

- One of the spouses wants to reconcile.
- One spouse has personal reasons (social, health, financial).
- One spouse wants to exact revenge by making the divorce as difficult as possible.
- One spouse is tired of giving in.
- One spouse wants time to hide some assets hoping that they will not be subject to distribution in the final divorce agreement.
- One spouse's religious faith does not sanction divorce.
- One spouse philosophically believes that marriage is a lifetime commitment that cannot be canceled.

ALTERNATIVES TO THE ADVERSARIAL DIVORCE

What if you feel stuck? What if you don't want a contested divorce and you don't think there is much chance of reaching an agreement without it? Are there any other options? Yes.

Alternatives to an adversarial divorce include:

- Mediation
- Arbitration
- An interdisciplinary committee

However, since our court system does not require these alternatives, you will have to investigate them yourself. We have observed that judges look favorably upon a mediated divorce agreement and will move more easily into issuing the divorce decree.

If you use any one of these resources, it does not eliminate the need to present the court with your final separation agreement in order to receive a legal divorce decree. These are simply alternatives to help you reach that point.

Mediation

Mediation is used by divorcing couples who deplore the prospect of a court fight or of allowing the mechanics and biases of the legal system to make binding decisions about their future. These kinds of couples want professional guidance in order to maximize their input into the separation agreement. Even when mediation does not result in an actual agreement, many couples will have developed a greater ability to cooperate and compromise through attorney negotiations.

A Mediator's Job

A mediator does not make decisions. Instead, a mediator's job is to:

- Have a knowledge of local family law.
- Consider the needs of each family member.
- Get both spouses to discuss their objectives.
- Bring all the facts out into the open.
- Equalize the bargaining power of the spouses.
- Give a crash course in negotiating skills.
- Create and explore options.
- Seek alternatives.
- Support the development of a written separation agreement.

If family court services are available in your state, they may provide basic mediation free of charge. Meetings are usually limited to three or less and you would not usually have a choice of mediators. Private mediation is not free but gives you a choice of mediators and an unlimited number of meetings.

Reviewing a Mediated Agreement

When the mediated agreement is drawn up it should be reviewed by each spouse's attorney to make sure that:

- The document is legally correct.
- Individual rights have been protected.
- Tax implications are recognized.
- Every proper consideration is included.

At this point, corrections or modifications are agreed upon and made.

Some Reasons for a Mediated Divorce

Here are some reasons for engaging in mediation:

- Provides a structure and forum for resolving settlement disputes.
- Develops communication in common areas of concern.
- Allows maximum participation of both partners.
- Burns up less energy in hostility and retaliation.
- Supports creative and innovative thinking.
- Uses less time for discovery and negotiation.
- Minimizes feelings of victimization.
- Stresses a win-win approach to negotiations rather than win-lose
- Assures greater success in carrying out agreement (less likelihood of future litigation) since both parties make compromises voluntarily.
- Minimizes attorney fees and court costs.
- Minimizes trauma for children.
- Avoids "public" fighting.
- Enhances ongoing relationship and individual ability to resolve future problems.

Some Reasons against a Mediated Divorce

There are several reasons to decide against using mediation to settle the terms of a settlement. These are listed below:

- Mediation presumes good faith between partners. (Information cannot be taken under oath and there is no penalty for lying.)
- Mediation is only a step toward divorce; its conclusions and agreements are not legally enforceable.
- Unsuccessful mediation can be expensive because the work must be undone and reorganized by attorneys.
- Some couples try to use mediation instead of legal counsel.
- Emotions may be too strong to allow rational conclusions to mediation.
- Mediation doesn't work when couples really want public justification or revenge.
- When one spouse is the dominant partner and the other will not be assertive, the mediator is forced to lose objectivity and/or neutrality.
- Neutrality is not appropriate when one spouse truly needs a strong backup — as in the case of retardation, brain damage or severe character disorder.
- Mediators aren't always fair and unbiased.

Arbitration

Arbitration is less formal than a regular court hearing. There is a third-party panel that acts as a surrogate judge to render a decision after hearing both sides of the divorce issues. It is a speedier process than a court hearing and usually will have greater relevance to the couple's specific needs.

The couple contemplating arbitration must be willing to accept a decision over which they have limited control. They will each be asked to make a full and honest disclosure of all information vital to the divorce agreement. Both must be represented by independent legal counsel. In some cases, the children will also be represented by counsel.

Although the arbitrator's decision is final, it has to be attached to the divorce complaint filed in court before it is incorporated as part of the final divorce decree.

Interdisciplinary Committee

An *interdisciplinary committee* acts as a third party performing the decision-making function of arbitration or litigation instead of the purely voluntary nature of divorce mediation.

The committee might include, for example, an impartial attorney, a clergyman, a child psychologist, and an educator. Ideally, these people should be acquainted with the family and its needs. If the issue is custody of children, an interdisciplinary committee is usually chosen by the parents.

The findings of the committee can become part of the legal proceedings.

Chapter 4
IMPLICATIONS OF A DECISION TO DIVORCE

Do you honestly have any idea what life is going to be like from here on? Major changes are coming in the following areas:

- Finance.
- Lifestyle.
- Children.
- Friends, relatives, coworkers, and community.
- Interaction with spouse.

Change can be for "better or for worse." It depends upon how you accept and deal with it. You can be as emotional as you need to be in your moments of privacy and counseling. When it comes to the business issues of divorce, you must be incredibly practical. For each spouse, there is bound to be:

- Economic upheaval—how to deal with the budget, finances, and assets and liabilities.
- Career disruption—time away from work to handle divorce matters and one's mental state during divorce (inability to concentrate, possible loss of self-esteem, lack of get-up-and-go, and so forth).
- A mourning process—feeling sad and lonely; regretful; disinterested in life; overly sensitive; and looking back, not forward.

- The loss of a partner—help with household chores and maintenance, coparenting, sexual needs, companionship (such as it may have been), social activities, and obligations.

FINANCIAL CHANGES

The tremendously high cost of breaking up a marriage can cause astronomical financial damage. Financial discussions, in the midst of everyday divorce tensions, are almost always awkward. Some of the discoveries can be very painful. On the other hand, a lot of liberation can come from knowing. Unfortunately, from a timing standpoint, these discussions are imperative at the same exact time that you are trying to plan for your whole life, not just for your financial security. In addition, you are probably in no mood to do either.

Separate Financial Needs

Stop thinking in terms of *our* budget and *our* property. You and your spouse now have separate and, for the time being, competitive financial needs. Two cannot live as cheaply as one. Some divorcing adults find themselves spending freely, while others are forced into frugality. Both parties are learning new consumer habits.

Regardless of previous involvement in handling family finances, each spouse now has the responsibility to organize and document prior and current financial activities. This has to be done to obtain your legal divorce and gives you a head start on preparing your financial plans for when you are single again.

The economic climate of the early 1990s has witnessed dramatic declines in the net worth of many families. When they begin the financial paperwork for the divorce, couples are often surprised to find out just how much money they have lost. Three particularly troublesome areas are the sinking value of homes, job cuts and layoffs, and the inability of the economy to absorb divorcing women into appropriate levels of employment.

Some statistics indicate a decline in the number of divorces. There is a debate about whether the current economic climate is actually resulting in the cancellation of divorce plans or merely delaying them.

Although divorce is a personal and financial blow to both sides, an ex-husband probably doesn't have to change his legal identity, apply for new credit ratings, or prepare for a different occupation. An ex-wife may have to do one or more of these things.

In the business and commercial world, where a woman's former married status was treated with respect, she may discover that she is now a financial nonentity.

The most common financial myth-conceptions are that:

- Money can make you whole.
- You are entitled to your fair share and the divorce court will see that you get it.

Note Socioeconomic factors that are typically disadvantageous to women in the marketplace simultaneously favor their assumption of the major domestic responsibilities.

PLANNING FOR YOUR FUTURE

In planning for your future, you have to throw away past expectations. There is no room for what might have been. You are beginning a new life. You are breaking new ground. You are going into a new way of juggling your personal, social, and business lives with family responsibilities.

Being divorced may resolve some problems and it will most certainly produce others. The original fantasy of sharing one's life fully and intimately with this spouse is over. Saying "good-bye" to the couple and "hello" to yourself may be very hard. Divorce can cause a powerful identity crisis.

Societal pressures notwithstanding, both spouses have to learn how to stop feeling married. Let's face it: Both of you have decisions to make and a single adult life to create. Where do you want to go? What do you want to do? Who do you want to be? This book has been designed to help you address each of these issues.

The rest of this chapter describes the possible effects of your divorce on others and the typical reactions you can expect from them. Specific suggestions of ways you can discuss your divorce and thereby gain some control over the reactions and behaviors of others will be found in Chapter 7.

CHILDREN AND DIVORCE—*LIKE ME, NEED ME, NOTICE ME*

Parents and children belong together. They need each other physically, emotionally, and psychologically. Breaking this bond is traumatic.

Adults can recover from the divorce games they sometimes play. Children are seldom as fortunate. At the Children's Divorce Center in Woodbridge, Connecticut, there was an art exhibit showing pictures drawn by children ages 4–15, all from divorced homes. The art was said to represent the sadness, confusion, anger, and eventual adjustment those children went through when their parents split up.

Children are affected by the various stages of divorce as much as you are. They are facing not only the loss of a parent on a daily basis, but also the cessation of family traditions and an uncertain future.

They have trouble acknowledging the reality of a marital separation. It is difficult for children of all ages to comprehend the permanence of divorce. They usually harbor expectations about their parents getting back together or that the divorce won't go through. Many children become confused by parents who say they are friends and yet still get divorced.

Children would urgently like to disengage themselves from any and all conflict in order to resume their normal lives. If they are unable to do so, you will see various types of reactive behavior showing their hurt and resentment.

Children's Worries

Children see divorce through tunnel vision. Their main concern is "What is going to happen to me?" Parental unhappiness takes second place to their threatened security. Most children see parents as an extension of themselves existing to supply their needs, not as individuals having separate and distinct lives of their own.

Children of all ages worry. Some of their comments have been:

- "I caused the divorce."
- "What did I do wrong?"
- "My parents spend more time getting a divorce than they do with me."
- "My mom/dad left the house, so that means she/he hates me."
- "My mom/dad won't want to see me again."
- "How can I be loyal to both of my parents?"
- "What will happen to me if they both leave?"
- "We're going to starve now because mom/dad says we don't have any money."
- "My grandparents won't love me any more."
- "What's going to happen next?"
- "Where is my room going to be?"

Children's Behaviors

The behavior of children often becomes exaggerated as they try to take care of themselves throughout the emotional crisis of divorce. In attempting to stop the inevitable movement of the process, they use everything in the book: tears, hysteria, psychosomatic illness, and even feigned or intended suicide.

Most of the divorce books for or about children indicate that they get very little support from adults as their world falls apart. Apparently, during this time, adult friends, relatives, and teachers are hesitant to interfere.

Use **FORM-ula 2: Observing Children's Divorce Behavior** to check for signs of trouble and indications of psychological stress that your children may be experiencing.

Recognize, however, that there is a tendency for adults to attribute all difficult behavior exhibited by offspring to the trials and tribulations of divorce and to ignore other relevant factors. It is wise to consult a professional if you feel that any of the behaviors apply to your children. For a detailed discussion, see Chapter 12.

When children are hostile, it is an expression of fear for their survival and fear of abandonment. Be-

neath all of that is the growing suspicion that you no longer love them, not that they hate you.

Basically, your children are watching *you*. They will continue to feel loved and respected if you:

- Keep them informed of your decisions.
- Are consistent in your own behavior.
- Can act as calmly as possible.
- Continue to set guidelines for appropriate behavior.

Eventually, most children settle into whatever new routine is provided. Hopefully, this will include lots of love and laughter.

Children's Stages by Ages During a Divorce

The way your children adjust will strongly correlate to your own adjustment. However, children in the same family may react quite differently in accordance with their personalities, ages, and gender. A lot will depend upon the emotional support they are getting, the amount of conflict going on, and how temporary custody and visitation arrangements are working.

Dealing with the parent who holds the purse strings can cause children to become either skilled manipulators or whining complainers. On the positive side, they can develop self-sufficiency and maturity that is not influenced by bribery or intimidated by unwise parental control.

The following lists provide insights into the types of reactions to expect from children. They are divided into age categories.

Youngsters (4–12 years)

- Younger children seem to be generally less troubled than older ones at the time of separation and divorce.
- Their three greatest fears are rejection, abandonment, and not being taken care of.
- The younger child often blames herself or himself for not being sufficiently lovable or well-behaved.
- Without specific guidance, the young child has trouble understanding the loss of the other parent and never stops waiting for a return, especially if that parent has been routinely away a great deal.
- A small child feels threatened by either parent's change in behavior and daily patterns and reacts by acting out.

- The preschooler may demonstrate anxiety by regressive behavior, reverting to an earlier period, or becoming destructive.
- Daddy/mommy "shopping" is heaviest when children are between 10 and 12 years old.

Adolescents (12–18 years)

- Taken as a group, adolescents are much angrier initially than the younger children.
- Teenagers are also much more inclined to become depressed and withdrawn.
- Already suffering the slings and arrows of outrageous puberty, the emotional stress of divorce often destroys their concentration and forces emotions to the boiling point.
- Close to adulthood, adolescents take on an exaggerated sense of adult responsibility which, in turn, fosters authoritarian behavior.
- Frequently, adolescents compete with parents who have started dating again. These teenagers face the insidious inner question of their own ability to have a lasting and healthy relationship.
- Adolescents can also become inordinately embarrassed by their parents' sexuality at a time when they are having a hard enough time with their own newly raging hormones.
- Teenagers usually maintain good rapport with the teachers they like. There is also little or no change in other adult or peer friendships.
- Divorce often speeds up the normal process of de-idealizing parents. The result is the assumption of greater personal decision-making than the real maturity level might warrant.
- If one parent has been more hurt by the divorce than the other, the adolescent is capable of showing sympathy and great loyalty in spite of the inner conflict of torn allegiances.
- Division of time and self becomes particularly difficult during holidays, vacations, and personal and family celebrations.
- Far too many adolescents translate their unhappiness into bad adult behavior such as sexual promiscuity, perversion, drug or alcohol abuse, or running away.

The adolescents who cope the best are those who have always demonstrated moral courage, reasonable behavior, and good relationships with one or both parents.

College-Age and Adult Children

Virtually all states recognize age 18 as the age of emancipation. (Some states do recognize the court's right to order support for adult dependent children, ages 18–21.) From this point on, parents no longer have legal or financial responsibility for their offspring.

Adult children of divorce have emotional reactions that are just as strong as those of younger children but they seem to suffer from financial worries more than anything else. Those in school question getting sufficient financial support from one or both parents. Conversely, independent adult children are concerned about being called upon for giving financial support for either or both parents. Issues relevant to college-age and adult children who face their parents' divorce are summarized below.

- The college-age young adult is likely to experience uncertainty and trepidation about continued or future education if there is no explicit written agreement regarding support (which is usually incorporated into the divorce decree but rarely counted as a child-support requirement because of the child's emancipated age).
- A common dilemma of the maturing adult is determining how much to confide in one parent or the other.
- Adult children have to consciously avoid being "used" by parents to relieve their hurt, pain, or anger.
- Feelings of being torn in half are not uncommon to the adult child of divorce. College graduations, weddings, and the birth of children are particularly difficult moments. (How much time is fair to spend with each child? How much of a vacation should be spent with each parent? Which parent comes first?)
- When a divorced woman chooses to use her maiden name or sells the family house, her children may take it as an implied rejection.
- Problems of etiquette arise. Does the young son escort his mother to social events? Should a daughter living with her now single father act as his hostess? How do adult children relate to a parent's new lover or spouse?
- Young adults tend to be extremely apprehensive about repeating the pattern of an unsuccessful marriage. They develop high ideals and a more practical than romantic view of wedlock.
- Older children are often under terrible pressures from competitive parental demands and expectations.

Counseling can help manage these problems. Unfortunately, while college counseling directors generally agree that help should be available to students of divorcing or divorced parents, the actual availability of such services is minimal. The only solution is outside counseling. Once again, parental guidance, love, and support will do much to ease the young adults' worries.

A Lifetime Effect on Children

There is no doubt that divorce plays an integral part in the shaping of a child's psyche and may affect a lifetime of values, emotions, and habits.

Advantages of Having Divorced Parents

From the children's standpoint, divorce can actually have some positive benefits, these include:

- Having parents who don't fight as much anymore.
- Relief from involvement in parental conflicts.
- More attention from *both* parents.
- Feeling stronger and more independent.
- Establishing a better support network between brothers and sisters.
- Looking forward to and enjoying visits by the noncustodial parent.
- Receiving more presents.
- Double celebrations of birthdays and holidays.
- Being cared for by a larger circle of people.
- Broader exposure through "weekend culture."

Disadvantages of Having Divorced Parents

The disadvantages to children of divorce include:

- Frequently being called upon to assume a very heavy load of household and caretaking responsibilities.
- Being forced to grow up a lot faster and sometimes lose their childhood and adolescence in the process. (Growing up faster is fine; having to always be "little adults" is not so good.)
- Additional pressure of trying to assume the role of the missing parent.
- Hurt and resentment from the inability to have some kind of control over what is happening to themselves.
- Playing one parent against the other. (This can happen in even the best-functioning of divorcing households.)

- Financial pressures that curtail normal recreation and social activities which, in turn, create resentment.
- Social stigmas to deal with through changes of financial status, school, and/or neighborhood.
- Dealing in doubles: two different living arrangements, social lives, mailings from school, church and community activities.

Probably the worst dilemma for children of all ages is feeling that they must take sides. It is even worse if parents actually force them to take sides. A division of loyalty can cause deep suffering.

If parents will treat each other civilly, love their children, and continue to be a part of their lives, the experience of divorce can be just another one of life's unfortunate wrinkles. When children of divorce are treated humanely and fairly, they grow up to be healthy, mature adults who face their parents' mistakes honestly and move on.

IMPACT OF YOUR DIVORCE ON OTHERS

No matter what kind of divorce you are experiencing:

- the so-called "amicable" divorce
- the surprise "Gotcha!" divorce
- the "significant other" divorce
- the "abusive" divorce, and so on,...

there are certain predictable responses on the part of those around you.

Every person you meet has been touched by divorce—if not personally, then the divorce of a relative, friend, coworker, or acquaintance. If you meet with hurtful responses, acknowledge prejudice as a part of living and move on to live as you see fit.

Impact on Extended Family

For our purpose, we define *extended family* as including parents, grandparents, sisters and brothers, aunts and uncles, cousins, and step- and foster relatives. Members of this group are probably going to:

- Take sides.
- Claim ownership directly (or indirectly) to specific family properties.
- Interfere, or at least try to.

- Feel confused about interim etiquette.
- Make use of grapevine communications ("What I heard is that...").
- Offer unwanted advice and even be judgmental.

With the older relatives, especially grandparents, there is the additional consideration that family is frequently the nucleus of their lives. Therefore, questions arise:

- What arrangements can be made to spend time with the family members they love?
- How can they continue to be emotionally or financially supportive to the divorcing adults without interfering in or undermining the process?
- Will they preserve or destroy their links with any or all members of the original family which is now splitting up?

Note Support systems are growing for the extended family. For example, Arizona State University offers a twelve-week course titled "Becoming a Better Grandparent." It focuses on understanding what life is like for single parent sons and daughters who are raising children alone. Also, some travel agencies run special trips for grandparents and their grandchildren.

Impact on Friends

"A friend is someone who likes you." During a divorce, friendships take on a new perspective. Some friends will feel helpless or that they are being put in an awkward position. Others come out of the woodwork to be pillars of strength. A few are the kind of friends who last a lifetime; others become fond memories.

Friends Can Be Wonderful

At their best, friends can:

- Give you support, when and where you least expect it.
- Blow the whistle when you are acting purely insane or overdoing the grievances.
- Be solid enough to stay friendly with both you and your former spouse.
- Will tolerate your depressions and soul-searching.
- Stick with you during crises.
- Keep in touch with you regularly to make sure you are okay.
- Be counted on, when appropriate, to keep their mouths shut to other friends.

Friends Can Be Disappointing

At their worst, friends:

- Are apt to take sides or are afraid that you will ask them to take sides.
- May interfere, particularly with their own version of pseudo-counseling.
- May tend to withdraw because you are no longer a couple.
- May perceive a divorcing woman as a threat to their own marriage, which she may not be.
- Often perceive a divorcing man as an eligible single, which he may not be.
- Can become too attentive, thereby creating an unhealthy dependency.
- May refuse to accept your decision because you seemed to have the perfect marriage.
- Could be frightened because you make them think about their own marital problems.

It is important to remember that as a divorce progresses, what you need from and can offer to friends will change. While the attitudes of your friends may vary, you will also be seeing them through different eyes.

Impact on Coworkers

Divorced people are not uncommon in the work place. Whether or not your coworkers have been through it themselves, they usually know enough to allow for some of the emotional spill-over that is bound to occur. Clients tell us that they will also let you know when they have had enough!

When you do begin your divorce, coworkers will usually give you a lot of support, especially if you have had a good business relationship with them. Frequently, they will be gracious enough to cover for you when you take time off to do your divorce business. They will be patient with your lapses in productivity and often fill in.

In most cases, coworkers will keep confidences and protect you from unwanted phone calls. They express an amazingly strong loyalty regardless of "who done what to whom."

However, if you have any control over the situation, try not to be in the middle of a divorce when it is time for a promotion. You will not be functioning at your best. And, for heaven's sake, if you are involved in any "office politics," be particularly circumspect in keeping your divorce business out of the work environment.

Community Reactions to Divorce

Divorce has become a fact of life. Evidence of this is everywhere from TV sitcoms (including a proposed show called *The Divorce Game*) to a whole new industry servicing singles.

Divorce has overloaded our family court system. Reforming it is going to take years. Grass-roots community programs are playing a large role in telling "the system" what is needed.

Typical Perceptions

There are always going to be people who believe that divorce is *bad*. For them, the divorce "stigma" symbolizes personal failure, poor judgment, and unwillingness or inability to adjust and "do the right thing." This kind of intolerance can cause feelings of inferiority and unworthiness at a time when self-esteem is already suffering.

Many organized religions deliver mixed messages on the subject of divorce.

The degree of negative pressure from the community depends primarily upon its size. In cities, divorce gets lost in the shuffle, whereas, in a small town, your divorce becomes everybody's business.

A woman is typically perceived to be the caretaker of the relationship. A divorce says she couldn't hold her marriage together. Without the backing of "Mrs.," she often becomes less than welcome wherever the loss of access to her husband's economic status or prestige is important.

A man is perceived to be the head of the household. A divorce says he couldn't control the situation. In the workplace, this is frequently seen as a negative for advancement.

Since the children of divorce are no longer in the minority in schools, they are less subject to prejudice than in prior years. There is even growing recognition that the children of divorce aren't necessarily "damaged goods." Unfortunately, there is relatively little guidance training for school personnel in how to deal with the emotional and practical issues resulting from divorce.

Support Systems

Support for the traumatized family is readily available through:

- Expanded public service agencies.
- Support programs sponsored by religious organizations.
- Specialized speakers, seminars, and talk shows.

- Increased divorce counseling and family therapy.
- The proliferation of relevant written materials.
- Singles organizations for:
  Dating or matchmaking
  Single parenting
  Recreation
  Vacation packages
  Education

INTERACTION WITH ONE'S SPOUSE DURING A DIVORCE

Divorce tends to bring out a couple's absolute worst behavior. In hot pursuit of possession or priority, both sexes may utilize any or all available power techniques. We have observed that these techniques generally differ by sex and usually reflect the gender socialization of our society.

Women tend to behave submissively. They often try to manipulate the situation by exhibiting a sense of moral superiority, reproachfulness, and helplessness. Women also tend to be less well-informed about the realities of the system. Once aroused to rage, they become less reasonable in both demands and responses.

Men tend to use dominance to coerce and manipulate. Men do this from a position of strength by using physical or mental abuse, economic power, and social sanctions as their major weapons. When caught unawares by a well-prepared spouse, they tend to fall back or fall apart.

You and your spouse have to reach a fair and reasonable agreement in order to have a successful divorce. You need to establish a format for negotiations that will keep you on track and get the divorce over with as gracefully as you both can manage it. This subject is addressed in Chapter 25.

Specific Cautions

Here is a list of cautions to consider when entering the divorce process:

- Do not give out personal information that could later be used to weaken your negotiations.
- Information you have on your spouse's personal life and finances should be shared only with your professional support team.
- Do not let yourself be drawn into arguments or conflicts with your spouse.

- Do not make any private agreements with your spouse or sign papers that you haven't discussed with your attorney.
- Be polite to everyone involved in the divorce process.
- Do not be taken in by attempts to win you over. Make informed decisions.
- Be open to a friendly relationship after the divorce.

Successful divorces are on the rise, helped by new concepts in family law such as no-fault divorce, equitable distribution of property, mediation, and joint custody of children. In many instances, divorced couples develop a genuine friendship with each other, sometimes for the first time.

GETTING PERSONALLY ORGANIZED: WHAT TO DO

"Alice was looking for direction and was startled to see the Cheshire Cat sitting on the branch of a tree.

'Cheshire Cat,' she said. 'Would you tell me please, which way I ought to go from here?'

'That depends a good deal on where you want to get to,' said the Cat.

'I don't much care where,' said Alice..

'Then it doesn't matter which way you go,' said the Cat."

LEWIS CARROLL
Alice's Adventure in Wonderland

Inadvertent describes the activities in lots of lives. We don't know many people who can say that where they are today is exactly where they set out to be.

Are you the kind of person who wonders what happened, watches things happen, or are you the sort who makes things happen? You've heard plenty of divorce war stories and know that months of business negotiating are about to take place. "One of these days I've got to get organized" is your second favorite saying, but where to begin?

GETTING STARTED

Action precedes motivation. If you are in a state of lethargy, you must prod yourself to act. A careless or disorganized person is easy prey. Don't agonize—Organize! Tension (not hard work) and worry (not doing) are what will drain you. The more you become enveloped in the divorce process, the more decisions you will have

to make. Organizing gives you the tools for managing multiple priorities.

Gathering Together or Purchasing Supplies

We encourage you to follow our system for organizing your materials and information. Specific types of products will make the business part of your divorce much easier. **FORM-ula 3: Divorce Business Supplies** is divided into two parts: *Basic Office Supplies* and *Paper Products*. Use this as a checklist to gather together the items you already own and as a reference while shopping.

Setting Up the System

A unique feature of *The Divorce Decisions Workbook* is its organized system for the business of divorce. All of your divorce information and the FORM-ulas go into your portable file box. Use this as a master filing system. The accordion file holds expense information and the step rack will be used for what you are working on currently. The beauty of this system is that, once set up, all of your important information will be at your fingertips.

Master File Box
Label your Pendaflex® files as follows:

Personal papers   Children

Education   Credit card list

Household inventory and appraisals	Personal banking
Money loaned to others	Money borrowed from others
Investments	Applications and financial statements
Titles and deeds	Medical insurance
Life insurance	Personal property insurance
Tax returns	Employment history and resumes
Employer policies and benefits	Proprietorship, partnership, professional corporation, family-owned business
Income records	Retirement dollars

When the files have been set up, store the two FORM-ulas that you have already completed. **FORM-ula 1: Marriage Assessment** is filed in Personal, and **FORM-ula 2: Observing Children's Divorce Behavior** in the file labeled Children.

Accordion File

Your accordion file will be for collecting expense information. The data will be used to develop your divorce agreement worksheets. Set up this part of the system by labeling the accordian file for paid bills and canceled checks in the following categories:

Banking	Children's expenses
Clothing	Contributions
Education	Entertainment
Food	Gifts
Housing	Household maintenance and services
Household, major purchases	Insurances
Loan repayments	Medical and dental
Miscellaneous	Special expenses
Taxes	Transportation
Vacations	

Step Rack

Label file folders for your step rack as follows:

Action

Current banking

Current bills

Pending

To be copied

Rolodex

Use your Rolodex to record names, addresses, and phone numbers. Designate a different color card for each of the following categories:

Personal friends

Divorce professionals

Relatives

Family professionals (business, medical, etc.)

A personal *Who's Who*

Transfer existing systems to this new format; staple old to new, if it seems easier. This may be a good time to update your information.

Note As you are proceeding further into the divorce process, be sure to record your increasing network of names and resources onto your Rolodex.

Note You can order *110 Ideas for Organizing your Business Life* and *111 Ideas for Organizing your Household* from:

Organizing Solutions, Inc.
226 Winding Lane
Bedford Hills, NY 10507
1-800-666-DESK

STARTING YOUR DIVORCE BUSINESS

If you want a better life, you must assume that you not only deserve it, but will find the way to get it. Getting it is going to be some of the hardest work you have ever done. Whether you have made the decision to divorce or it has been made for you, begin now to use this book to help your preparation.

By following each chapter in its entirety, you will organize both your divorce and your life. The workbook will also assist you in evaluating what you need and what is likely to happen in your divorce as opposed to what you may desire or expect. This preparation will allow you to make educated choices.

Chapter 5
DESCRIBING THE PLAYERS IN YOUR DRAMA

Introspection is imperative to your direction and survival in the divorce process. We have designed *The Divorce Decisions Workbook* to make the task possible instead of overwhelming.

For the purpose of organizing the business ahead, you need to take a look at basic information about yourself and your family. The FORM-ulas in this chapter present a format for organizing your family data. They will be your private resource from which you can draw information as you need it. These FORM-ulas will be kept in your master file labeled Personal. When there is missing data or information that you are waiting for, make note of this in the Pending section of your step rack.

FORM-ula 4: PROFILE SELF AND SPOUSE

By completing **FORM-ula 4: Profile Self and Spouse** (one for each party), you will be forced to think from both sides. The clearer psychological perspective will give you greater leverage in decision-making and negotiating.

As you read the forms, start right in and put down as much information as you can. You can finish these FORM-ulas as you become more organized and progress with your divorce business.

FORM-ula 5: MYSELF

Begin to think about "The Me Nobody Knows." By completing **FORM-ula 5: Myself** at this time, you will get in touch with ideas that will become part of your thinking as you work your way through the rest of this book. The cumulative effect of what you are learning about yourself will be especially helpful when you come to Chapter 22.

FORM-ula 6: PROFILE CHILDREN

During times of stress, the tendency to draw a blank on information is always present. It is important to have the vital statistics on your children readily available. The profile for each child provides an excellent starting point for negotiations about custody and financial arrangements.

Fill in a copy of **FORM-ula 6: Profile Children** for every child in your household. Include stepchildren, adopted children, children from a previous relationship (marital or not), and children for whom you or your spouse have legal responsibility (guardianship or foster relationship).

If any of these children do not yet have their Social Security numbers, apply for them now. Find the local Social Security office number in your phone book and call for current procedures. Getting a Social Security number always takes much longer than anticipated. Be sure to have it by the time you claim the child as a dependent/tax deduction. It is also used for the enforcement of support orders.

FORM-ula 7: CHILD IDENTIFICATION

It is important for each child to be easily identified. Use **FORM-ula 7: Child Identification** to gather pertinent information. Keep the original document in your Children file and use copies as needed. Attachments to this FORM-ula should include a:

- Current photo of the child.
- Copy of the child's signature.
- Set of thumb or fingerprints

FORM-ula 8: EXTENDED FAMILY

If you have one or more extended family members living in the home with you or closely involved in family activities, you will want to fill out a copy of **FORM-ula 8: Extended Family** for each of them. This is especially important if you are financially interdependent.

FORM-ula 9: CHRONOLOGICAL MARITAL HISTORY

Throughout the book we deal with both the practical issues of divorce (ending the marriage and beginning a single life) and its legal dimensions (court-related activities and judgment rulings). A comprehensive description of your marriage will help you to develop your personal objectives as well as provide important information for your attorney.

Just the Facts, Please

In any piece of reportorial writing there might be the tendency to deviate from the old rule of Who, What, When, Where and Why; that is, to try to rewrite the marriage from *your* point of view. (When we hear two personal accounts about the same marriage, we begin to wonder about history itself.) Short memories may preserve good consciences, but please write the facts and include as many dates as possible.

To jog your memory, don't overlook old address books, calendars, letters, family photos, and old greeting cards. You will be sorting through memorabilia anyway. The touches of humor and reminders of happier times that you may uncover will help you regain your perspective.

A Family Review

Use **FORM-ula 9: Chronological Marital History** to record information. Begin your story with the time prior to your marriage. Tell about your meeting, courtship, dreams, and plans. Go on to describe your wedding, honeymoon, and activities during the early years.

Note the various changes in circumstance that came about during the marriage. Write about moves, jobs, becoming parents, changes in your sex life, health problems, and unforeseen difficulties. Write about relationships with your extended family.

It is important to show the development of your present lifestyle. Include the current division of labors and responsibilities in your household and family and how they may have changed over the years. Write about your social life.

Develop a history of your family finances. Who makes the decisions and who handles the checkbook? What assets and liabilities have you accumulated along the way? How were they acquired or lost? Don't forget to include gifts and contributions from family or friends.

If you or your spouse have received counseling, separately or together, write about why you sought it and what you feel the results have been.

Highlight Important Information

When you are finished, use different colored highlighters to mark the following:

- Important data to retain for business purposes.
- Important data to retain for sanity and self-esteem.
- Important data to let go of emotionally.

FORM-ula 10: CHILD CARE

Decisions will have to be made for support and custody of the children. **FORM-ula 10: Child Care** will indicate who has been responsible for the needs of the children, past and present: mother, father, sibling, relative, neighbor, friend, or paid caretaker. This type of information is used to determine future child care responsibilities that will be incorporated into the separation agreement.

Chapter 6
RECOGNIZING EXTENUATING CIRCUMSTANCES

There are some special issues of life that must be faced as quickly as they are recognized. They must be dealt with before they cause any more harm. Such issues include:

- Substance abuse and addictions.
- Physical or mental abuse.
- Marital rape.
- Abandonment.
- Overpowering pressure from spouse for divorce.
- Insufficient legal support.
- Inequities:
    Financial control.
    Earning capacity.
    Education.
    Professional or family power.
- The use of personal blackmail

If you recognize any of these as an underlying cause of your divorce, you need legal help and emotional support to formulate a clear plan of action. Therapy is suggested.

As you read this section, keep the following questions in mind:

- Is there a continuing danger of physical injury to you or your children?
- Do you feel that you or your spouse need psychological help?
- Is such help available to you? Do you have the power to see that your spouse gets help?
- Are there resources in your community that are readily available to you and your spouse?

As unpleasant as it may be, consider each of the following topics in terms of whether or not they apply to you or your family. If they do, be sure to read about the preliminary steps to be taken.

SUBSTANCE ABUSE

Substance abuse is a growing problem. Alcohol is the *number one* drug of choice for all ages. One out of four American adults (65 million) admits that alcohol or drug abuse has created family troubles.

"The stereotype of the alcoholic as a drunk, lying in a gutter on skid row is a myth. 95% of all alcoholics are employed. 45% of them have management positions. 50% of them have college degrees." This information was published in a 1989 Alcoholism and Drug Dependency Newsletter.

Addiction

What is addiction? *Addiction* is defined as an irresistible compulsion to use a drug habitually and regularly (usually increasing both dose and frequency) despite knowing the serious physical or psychological side-effects and accepting the real possibility that it will totally disrupt one's system of values and personal relationships.

Drug **use** leads to

tolerance which leads to

abuse and finally to

chemical dependency and

addiction.

The saddest fact about alcohol and drug dependency is that they are *treatable* diseases, but often the one with the problem refuses to acknowledge that it *is* a problem. Nothing can be done until that person admits to having a problem and seeks treatment.

Sometimes a couple will marry without knowledge or understanding that there is a problem with substance abuse. When one spouse has a problem with some type of substance abuse, eventually the other spouse does become aware of it.

Denial of Abuse and Addiction

Denial is one of the major symptoms of alcoholism and drug abuse. Both types of users say, "I can stop any time I want to." "I don't have a problem." And the ones who say this genuinely believe it! Because of the marital relationship and the desire to preserve it, the spouse of the addicted one is usually talked into believing it, too. In the beginning, the nonaddicted spouse denies that it is seriously affecting the relationship, or the relationship with family and close friends. Sometimes the denial goes on for such a long period of time that it becomes hard to remember life before the habit started.

An enormous amount of time and energy is spent reinforcing this "lack of a problem." The mate of the spouse in denial might just as well be an abuser, too, because neither one is going anywhere but *down*. This is called enabling or codependency. Both spouses have been gradually capitulating to the addiction.

Recognizing the Addiction

If you even suspect yourself of having an addiction, by all means seek help. Whatever the addiction, today there is a group for it. Best known are the twelve-step programs of Alcoholics Anonymous, Al Anon, and Alateen.

Resources for Information

There are excellent basic pamphlets available for almost every kind of addiction: so called street drugs (cocaine, marijuana, crack, and so forth); prescription drugs; alcohol; overeating; sex; gambling; and codependency. You can get them from:

- Drug and alcohol abuse centers.
- Churches and social work organizations.
- Counselors, psychologists, and therapists.
- Hospital outpatient clinics.

These pamphlets provide pertinent information describing addictions in all stages. They tell where treatment can be obtained and usually provide a questionnaire to help the reader identify an addiction. Whether or not the addict is ready to stop, the material frequently plants a fertile seed.

Painful Family Systems

Here are some guidelines that describe a marriage troubled by an addicted spouse, as suggested by material from the *National Council on Alcoholism*:

- Little or no communication.
- Internalized feelings.
- Dependency in relationships.
- Use of manipulation and control.
- Jealousy and suspicion.
- Unpleasant and tense atmosphere.
- Frequent illness, apathy.
- Disorganization, undependability.
- Disintegrating values.
- Denial of problems.
- Away from home a lot.
- Erratic spending.
- Pointless and continual arguing.
- Unwillingness to face facts.

Divorce and the Addict

Even if there is a genuine attempt to stop the addiction and change the patterns, there may still be relapses or the taking up of another type of addiction. According to statistics, full recovery is unlikely to occur unless there is a 24-hour-a-day support system available to the individual.

Divorcing an addict can be difficult and even dangerous. The longer you have been in an addicted relationship, the stronger the support network you will require.

Referral Services

Drug and alcohol dependency councils exist everywhere today. Just pick up a phone book in any town in the United States, Canada, and many foreign countries to get a hot line (emergency) number. Services that are available include:

- Information and referral.
- Individual counseling for substance abusers and their families.
- Intervention services.

The first thing you must be able to do is recognize abuse. Studies indicate that when there is a pattern of abuse over a long period of time, victims no longer recognize it or feel that they have been in such a situation. They may also feel that they are currently doing something to deserve such abusive treatment. Too often the pattern of behavior has become so ingrained that it is an accepted part of life.

EMOTIONAL ABUSE

Emotional abuse (sometimes referred to as mental cruelty) is harder to recognize than physical abuse, but that does not eliminate the likelihood of injury or permanent damage. Physical wounds are obvious and can heal but mental wounds must first be detected.

Normal Behavior or an Abuse Syndrome

Almost everyone is abusive at one time or another. There is a fine line between being emotionally volatile and being abusive. Many couples hurl insults at each other, throw things, even strike out at one another as a means of expressive communication. To a degree, this behavior is acceptable as long as neither spouse feels like or becomes the "victim."

In an abuse syndrome, the abuser behaves in a repeated pattern:

1. Tension and anger
2. Explosions of violence
3. Tenderness and offers of apology

Both abuser and victim often convince themselves that *it won't happen again.*

Telling the difference

Use **FORM-ula 11: Emotional Abuse** to evaluate the emotional condition of your marital relationship. Abuse is prevalent. That does not make abuse normal or acceptable.

Note In states that recognize a fault divorce, so-called mental cruelty is often used as the reason. Courts often seem willing to accept minor problems as sufficient evidence to justify grounds for divorce.

PHYSICAL ABUSE

According to FBI statistics, violence between lovers erupts continuously. Ninety-four times out of 100, a woman is the victim. Although all physical abuse does not result in death, a woman is more likely to be killed by a male partner than by any other person.

Note Marital rape and willful exposure to sexually transmitted diseases are now recognized as spouse abuse.

How to Handle Spouse Abuse

If you are living with an abusive spouse, there are a number of things to do for your own protection:

- Find a safe place for emergency money, car keys, and important documents so you can get them in a hurry.
- Arrange for a safe place where you and your children can go on a moment's notice, such as the home of a close friend or relative, or an emergency shelter.

- Memorize the phone number of the local police department.

Asking for Help

The only behavior you can control is your own. Asking for your own help is an important first step. Help is available through crisis intervention centers, social service agencies, most religious institutions, and counselors and therapists. (If the only advice you receive is to "Go back and make your marriage work," go to another source of help. You need concrete information.)

The Domestic Violence Hotline is 1-800-333-SAFE (7233). The hearing impaired can call 1-800-873-3636 (equipped with T.D.D.). These lines are answered 24 hours a day, seven days a week and can refer callers to local resources throughout the United States, Puerto Rico, the Virgin Islands, Hawaii, Alaska, and some overseas locations.

Hotlines were established to network shelters and legal safeguards for women in abusive relationships. (We are not aware of comparable resources available to men.) This grass-roots form of survival has come about in recognition that:

- Police are limited in training and authority.

- The court system is slow.

- Judges are often disbelieving when the accused adult "looks normal" or is a community professional.

- Evidence is frequently suppressed during hearings.

- Many attorneys won't touch the issue (it's a lose-lose situation for them professionally and financially).

The Domestic Violence Hotline refers you to organizations that will help you work within the legal system to the extent that it is possible. These organizations offer access to court advocacy programs where trained lay persons go through the legal process with you. They also have access to higher authorities, as needed.

The availability of these shelters and support systems is the good news. The bad news is that when women take the initiative to help themselves (and thereby break the power that their men have had over them), the men feel this immediately and often react with increased rage.

Recognizing this fact, there is an underground protection system that can be put into effect when all other measures have failed.

To take advantage of these resources, you need to contact the Domestic Violence Hotline and identify yourself and the kind of help you need. If you are not known to them, they cannot help you.

Protective Action

Here are some other immediate steps to take when confronting domestic violence:

- Act quickly and decisively.
- Save evidence.
- Never take the law into your own hands.
- Seek legal assistance.
- Ask about a court temporary protection order.

Act quickly and decisively. Failure to take action may be seen by the courts and others as evidence of your acquiescence towards abuse. It will also encourage increased and worsening attacks and prolong your misery.

Save evidence. Seek immediate medical assistance and advice for any traumatic episode. Be sure that injuries are documented in writing by the medical professionals. Whenever possible, include color photos of injuries and damage to any property. Save as evidence such items as torn or bloody clothing. If there were witnesses, notify the authorities so that legally acceptable testimony can be obtained. Incidents of spouse abuse should be officially recorded.

Note The burden of pressing charges or seeking redress will be on the victim.

Never take the law into your own hands! You could face possible criminal charges and a jail sentence if you do. Always check with your local hotline for directions about the best way to proceed in your particular area. If you have been attacked, call the police for immediate legal protection.

Note It is only recently that married individuals have been granted the right of police protection from a violent spouse.

Seek legal assistance immediately. The threat of court action appears to be a major deterrent to a repeat performance of physical abuse. Before beginning court action, consider having an attorney send your spouse a warning letter. The letter would advise your spouse of the steps you intend to take if the abuse continues.

Note Spouse abuse is considered a crime in most states. Once recorded, district attorneys can prosecute even if the reporting spouse subsequently decides not to press charges.

Ask about a Court Temporary Restraining Order. This is issued by the family court in your county. While not a final solution to the problem, it sometimes gives temporary relief and may help you to maintain a degree of peace while you are moving forward with your divorce. This order instructs the abusive spouse to refrain from any and all contact for a specified period of time. (Tragically, it doesn't always work.)

CHILD ABUSE

While child abuse is seldom the primary reason for seeking a divorce, if it exists, it is a major factor in custody arrangements.

No Reasonable Explanation

Child abuse is damage to a child for which there is no reasonable explanation. Some of its aspects include:

Nonaccidental injury

Severe beatings resulting in fractures or bruises

Burns or other disfigurements

Bites, shaking, choking

Neglect (failure to provide basic necessities)

Inadequate food, clothing, shelter

Inappropriate medical care

Improper supervision (including from sitters or relatives)

Abandonment

Sexual molestation

Rape

Incest

Genital fondling

Exhibitionism

Emotional abuse

Constant teasing or belittling

Verbal attacks, including shouting and threats

Lack of love, support, guidance

Nonverbal Signals

Children who have been abused may not talk about it, especially if there is already tension in the household or if they have been threatened into secrecy. Frequently related nonverbal signals include:

- Withdrawal, secretiveness.
- Self-destructiveness.
- Neglect of body and clothing.
- Play-acting abusive behavior (for a tot, use of toys and dolls; for an adolescent, taking on a new role).
- Noticeable deterioration of health.
- Manic need for security and reassurance.
- Regression to former behavior or quantum leap into "adult" behavior.
- Expressions of specific suspicions from others.

If you suspect that your child has been abused, seek immediate professional support. A full page of community service telephone numbers is in the front of your phone book.

Once you have found the professional help that you need, the procedures will be essentially the same as described in the preceding section on spouse abuse. If speed is of the essence or the situation is particularly complicated, remember that there are underground resources. You will discover these contacts through networking.

A Two-Edged Sword

Legally, child abuse is a two-edged sword. It is hard to prove, but once a case goes to court it becomes doubly difficult to disprove. Children today are precocious. While they seldom want to lie, either to incriminate or to protect, warring spouses leave a wide open space in which a child can practice clear-cut manipulation. A child can also be coached by a vindictive spouse.

Even when child abuse is strongly suspected by people from outside the immediate family (neighbors and teachers have a particularly good vantage point for observation), others are often reluctant to report suspicions or testify against adults. Very often, they are parents themselves. They are in the position of balancing the need for the child to be in a safe environment with the possibility of wrongfully accusing someone of child abuse. There is also the fear of being sued by the accused parent and a desire to avoid becoming involved in a complicated criminal trial.

When seeming evidence of child abuse becomes a legal issue, the child-protection system of the courts has the ability to take over. The quality of these systems varies.

CHILD SNATCHING

The major reason for child snatching is animosity and retribution against the ex-spouse. It is rarely the child's welfare that motivates this action. In most of the documented cases, it is the noncustodial parent who abducts the child.

Circumstances Favoring Thoughts of Abduction

There is a higher likelihood of abduction when one or more of the following circumstances exists:

- Job mobility.
- Lack of roots in the community.
- Personal assistance from friends or relatives out-of-state.
- Job dissatisfaction.
- Frustration and anger over current custody arrangements.
- Disagreement over lifestyle and child rearing methods.
- Refusal to share parenting.
- Availability of financial resources.
- Pressure from creditors.
- Delinquent support payments.
- Resentment about having to make support payments.

Preventive Measures

If you feel that your spouse might be thinking of abducting your child (based upon threats or past or present behaviors), recognize that it could happen and take preventive measures. We suggest the following Action Checklist:

- ☐ Instruct the child's teachers, sitters, and anyone else who might function as a substitute guardian for your child to follow explicit directions regarding:

    Daily schedule and unexpected changes.

    Adults who are authorized to spend time with children.

- ☐ Schedule regular updates for contact list.

- ☐ Talk with your child. Children usually sense when something is afoot.

- ☐ Teach your child to keep you informed of her or his whereabouts and of the phone numbers of places they are visiting, particularly when there are changes in plans.

- ☐ For emergencies, consider giving your child a telephone credit card and making sure that the child memorizes it. (People don't readily allow children to make long distance phone calls).

- ☐ Develop an innocuous Mayday message for your child to use when unable to talk with you under normal circumstances. If you cannot be reached, is there someone who is always dependably available to take this message and search you out? For instance, a relative or close friend, or a pediatrician or clergyperson.

- ☐ Get information on the legal process in your community regarding child snatching. Find out what the law will allow you to do to protect yourself and your child.

- ☐ Obtain a family court decree. Properly drafted separation agreements protect the rights of both parents with respect to custody and will often inhibit illegal behavior.

- ☐ Update information on your child. Use **FORM-ula 6: Profile Children.**

Moving Your Child

If you think you have good reasons to move a child without waiting for legal sanction, or you feel that out-and-out abduction is the only solution to your divorce problems, get immediate professional advice and counseling.

THREATS

Threats are an outlet for the emotions and frustrations of a lost cause. They spew forth out of sadness, anger, and frustration. A threat may or may not be carried out. Some are more harmless than others. If a threat is the dragon's fire of some sudden and impulsive inner hostility, a well-placed dash of legal cold water can generally quench it quickly. If, however, a threat is symptomatic of a more serious problem that has existed throughout the marriage, it could signal trouble. Deal with it as you would with any other type of physical or emotional abuse.

The ordinary kinds of threats used during divorce aren't very original. In fact, they're almost clichés of the divorce process. Some common threats are listed below:

- *"I'll go to jail before I'll pay you a dime!"* In reality, there are a number of ways to enforce support obligations. There has even been legislation enacted which will reach out to a supporting spouse in another state. Contempt of court could mean a jail sentence, so the spouse usually pays voluntarily.

- *"Unless you play this my way, you'll never get a dime."* This person has not reckoned with the newer rulings on equitable distribution of money and property.

- *"I'll quit my job before I'll pay you that kind of money."* It is helpful to have a witness to this kind of statement. If a documented threat is carried out, the financial obligations are not legally eliminated.

- *"When the judge sees what my expenses are, he'll never give you the support you want."* Manipulated financial statements usually don't work.

- *"I will consider a reconciliation if you sign the agreement."* If so, why sign an agreement? No dice.

- *"Why are you doing this to me? I'll have nothing left and nothing to live for!"* The answer is that you are entitled to an equitable separation agreement.

- *"If you don't do this my way, the judge will make us sell everything."* The court will not order the sale of an asset unless there is an economic reason that is in the best interest of *both* parties.

- *"Your attorney is only out to get our money, so why don't we use one attorney?"* This is clearly a "divide and conquer" technique. Don't buy it. Just make sure you get the right attorney. We'll tell you how to do this in Chapter 25.

- *"I'll tell them all about _____ and then you'll never get the children!"* If you think that this could be a valid issue, be sure to discuss this threat candidly with your attorney. Do not ignore it and simply hope that this threat will go away.

- *"You'll never see the kids again!"* We have already discussed child snatching. Failure to allow visitation can be a justifiable reason for the courts to change the custody from one parent to the other.

If any of these threats are being used against you, it would be a good idea to keep a running diary of occasions, dates, times, places, any witnesses, and a summary of the conversations that occurred.

Note Never use a tape recorder without consent. The information is inadmissible in court and can also be a felony which carries a heavy fine.

If *You* Are Doing the Threatening

If you find yourself uttering threats, do two things:

- Get legal advice on the consequences.
- Arrange for counseling to deal with your anger and frustration.

A FEW ADDITIONAL CIRCUMSTANCES

There are a few additional circumstances that may affect the outcome of your divorce negotiations. You'll find them listed in our **FORM-ula 12: Current Perspectives.** Begin thinking about them now because the conclusions you reach will be helpful in making the decisions discussed in Section 6, "Big Picture" Planning and in Chapter 22.

Section III

PULLING YOURSELF AND YOUR FAMILY TOGETHER

Life is about change and making choices. Change is difficult because it means letting go of what was. Until we do, however, we can't begin to appreciate what is.

Everyone can use some "feel bad" time before moving on. This may be a necessary part of your divorce process.

The real world is still out there and the next test is whether you will settle for merely coping. Changes will begin when you see the next step. You will make mistakes. Plans will take the wrong turn. Learn from them.

PLANNING GOVERNED BY TIME

Getting organized goes hand-in-hand with *planning governed by time*. Let's face it—you get a 168-hour week just the same as everybody else. How will you manage to get the most out of this time? How will you handle your urge to procrastinate?

Getting organized can be a time-consuming pain-in-the-neck, but good planning is well worth the effort. There are certain tricks to getting and staying organized, including the following:

- Have a FORM-ula for just about everything.
- Make realistic lists of things to be done. Just seeing items crossed off gives a sense of accomplishment.
- Get to know your up and down times. Are you a morning or night person? When do you do your best work?

- Stay with your day-to-day schedule as closely as you can so things don't pile up.
- Give yourself permission to withdraw from the pressure (by sleeping, reading, watching TV or a movie). When things become overwhelming, *stop*.
- Be gentle, patient, and fair with yourself. At the same time, be persistent.

GIVING YOURSELF PEP TALKS

Problems have a way of surfacing at the worst possible times and always need resourceful solutions. While you can't give yourself hugs, you can give yourself pep talks:

- "I know getting organized is important."
- "I have the opportunity to do a really good job."
- "I can make my own plans."
- "I am a fully responsible person."
- "I can grow and develop on the job!"

A DIVORCE SURVIVAL AND GROWTH PROGRAM

For the purpose of helping you to organize a *divorce survival and growth program*, we are addressing

43

ways that will help you to prepare others for your divorce.

Personal growth issues are discussed by using a variation on psychologist Abraham Maslow's definitions of human needs:

- Physiological needs: hunger, thirst, rest.
- Safety: shelter, avoidance of pain and anxiety, general physical security.
- Need to belong and feel loved: affection and intimacy with family and friends.

- Self-actualization: to be fully what you can be; to engage your curiosity, explore knowledge, enjoy aesthetics.

The most rapid personal growth often takes place within the compassionate and professional environment of a counselor's office. This section would not be complete without a discussion of that possibility.

Those divorcing couples with young children will find both information and ideas relating to becoming a single-parent household in Chapter 13.

Chapter 7
DISCUSSING YOUR DIVORCE

"Rumor travels faster, but it don't stay put as long as truth."

WILL ROGERS, HUMORIST

Divorce is a paradox because it is both very public and very private. You must decide how you want to be perceived during this period. When you are out and about, people will be watching your behavior and your appearance. Your style will be evident in everything you say and do.

CONTROL OF YOUR DIVORCE INFORMATION

People like to talk about divorce. We recommend that you take control of divorce information before the gossip takes over. (No matter what goes wrong, there is always someone who knew it would.) Family and friends will want to be supportive. They need to hear from you personally instead of through the grapevine.

Promise yourself not to be pressured into discussing things you are not yet ready or willing to talk about. Take these steps:

■ Decide how much information you want to share and with whom.

■ Think about what you want or need from each person with whom you are talking.

■ Be prepared to guide people to sources of correct information – pamphlets, books, professionals, and so forth.

Try to anticipate how others will react to your news. You are right to be afraid that some people won't understand. They won't. Others will offer opinions and advice that might sound good and make you feel comfortable because you already agree with them or they come from someone you like and respect. Be aware that their ideas may not be right for you in your current situation.

TELLING YOUR CHILDREN ABOUT THE PLANS

If you have been contemplating divorce, your children have been experiencing anxiety. When the decision to divorce has been made, they deserve to be told by the parents who love them. Your children should not get this information from anyone else! The first decision is whether to be together when the children are told or for each parent to talk with the children separately.

Tell the Truth

Regardless of whether you tell the children together or separately, tell them the truth about what is going

45

to happen. Be clear in your statements. If you know for sure that the decision to divorce is final, reinforce that fact. At the same time, reassure your children that you will continue to love and care for them.

We mortals do strange things when we're in emotional pain. So, this is just a reminder that it is not a great idea to present your divorce decision to your children before bedtime, before an important event such as an exam or before they leave home for camp, school, or a trip.

How to Tell Your Children

Here are some tips for telling your children about your decision to divorce:

- Assure them that they are loved.
- State briefly your reasons for the divorce and avoid elaborate details of your marital problems.
- Try not to put down the other parent. Remember that you are divorcing each other, not the children.
- Stress that they are in no way responsible for the divorce.
- Describe basic changes to expect such as which parent is moving out and where the children will be living.
- Try to give them a time frame for the divorce.

Of course, if your children are infants or very small children, your method of communicating will be different; it will be a more direct expression of *feeling* than an articulation of thoughts and feelings. According to some psychologists, infants feel and react to changes in the atmosphere around them. Speaking gently and honestly, even to babies, has a positive affect even though what you will say to them is obviously much more limited.

What Could Children Learn?

A lot of divorced parents would really like to tell their children something quite different from what they actually say. If parents truly want to teach their children positive lessons about marriage, they should begin by debunking the myths of "magical happiness," effortless relationships, "opposites attracting," and the like. Personalities change in a marriage. "Stuff happens."

How much more would your children understand about marriage if you told them:

- "I thought marriage was like a romance novel or a sitcom, but I learned differently."

- "I grew up pretending to be one kind of an image and ended up marrying another image."
- "We didn't know how to share the responsibilities."
- "We didn't discuss our value systems."
- "Getting stuck in a marriage with the wrong partner is no fun!"
- "I thought my happiness was dependent upon someone else."
- "I shouldn't have gotten married right out of school. I should have spent time by myself first, getting to know the world, my work, and my own life."
- "My spouse was never my best friend. We fell in love and didn't wait to see if we could be friends as well."
- "We didn't learn how to deal with our conflicts or how to talk about them."
- "We didn't expect to change and find ourselves wanting different things from life."
- "I married because I thought I should, not because I was ready."
- "I wasn't honest with myself. I thought I could be what someone else wanted me to be."
- "I wish I had dated more. I really didn't know enough about marriage or the kind of person I wanted to marry."
- "I didn't realize how much children would change our lives. We didn't know how much time and responsibility it would take."

Could your children learn from your experience?

BREAKING THE NEWS TO YOUR FAMILY

Your Parents

It is never easy to tell the parents who raised you and watched you take your wedding vows that you are now getting a divorce. You certainly don't want them to hear it from anyone else, so tell them you must.

If you are fortunate enough to have parents who offer you unconditional love (and are sensible and wise in the bargain), you will have a good sounding board for your separation agreement. They will be there for you whether or not your divorce comes as a surprise. If you have had open communication with them all along, you will simply be keeping them informed of events as they evolve.

If there is emotional or geographic distance between you and your parents, it will be harder to decide how much you want or need to share about your divorce. They might not be able to give you the kind of support that you are expecting.

If your parents were divorced themselves, it is hard to tell what their reaction might be. Remembering their own experience, they are most likely to understand and empathize with you. But they could also blame themselves because they couldn't make their own marriage work. What you don't need right now is a double guilt trip!

It is sometimes hardest to tell the parents who have succeeded in making their marriage work. You don't know whether the reaction will be totally disciplinary, such as "You can make your marriage work if you really want to," or wistful, such as "I wish we had had the courage to do what you're doing."

You are taking one of the toughest steps of your life and you need all the support and love you can get. If your parents cannot understand or give you the support and sympathy you need, you might want to go elsewhere.

Your Spouse's Parents

From your point of view, it's a wait-and-see proposition. It stands to reason that if you have had a good relationship with your in-laws during the marriage, they will probably want to maintain some kind of connection with you, especially if there are children involved.

If your divorce is an amicable one, your ex-in-laws will probably remain friends with you even after your spouse remarries or until, under the normal course of events, the friendship fades.

If the divorce is adversarial, divided loyalties can become hard to live with. Even if you have had a positive relationship with your spouse's parents they cannot usually remain impartial. Most often, they will take your spouse's side. In any event, if there is "family" property involved, there will probably be ownership claims.

Sharing Divorce Plans With Other Family Members

It is always better for you to be the one to tell your brothers and sisters about your plans for divorce. Be prepared to tell them what they can do to help you.

If you have a special closeness with a sibling, you may even want this brother or sister to be with you when you tell your parents. You may want that sibling to tell the rest of the family members for you. If so, give them some notes to use. One thing you do not need right now is a lot of misinformation flying around.

If you choose to tell extended family members yourself, be careful not to accidentally leave someone out. Making a list in advance could save hard feelings later on.

FRIENDS AND CONFIDANTS

Once the decision to divorce has been made, you will not have a lot of time to spend talking about it. In addition to getting organized, you will need plenty of rest and privacy.

The reality of your plan to divorce is not usually a surprise to your closest friends. Either they have intuited that something was up, or you will have already taken them into your confidence. So, what do you tell friends who have been part of your social life?

Make a List

If it seems socially correct or "politically" useful that you notify certain people about your divorce, decide who gets a call and who gets a note. Make a list of these people and check off their names as you notify them.

Anticipate phone calls and choose times to discuss the divorce that are convenient for you. When anyone starts to talk at an inopportune moment about the circumstances of the divorce, learn to put them off. Say, "I'd prefer to talk about this another time." Protect yourself from personal opinions and emotional reactions. When telling about your divorce, keep your messages simple and direct.

Expect a Variety of Reactions from Near and Far

Soon after the news is out, you will get a variety of reactions. You will hear from people who:

- Think it is their duty to sympathize.
- Just want to try to dig up the *real* dirt.
- Have a romantic eye on you or your spouse.

Some of the people you least expect to hear from will become staunch allies. You'll find that your true friends are the ones who:

- Express concern for the welfare of you and your children.
- Offer sociability and entertainment.
- Offer empathy because they have been there and know what it is like.
- Admire your courage and offer support.
- Have specific services to offer as friends.

INFORMING COWORKERS

In your professional environment, you will be the best judge of who is friend or foe. What you tell about your divorce is up to you.

If you work in a close-knit team environment, you may wish to have a short meeting in which you can discuss the facts. At this time, you can ask that phone calls be screened and make arrangements for work coverage when you need time off to do your divorce business.

If you work in a more formal environment, you will need to make similar arrangements with a trusted coworker. Discuss your divorce plans only with those who need to know.

Regardless of your emotional state (be it happy or sad), the workplace is not a therapy support group and shouldn't be used as such. However, you may want to contact the personnel manager (or owner, in a small company) about the policy on employee assistance programs.

Chapter 8
PHYSIOLOGICAL NEEDS

It is going to take a while to adjust to your altered status. By first taking good care of yourself, you will be able to handle the tasks ahead and care for those who are dependent upon you. If ever there was a time in your life to treat yourself the very best that you can, this is it!

MENTAL AND PHYSICAL SURVIVAL

Keep life as simple as possible. Most humans don't know what every other animal instinctively does know, that it is necessary to back off and give yourself time to "lick your wounds." People also need time to think.

Fatigue

Fatigue is usually an everpresent companion, along with ragged edges and an unusual appetite that demands either too much or not enough food. A case of the slows is sometimes pure ole procrastination. However, it also may be your body's way of telling you that you need more rest, a better diet, some exercise, or more quiet time to relax your overworked

head. (Wouldn't it be nice if there was an old-fashioned Grandma service out there to bring you chicken soup and make it all better?)

Illness

Psychosomatic illnesses can run rampant throughout any difficult period and divorce certainly qualifies for that category. Emotional tensions turn into physical complaints (aching back, rashes, queasiness, frequent headaches, hair loss, etc.). Allergies flare up under stress. We all seem to automatically become tired when there is something unpleasant to deal with.

Manners of speech frequently reflect one's mental state: "...burned up," "...a pain-in-the-neck," "...a headache just thinking about it," and so forth.

About Those Physical Symptoms

One way to ease concerns about physical symptoms is to get a medical exam. That's a good idea for two reasons. First, it will reassure you that you are okay, and second, if you are not okay, awareness of your physical condition will be of major importance in developing your separation agreement. Your doctor's name and phone number and insurance information should already be on your Rolodex and in **FORM-ula 4: Profile Self.**

Note In the future, scheduling annual checkups in birthday months makes them easier to remember.

FEEDING FRENZIES

Divorce is not conducive to optimal digestion. Since good nutrition is essential for mental and physical balance, we suggest that you pay attention to your diet. We also assure you that it is possible for you to do little or no cooking and still eat very well.

Since your health comes first, the worst place to cut back is in the area of good food. Fortunately, the best diet is not an expensive one.

This is a good time to back off on caffeine, sugar, alcohol, and nicotine—not only because they are unhealthy and expensive, but because they are addictive and mind-altering. Divorce is no time to alter or numb your feelings. These feelings are useful indicators of the changes you are starting to make, or need to make.

Under stress, the body has a tendency to react with much more hypersensitivity to food and drink. (This fact is important to know if you suffer from any allergies.) Rather than being energized, alcohol and sweets are more likely to leave you sluggish and undisciplined. Too much coffee causes anxiety and irritability in addition to decreasing your performance.

If your knowledge of diet and vitamins is limited, this may be the opportune time to consult with a reliable nutritionist or to get hold of a doctor-recommended book on nutrition. There are so many impractical or faddish nutrition books on the market these days. Also, with medical costs so high, a lot of people have taken to using books to doctor themselves. So be wary.

Balanced Food Guidelines

The objective is to save yourself the trouble of constantly thinking about food and yet still take care of nutritional needs.

The medical profession tells us that there are five priorities for daily eating:

- Bread, cereal, pasta, rice
- Fruits
- Vegetables
- Meat, poultry, fish, beans
- Dairy (eggs, milk, cheese, and so forth)

How you eat your food can be almost as important as what you eat. For instance, try not to eat right after you have been upset. Eat in the most pleasant atmosphere you can create for yourself. If you have children, try to have at least one meal a day as a family meal.

Food can be an emotional subject between divorcing parents. Make healthy foods available and plan for balanced meals if you want to avoid the possibility of courtroom discussions about child nutrition.

Shopping Helpers

Here are some tips for food shopping, especially during trying times.

Rule 1: Never go food shopping on an empty stomach!

Rule 2: Shop smarter, not harder. (Coupons save food dollars.)

Rule 3: Everyone who eats, helps out. (You should not have to do all the food shopping and preparation; enlist the help of others.)

To make things easier right from the start, consider working with **FORM-ula 13: Grocery Shopping**. Keep a weekly copy handy in your kitchen for every member of your household to use. Each family member can circle both the items that they would like to have and those items that need to be replaced. (Sorry, we have found no cure for teenagers who leave one spoonful and don't consider the box or jar empty!)

TIME TO CLEAN UP

Daily routines always revolve around the basic problems of time, labor, and funds. It doesn't really matter which spouse remains in the home (or if both do) during the divorce process. There is still work to be done and a decision to be made about who is going to do it and when.

Recognize that there are options to doing everything yourself. Pay someone else to do the tasks you most hate. Spend the money even if you have to scrimp on another part of your budget. The relief will make it worthwhile.

If you are not living alone, other members of the household can participate in doing the chores. Since we all have different assumptions and expectations about how things should be done and to what degree, the definitions of "clean" and "finished" will vary by degree of finickiness. (If one of your "hot buttons" is unmade beds, consider using comforters rather than bedspreads. They're quicker, easier and hide blanket wrinkles.) You and your household members need to come to a common agreement of standards so that the performance of each task can be measured fairly.

Customize **FORM-ula 14: Household Chores** to meet your family's needs. Add on tasks that we have missed. Play with the schedule for a few weeks. Try rotating jobs. Try marking each individual's tasks in a separate color. One simple approach is to divide the house into sections, with one for each family member. Rotate sections. (This idea is compliments of Jim Bessent, our editor.)

Chapter 9
SAFETY

Going through a divorce inevitably opens you and your personal business to wider public exposure than you may have any wish to experience. It is important for you to feel safe.

Your comfort level may be threatened by pain, anxiety, and stress. It is important to have the physical and psychological security that comes from maintaining an appropriate shelter.

BEGINNING TO PROTECT YOURSELF

Consider using an answering machine to protect yourself against having to speak with people when you don't want to. You can also avoid missing important conversations by taking or returning calls during the best times for you.

Ask that your name be removed from junk-mail lists by contacting the Direct Marketing Associates, Mail Preference Service, 6 E. 43d St. New York, NY 10017. This will eventually eliminate the accumulation of unwanted print materials.

We have also observed that while going through a divorce, there is a tendency to lose or misplace things like wallets and handbags. If this happens, you may have to compete with the crooks to see how fast you can list, report, and replace checks and credit cards before they can spend, spend, spend!

Take a few minutes to list everything in your wallet or handbag that will require action if they are lost. This includes such items as your driver's license and bank, credit, and membership cards.

If you need to report a loss, note the time and date of your call as well as the name of the person who took your message. Some credit card companies require written notification, as well, in order to relieve you from liability of expenses incurred. Details on organizing your credit card information can be found in Chapter 15.

Your Own Personal "Yellow Pages"

There are additional things you can do right away to insure your personal safety. Complete **FORM-ula 15: Emergency Telephone Numbers**, **FORM-ula 16: Resource Telephone Numbers**, and **FORM-ula 17: Children's Whereabouts**. Many of these numbers can be found in your local telephone book or through your telephone information service. Put copies of these FORM-ulas in their appropriate locations (refrigerator, bulletin board, bedroom telephone, handbag, or briefcase). Be sure that this information is also on your personal Rolodex.

Since "911" or "0" are the quickest way to get emergency help, it is important that all members of the household know these phone numbers.

As we mentioned before, this is a period when "stuff happens." A little prevention goes a long way.

DEALING WITH YOUR PAIN

"A merry heart doeth good like a medicine; but a broken spirit drieth the bones."

Proverbs 17:22

There is a theory that forcing a smile, no matter how bad we feel, works the muscles that send blood to the brain and triggers a sense of well-being. Contrary to popular opinion, you do not have to hit bottom to start getting better.

Understanding your loss is the beginning of dealing with your pain. Pain is the beginning of healing. Don't deny the process. Let it happen. You need to feel the grief and hurt that a divorce brings with it. Don't, for goodness' sake, store up tears and never shed them! Cry when you feel like it. Your body won't let you cry hard for very long and that feeling of emptiness will go away much faster.

Be realistic about yourself. It's normal to have mood swings, to feel depressed, to be confused, and to have terribly mixed feelings about your former spouse. We call this *PDS—Pre-Divorce-Syndrome.*

When you can begin to let go of your fears, hurt, blame, resentment, rage, and numbness; when you can cry, yell and scream some of your frustration and follow it with a good laugh at how absurd it all feels— then you will mourn your loss, learn from your old mistakes and begin to make positive things happen for yourself.

Unless you are determined to be cynical and sour, you will start becoming grateful for life on its own terms. Your happiness will not be conditional upon everything being "just right."

CONFRONTING ANXIETY

Bravery is confronting your anxiety and doing something about it. Anxiety is normal. Without it, we wouldn't be truly alive. It keeps us alert and ready to trigger our "fight-or-flight" mechanism. It is a reminder that we need to do something to help ourselves.

You can expect to be anxious during the transition period of your divorce. You can expect those around you to be anxious, too. Old fears will readily surface as part of this rupturing process called divorce.

Help Yourself

Start with the premise that you can help yourself by becoming more aware of your attitudes, actions, and reactions when you are most anxious. What are your mental habits and patterns when you feel anxious?

- Do you usually blame someone else when things go wrong?
- Do you usually accept the blame when things go wrong?
- Do you try to get some balance?

It is a matter of observing yourself. When a situation seems to overcome you, try to look at it objectively. Is your mind trying to play tricks on you? Are you literally scaring yourself? Or, is your anxiety real and justified?

What becomes intolerable is trying to live all of yesterday's regrets and tomorrow's anxieties at the same time.

Meeting the New Circumstances

Perhaps the greatest anxiety of divorce has to do with how you are going to live and how much it will cost you. Very often, your usual expenses have to be changed to meet the new circumstances. If this kind of change is needed:

- Clarify and understand the financial aspects of your joint life.
- Begin to analyze and understand the rights and obligations you now have as a single person.
- Decide what you want for yourself, using legal standards as a guide.
- Plan how to live on a new income in a changed lifestyle.

Specific suggestions for accomplishing these goals are offered in Section IV.

OVERCOMING STRESS

"Whatever does not kill me makes me stronger."

NIETZSCHE

The ordinary irritations and hassles of daily life can give rise to a wide variety of physical and psychological ailments. That is because they are stressful. In fact, your daily stresses, laid end-to-end, can have a more damaging effect on you than your major source of stress, the divorce itself! An astonishing revelation, for sure, and one that needs to be put into proper perspective.

Throughout your divorce, stress is likely to take an enormous toll on your mind, spirit, and body. This is particularly true if you have become so used to stress that you have learned to ignore it.

Hassles and Reactions

The most common hassles seem no more health-threatening than the events of any bad day. Here are some that turned up in a variety of newspaper articles:

Personal

- Physical appearance
- Concern about weight
- Too much to do
- Misplacing or losing things
- Ill health of a family member

Household

- Interior home maintenance
- Yard work, or outside maintenance
- Property investment or taxes

General

- Crime
- Rising prices

The more hassles people have, the more susceptible they are to these kinds of reactions:

- Headaches, stomach aches, colds, and flu.
- Skin conditions such as multiple spreading warts, itching, hives, psoriasis, some forms of eczema, and acne.
- Depression, anger, low morale, low energy, and fatigue.
- Low self-esteem, an overall sense of malaise.
- Poor job performance and absenteeism.

Women are more likely than men to develop psychological problems, especially depression and psy-chosomatic illness. Men are more likely to experience heart attacks, car accidents, or to attempt suicide.

Coping Successfully

To successfully cope with stress is to understand that it is not just the series of outside events that you are grappling with. It is also the personal mechanics through which you deal with challenge and change. When hassles start to mount up and turn into stress, recognize the signs and stop yourself from falling under the spell. The positive features of stress help you to learn to:

- Strengthen your defenses.
- Sharpen your resolve.
- Prioritize your activities.
- Think more productively.

Escape-ades

When the alarms indicate your circuits are about to blow, it's time to take the pressure off. Find an escape hatch. This doesn't mean you run away or give up. This simply means that you give yourself a break. Staying in a mental or physical state which has stretched you to the limit is not an effective way to cope.

Quick and Simple Alternatives

Here are some alternatives that can begin to calm you down:

- Practice deep breathing.
- Talk out loud to yourself.
- Phone an upbeat friend whose life is just fine.
- Start a "spouse-is-a-louse" journal.
- Turn on some good music or the TV.
- Do a chore you've been putting off.

When you feel like doing something but don't know what, clean up the stuff in your junk drawers. You never know what you will find—it might be interesting.

Still in rough shape?

- Call a friend who gives you support.
- Exercise.
- Cry and get it out of your system.
- Pray for the restoration of your sanity.

Balancing the Good and the Bad

Frequent vacations from problem-solving are an important part of keeping in balance. Rewarding yourself is a tremendous step toward self-fulfillment. Escapades that last from five minutes to an hour can remake your day. For example, how about:

- Eating popcorn and watching a funny video (or two).
- Buying a toy (don't lose sight of the child inside you).
- Getting a massage or taking a long, tension-relieving bath or shower.
- Making a sports or lunch date with a friend.
- Taking a crack at a new hobby.

Imagery, Color, and Music

Imagery, color and music are wonderful tension relievers, particularly if one or more of them are used consistently. Don't worry if you can't achieve peace when you begin these methods. It will probably take more than a few regular sessions for you to be successful in discarding interfering thoughts. The more you are able to schedule this kind of relaxation on a daily basis, the more peaceful you will feel. You will soon be able to sense the before and after of your general state of mind.

Imagery is picturing in your mind the kinds of things that would give you relief. For example, feeling yourself lying in the sun on your favorite beach or skiing through a glade of fresh snow.

Color lets you close your eyes and imagine each of your favorite colors as lights moving to different parts of your body, relaxing and healing you.

Music works best when you will be uninterrupted. Sit or lie down in comfortable clothing and close your eyes. Focus your attention on the music that you find most peaceful.

Note Tapes and videos are available for each of these methods.

Rx: Laughter

Last but not least, the greatest Escape-ade is laughter. Laughter is internal jogging. Laughter is the prescription for almost any ill. In the beginning, it will be very hard. Nothing that's happening seems to be very funny. Even dark humor doesn't appeal. Nevertheless, making time in your day to find *something* to laugh about is good therapy.

We all have a tendency to take ourselves much too seriously. Lighten up. Even the worst trouble has its absurd side. If you lose your sense of humor, the divorce process is guaranteed to get you down. If you can see the ridiculous side, you'll keep your equilibrium and come up a winner.

Start with a joke book, your favorite sitcom, the late night stand-up comedy and talk shows, anything to put a smile on your puss. You may find yourself with a better sense of humor than you ever gave yourself credit for in your "happily married" days. There are hundreds of ways to keep laughing. Just a few of them are:

- Cartoon books.
- Puns and jokes.
- Humor magazines.
- Comedy and slapstick movies.
- TV sitcoms, stand-up comedians, humorous specials.
- Funny radio tapes (especially from the early days, before TV).
- Political humor.
- Newspaper comics.
- Night clubs and cabarets.
- Joke-writing workshops.
- Things your kids say.
- What the neighbors tell you.
- Favorite cartoons taped up around the house.

Actual "smileage" may vary, but if you totally lose your sense of humor, the divorce will crack you.

Be Kind to Yourself

To take up arms against stress, there are a number of changes you can make starting right now:

- Learn to live with less.
- Plan fewer things to do in a day.
- Don't try to be so many things to so many people.
- Make time for yourself.
- Remember the things that went well.

SECURE AND APPROPRIATE SHELTER

The period between filing for divorce and receiving the actual decree is a time when life is most insecure. Because of the increased pressures and responsibilities of divorce, it is imperative to have a secure and appropriate place to live, particularly if there are children involved.

Moving Out or Living In

Traditionally, when a couple decides to split up, one spouse temporarily moves out of the family home. This kind of move requires at least minimal household effects for the departing spouse, which are taken from common property. The new place is usually a temporary "camp out" and frequently represents a significant difference in lifestyle. The spouse who remains in the home is left alone to face the uncertainty of how the mortgage and utility bills will be paid plus the costs and responsibilities of general maintenance.

Lately, the *live-in* divorce has hit the scene compliments of the tough housing market, high cost of living, new laws and court decisions on the division of property, occupancy rights, and custody and child support. For all practical purposes, living in means that:

- Both spouses are attached to the home and are determined to stay.

- Separate residences are not affordable during the interim.

- Both can lose money by selling the home in a down market.

- Each must maintain primary residence to prevent future penalties from the Internal Revenue Service.

- Courts are less likely to award custody to a parent who leaves.

- A spouse cannot be forced to leave unless there is proven physical violence. (The law requires clear evidence.)

Your Own Space

Whether you are sharing housing with your children, a roommate, or your soon-to-be-ex, there should always be a space that is singularly *yours*. Make it your own by what you put in that space (or what you take out of it). Consider the atmosphere you want to create for yourself.

Note You might want to buy yourself the standard divorce greenery—the fichus tree. It looks pretty and if you forget to water it, don't panic. It's used to "near death experiences."

You have to be very realistic about your budget—whether you stay in your home or leave it. Remember the beginning days of marriage when you furnished with "early attic"? Now you are faced with the prospect of "late divorce" decor.

Making Repairs

Chances are you will be making a lot of your own home repairs. We suggest that you buy high quality tools since, as the saying goes, you get what you pay for. See FORM-ula 18: for Household Supplies for a list of basic tools to have available.

Home Security Action List

If, for any reason, you are afraid for your safety at home, here is a list of ways to protect yourself:

- Be sure to lock your doors (day and night).

- Account for all keys, or have the locks changed.

- Add a dead-bolt lock.

- Find a new hiding place for the emergency key.

- Put dowels in glass sliding doors.

If you live in a house or condominium, depending upon your level of concern, it may make sense to:

- Join a neighborhood watch group.

- Install a garage door opener, so you don't have to get out of your car at night.

- Install floodlights to illuminate the darkest areas around your home.

- Install an intercom for your front door.

- Install a burglar alarm or security system.

- Hire a security service to watch your house.

If you are afraid to go alone into your cellar (have "cellarphobia"), you have three choices: (1) get over it, (2) continually call upon friends and neighbors or, (3) have electric panels and water valve cut-offs installed upstairs.

Smoke and Fire Safety

If you have children, plan a couple of drills so they know what to do in case of fire.

- Buy a fire extinguisher for your kitchen.

- Be sure you have smoke detectors, and they are working.

- If you have a two- or three-story house, buy a rope ladder to use for a quick escape.

General Safety Precautions

Here are some additional safety measures:

- Tape emergency and hot-line numbers to the phone.
- Teach your children the emergency numbers.
- If you can and it suits your temperament, get a watchdog.
- When answering the phone, don't give your name until the caller is properly identified.
- Put trash out in the daytime, not at night.
- If the same unknown car is regularly near your home, get the license plate number and phone the police.
- Get a service contract on your heating system and major appliances.

If you are justifiably afraid of retaliations arising from the divorce process, your safety must be a first consideration. Get advice and support from professionals.

When Leaving Home Overnight or Longer

Traveling away from home necessitates taking special security measures. Here are a few:

- Put excess cash and jewelry in a safety deposit box.
- Disconnect TV, computer, and appliances.
- Set automatic timers on lights, radios, stereos, TVs, and so forth.
- Discontinue home deliveries.
- Have mail held at post office.
- Turn down heat and air-conditioning.
- Check stove and refrigerator temperature.
- Lock windows and doors.

Basic First Aid

Keep separate first-aid kits for your home and automobile. Check both kits from time to time for replenishment or replacement. **FORM-ula 18: Household Supplies** contains a list of recommended first-aid items. You can also purchase prepackaged first-aid kits in a variety of sizes.

Periodically go through your medicine chest and dispose of all expired prescriptions. If you have doubts about any medication, consult your local pharmacist.

Note Many pharmacies have free booklets of first-aid tips.

Emergency Precautions

Should an emergency be declared because of storms or other natural disasters, immediate preparations include:

- Putting a full tank of gas in your car.
- Boarding up or taping glass doors and windows with an *X* pattern (glass can still break but this will prevent it from shattering into tiny pieces).
- Filling containers and bathtubs with water (emergency bottled water is even better).
- Keeping handy flashlights and extra batteries for each person in the family.
- Keeping ready a change of clothing. Store it in a pillow case because suitcases are heavy and paper or plastic bags break. Each person should have a complete change of clothes. (Also consider preparing a small bottle of water, a book, a nourishing snack, and possibly a whistle and favorite toy for each child.)
- For a baby, a standard diaper bag packed for a day trip, include extra formula and food. (If it is truly a disaster, it will be easier to wash out cloth diapers than to obtain disposable ones.)
- Turn up refrigerator temperature and open as little and infrequently as possible. If power goes, the cold will last longer.

If it is okay to remain at home, teach everyone to stay together. Remember that you're safer away from glass and where the house has extra reinforcement such as doorways and basements. Heavy tables or desks will also offer some protection.

If you are told to go to a shelter, *go!* When you evacuate, shut off the utilities and take with you valuables that you can carry (financial and insurance papers, jewelry, and so forth). Local radio stations will usually indicate the safest evacuation route.

It can be really dangerous after a storm, so it's best to be "mean" and keep the children in the house. Roaming the neighborhood opens the opportunity for contact with live downed wires and gas leaks. Power companies usually have booklets on safety during and after storms, hurricanes, tornadoes, and earthquakes. Consult these for additional information.

FORM-ula 18: Household Supplies also provides a list of items you should have on hand in the event of a bad storm or a natural disaster.

PAY ATTENTION TO YOUR AUTOMOBILE

"Wheels" may be vital to your independence and livelihood so pay attention to your automobile. As part of your basic organization process, you can prepare yourself for circumstances ranging from lost keys and breakdowns to automobile accidents. Use **FORM-ula 19: Functional Automobile** as a specific checklist for "General Preparation," items to "Carry in the Car" and "Automobile Maintenance."

Service and Maintenance Tips

Maintenance suggestions have been provided by Charles Craven, an entrepreneur who has developed a record-keeping kit designed to be attached to the car dashboard or door interior. The kit consists of a small leather holder containing three automobile maintenance cards to assist everyone from novice to experienced driver. The reusable plastic cards cover causes of highway breakdown, information on the frequency of maintenance servicing, and tips for periodically mileage checking and time. They are a service reminder used to minimize worry and save dollars.

To obtain a Safe Wheels™ kit ($6.95), write to:

Car Craft Products
PO Box 552
Lexington, MA 02173

Expired Warranties

According to a consumer-advocacy group, a major problem with your car, after the warranty has expired, does not always mean gloom and doom. To find out whether a specific problem is covered by a so-called "secret" warranty, write to:

Center for Auto Safety
Department RD, Suite 410
2001 S Street, N.W.
Washington, D. C. 20009

Enclose a self-addressed envelope with double first-class postage. Indicate your auto's make, model and year and the problem you're having with it. You might get lucky.

CHILD-CARE ARRANGEMENTS

During a divorce, finding safe and affordable child care is an additional concern. Both spouses are aware that this is a sensitive issue, especially if custody is not yet legally established.

Budget changes and single parenting will probably alter preexisting child care arrangements. Under the circumstances of divorce, you will need to consider the ages of your children, their activities, and your available dollars before you can list the alternatives you have for short- and long-term child care.

Resources for Child-Care Information

Resources to help you form this list are:

- Family-service agencies.
- State hot line for licensed sitters.
- *Yellow Pages,* under Child Care, Sitting Services, Day Care Centers.
- College child-development programs.
- Ads in local newspapers. (Check the references of any group or program you are considering using.)
- Other working parents (networking).

The National Association of Child Care Resource and Referral Agencies is located in Rochester, Minnesota. Call (507) 287-2220 for the agency to provide you with names of resources in your area.

Your Personal Philosophy About Child Care

Think about how you are raising your children before you choose child-care services. In your new position as a single parent (custodial or not) you will need a consistent philosophy to help maintain a nurturing environment.

Personal Thoughts About Child Care

Here are some thoughts to consider while developing your child-care philosophy:

- How are your children disciplined?
- Are you relaxed and accepting of your children's moods and behaviors?
- How important is it that your children have a set routine?
- Do you want the routine to be structured or unstructured?
- How much are you willing and able to spend for child care?
- What would be the ideal situation for your children?

Child Care Inside the Home

Professional child care in your home will require instructions on a number of issues. This is true for full-time day care and short-term sitting. Make clear to the child-care professional your feelings about the following issues:

- Nap and bedtime routines and hours.
- Meals and snacks for children and the sitter.
- Rules for visitors of children and sitters.
- Permissible TV programs.
- Special activities for the sitter to do.
- Expectations for cooking and cleaning up.
- Emergency measures and phone numbers.
- Where you can be reached.

Note Be sure to establish hourly fees in advance.

Child Care Outside of the Home

For selecting child care outside of the home, we have prepared FORM-ula 20: Child Care Outside of the Home. Complete one for each child-care home or facility you visit. The information will remind you of both basics and details when you are ready to make a decision.

Latchkey Children

If the decision regarding child care is for the children to remain alone at home, they need clear-cut procedures to follow. This mutual understanding will give parents and children a greater sense of security.

Basic Procedures for Latchkey Children

Be sure your children understand the following procedures if they are to stay alone at home:

- Lock the door when you get home.
- Call me (custodial parent).
- Don't let any unexpected person into the house.
- Don't let strangers know that you are alone (say that the parent is busy, in the shower, napping, and so forth).
- Tell phone callers parent is "busy" and will call back.
- Don't use appliances, including stove, without permission.
- In case of emergency, call me (custodial parent) or neighbor immediately.

Telephone contact between parent and latchkey children is the only means of keeping open the lines of communication and maintaining security when children are home alone. Even though your children should be instructed to call you only once after school, they should feel that you are available for anything they consider important. If the calls become too frequent or indicate trouble at home, you will have to think about making other arrangements.

Child-Care Evaluations

Regardless of which option is used—home with sitter, outside care, or latchkey—you need to be sensitive to how you and your children feel about it after a reasonable trial period. Ask yourself the following questions:

- Are your children being well cared for?
- Do your children talk about what happened during the day?
- Are your children enthusiastic about the care-giver?
- Are your children generally happy in the morning?
- Do your children seem relatively cheerful and happy?
- Are your children learning new things and eager to explore?
- Do your children seem to be progressing?

If Child-Care Arrangements Aren't Working

If current child-care arrangements aren't working, be careful not to blame all the problems on the divorce. If you or your children feel that things are not going well, move quickly and talk honestly with the sitter or care-giver.

Recognize that some children settle into latchkey routines very happily and enjoy the time of solitude and privacy it brings, while others become nervous and resentful and need more access to the outside world. These children usually require a supervised after-school activity.

You owe it to yourself and your children to be caring and assertive about what you think is needed and lacking.

Chapter 10
NEED TO BELONG AND FEEL LOVED

"Being alone is a good place to begin a very full life."

PHYLLIS HOBE
Never Alone

Loneliness is when weekends expand into an infinite amount of time with no structure, no festivities, and no intimacy.

ALONE VERSUS LONELY

The overwhelming reality of divorce is its state of aloneness. Most divorcing individuals are left alone and bereft for a period of time. The spouse who has initiated the divorce (and seemingly has the easier life) may or may not be feeling the effects of the "amputation." Chances are, sooner or later these feelings will crop up.

Aloneness during and immediately after a divorce is time to take stock. Being alone as much as you really need to be is sensible. Going it alone, however, is rarely the answer. Climbing into a shell and shutting out the world is regrettable.

Filling the Void

The human soul always welcomes the chance to be revitalized. It is important to have friends to hold and by whom you can be held. Every human being benefits from Vitamin T, for *touch,* so ask for and offer hugs.

A Vulnerable Period

Reaching out to new situations and individuals can have its own excesses. In the process of replacing what is needed, you are vulnerable to new ideas and activities. You may have a tendency to overdo, or become overwhelmingly involved, in your new interests. Some groups might even take advantage of your need to belong.

Pets Give Unconditional Love

Divorce may be a good time for a pet if you are willing and able to assume the additional responsibility. Research indicates that cats and dogs help buffer stress in addition to being a wonderful source of affection.

A word of caution in selecting a pet. Some breeds of cats and dogs become extremely attached to their primary caretaker and may not adjust well to a future significant other.

FRIENDSHIPS DURING DIVORCE

During a divorce, you need friends who can provide spiritual and emotional nourishment. Never underestimate the power of a solid friendship. Some people would even go so far as to say that friends are more important than romances. Adoring the opposite sex is great, but it's usually same-sex friends who hold your life together and stay with you throughout your lifetime.

Divorced Friends

Those who are already divorced can become very supportive friends. However, there are two types of divorced people: those who have successfully moved on, and those who haven't. The ones who have adjusted well, even grown and prospered in their new state, are the ones you want to emulate.

Expect to have conflicting reactions to these pathfinders. On the one hand, you can feel strong and empowered by what you learn from them. On the other hand, when you are feeling that you aren't moving fast enough and are temporarily stuck in the old life, these same people can make you feel depressed and backward.

Finding New Friends

What do you do about making new friends? You don't just go out on the street and whistle for them like taxicabs. Where do you look?

Potential sources for new friends could be:

Family members	Divorce-adjustment workshops
Therapy groups	Revival of old relationships
Singles groups	Special-interest groups
Singles clubs	Church activities and committees
Local clubs	Hobby- or sport-groups
Business associations	Dances
Touring clubs	Special singles vacations
Parents of other children	Community centers
Adult-education courses	"Better" singles bars

From a purely practical aspect, use the Rolodex to make your own "Who's Who" section. Include the people who are coming through for you. Pull out the names and addresses of the people who have walked away.

Note Willful helplessness will make friends leave faster than anything else while you're going through a divorce.

"Deebest" and "Deevorced" Things for You

When your family and friends ask how they can help, be prepared to tell them "Deebest" and "Deevorced" things they can do in the care and treating of *me* during my divorce:

Deebest things you can say and do

- Give me unconditional love.
- Be willing to listen.
- Offer your good-natured companionship.
- If you think I'm off base, tell me honestly.
- Encourage me to do my own thinking.
- Share information and resources.
- Keep in touch.
- Ask me what you can do *and* when you can do it.

Deevorced things you can say and do

- Give me unsolicited advice.
- Tell me about your problems and suffering.
- Make empty offers of help.
- Renege on specific offers of help that I counted on.

COMMUNITY INVOLVEMENT

Your community is a great place to start when you need to accelerate your involvement with the world around you. You can use your community to increase the number of people you know and your areas of interest. It is important, however, to be selective in your choice of community service or activity to fit your interests, time, and energy.

Some guidelines to finding new activities are:

- Listing your current interests.
- Determining activities you'd like to do on weekends.
- Knowing when and how much time you have available.
- Understanding whether you prefer to be alone or in a group.

Volunteering

There are a staggering number of services that rely on good volunteers. Volunteering is a constructive way to meet people and to learn about new job and career opportunities. Whatever special skills you have to offer are always needed in your community.

Professional Opportunities

As a professional, consider putting aside short blocks of time or working on a project basis by offering pro bono services in law, medicine, management, finance, taxation, real estate, psychology, or business counseling. Clerical and office skills are welcomed at almost every level of community service. Word processing and computer knowledge is invaluable to nonprofit agencies, as are personnel interviewing and testing, job training, and language interpreting skills.

Parenting Skills

Parenting work is in great demand at community centers, schools, and hospitals. Everything from reading programs to teaching crafts and supervising sports are open to volunteers these days. Working with the handicapped or retarded children demands special skills and patience, and offers a great way to forget your own troubles for a while.

Organized Programs

Consider one of these less obvious community contributions:

- Docent (tour guide) in a local museum.
- Receptionist at almost any community building.
- Trail guide in a nature park or preserve.
- Assistant to animal keepers in a zoo or animal shelter.
- Gardener, landscaper, or groundskeeper for public buildings.

- Cook for soup kitchen, shelter, meals-on-wheels program.
- Receiver at a recycling center.
- Member of an inner-city clean-up project.
- Member of a voter-registration committee.
- Blood-pressure taker for a community-health campaign.
- Youth-club organizer.
- Walkathon participant.
- Usher at local performances of music, dance, or theater.
- Performer in community theater.
- Teacher at local hospitals, prisons, or schools.

Care of the Less Fortunate

There is a wide variety of volunteer service available for helping less fortunate individuals; these include being:

- An ombudsman for a person in a nursing home.
- A candy striper in a hospital.
- A buddy to assist someone with AIDS.
- A crisis center worker.
- A housing rehabilitator for the elderly and disabled.
- A facilitator to help relocate families who have lost their homes.
- An assistant in exercise and therapy for the handicapped.
- A worker for the Special Olympics.
- A telephone communicator to homebound elderly or retarded individuals.

Any way you choose to develop new interests while touching and being touched by others will inevitably help you to learn more about yourself and what it is you will ask for your new life.

ACTIVITY CALENDARS

Divorce makes you a prime candidate for forgetfulness. Even the most compulsively organized individuals miss appointments and double schedule their time.

If you have not already begun to do so, now is definitely the time to actively use your wall and pocket-size calendars. Throughout *The Divorce Decisions Workbook* we encourage you to include additional categories of information on your calendars.

At this time, you will want to have recorded all of the personal and community-related activities and appointments for yourself and your children, including:

- Courses, classes, and workshops.
- Leagues and teams.
- Social engagements.
- Holiday and birthday plans.
- Afterschool activities.
- Medical appointments.
- Religious functions.
- Clubs and organization meetings.
- Volunteer projects.
- Children's visitation times with noncustodial parent.

Chapter 11
SELF-ACTUALIZATION

"Sometimes our fate resembles a fruit tree in winter. Who would think that those branches would turn green again and blossom, but we hope it, we know it."

GOETHE

You can turn your distress into success because adversity has a strange way of breeding creativity. Growth is a mysterious process that comes at the darnedest times. Expect to experience setbacks. Sometimes you will feel as though you are making every possible mistake. The objective is to learn from your mistakes.

CHANGE AND GROWTH POTENTIAL

Divorce is almost a modern day rite of passage. It has to do with a renewed commitment to build your own life so that you claim a rich and fulfilling existence while reestablishing your singular identity.

Understanding Change

The initiation stage of this rite of passage is a hard one. It often requires intensive examination of long-held beliefs and behaviors which may end up having to be changed. These changes may have a negative domino effect on everyone, from your children to your community, depending upon how willing they are to accept your changes.

It may be difficult to convince yourself that certain kinds of thoughts and emotions can work against you. For example, are you too busy being angry with your spouse to plan how to take care of yourself? How many of your thoughts and emotions have led to your present condition? How would getting them under control help you? We are not talking about repressing thoughts and emotions. We are talking about the lengthy and often painful process of dealing with them, possibly with professional help. Make a conscious effort to stop worrying about things that you cannot control.

Eliminate Self-Pity

A major requirement for personal growth is the elimination of self-pity. Life is not fair. In order to manage the practical divorce, you need to draw a realistic picture of your situation.

Some simple affirmations to use as a daily pep talk to yourself might be:

- "I am my own human being, worthwhile and needed by myself and others."

- "I am working for my own personal growth and am able to decide what is best for me."

- "I can make any change in my life that I need to in order to achieve my goals."
- "I am not alone. I can ask others to help me."

Finding Opportunities for Change

Now is the time to think about the kinds of things you have always wanted to do. This may be your chance to consider new ideas and to begin rearranging your life to suit your own needs. You choose and make the self that you want. You may not realize all of your ambitions but you are more likely to realize all of your plans.

Very few of your future plans can be acted upon immediately. You have too many other things to do right now to get your divorce properly organized. The divorcing period is not usually a good time for other radical changes (unless you are being forced into them), but it sure feels good to have something to look forward to.

At this point, all we are asking you to do is think about change. Don't *not* consider the possibilities because you are convinced that they will never work out or even be feasible. Hopes and dreams can be fun again.

Being a Class Act

First impressions count! You are going to be scrutinized by those you already know as well as meeting a lot of new people. You certainly won't want to pretend to be someone you are not. You will, however, want to show the best of who you are.

If you have a yen to get your life reorganized, and your daily schedule on a good track, now is as good a time as any to begin.

Appearances Count

Take a long look at yourself in the mirror. Don't underestimate the importance of your appearance. Are you well groomed? Are your nails filed and clean? Is your clothing neat? Do you need a haircut?

Is there anything within reason that you would like to change? This is a good time to try on some new looks and styles. Reprioritizing your budget might allow for a few purchases that may do wonders for your morale.

We've observed that newly separated and divorced men and women do tend to change their appearance, through changes in hair color or style, cosmetic surgery, or weight gains or losses. (The weight losses were usually due more to depression than conscious effort, however.)

Within a relatively short period of time (six months to a year), separated and divorcing individuals often look more attractive and appear healthier and more vibrant. When they have been working to resolve emotional problems, the overall change in attitude can be significant and apparent.

FOCUSING ON YOUR CAREER

Work has a valid function in the arena of divorce. It gives continuity to life and keeps the mind from turning in on itself. Doing good work can make one feel a sense of honest achievement at a time when self-esteem tends to be very low.

Changing Work Patterns

How will the divorce affect your work status? Are your dollars the primary income, the secondary income, or are you the primary caretaker of the home and children?

Will your divorce require changing work patterns? What is going to change?

- Will you have more or less time available for work?
- Will you have to earn more money to make ends meet?
- How will this need impinge on your career development?
- Will you have to start all over again in the workplace?
- How will you maintain an acceptable standard of living without neglecting your children?

Research Your Options

Whether you are making a work change by force or by choice, you should take the time to research your options. This is another important part of self-actualization.

If you are satisfied with your current work and it is compatible with the changes divorce brings, your thoughts may run more toward setting higher goals and earning advancement. Perhaps you are more interested in earning money at home or on a part-time basis.

Begin to assess the kinds of work you are interested in and evaluate the strength of your talents and skills. Achievers are the people who can recognize and use resources. Information can come from:

- Career counseling professionals.
- Books, periodicals, and trade journals.
- Networking.
- Business development counselors.
- Professional associations and organizations.
- *Yellow Pages*.

People love to give advice. So, make phone calls and appointments. Use your spiral notebook for strategic planning to take notes on your meetings and conversations. Keep track of your contacts by including them in the personal "Who's Who" section of your Rolodex.

Chapter 12
WOULD COUNSELING HELP?

"Ever you remark another's Sin, Bid your own conscience look within."

Poor Richard's Almanac

Sometimes, if you grapple with a problem and try very hard to see it from all angles, including the opposing ones, and if you wait long enough, the problem might correct itself. The wisdom lies in knowing when it is time to stop waiting.

Almost everyone can use counseling at some point in life. It is a fact that at times we all exhibit a bit of neurotic and inappropriate behavior, particularly during a divorce.

On the premise that many inappropriate behavioral patterns were set up in childhood and could have been further exacerbated by the marriage, should you not at least try to understand the psychological mechanisms that helped determine them? What can be changed? What is most valuable to you? Have you been fighting against odds? Would counseling help you?

REASONS TO THINK ABOUT COUNSELING

It is never too soon in a divorce to latch on to the kind of support that you need for mental and emo-

tional stability. The strains of breaking off a relationship are painful. Mixed feelings, stress, and uncertainty don't do much for your self-esteem. If you feel that you are a failure, you can only gain by trying to figure out what happened so that you won't do the same things again.

Support Groups

If you are you are afraid of therapy, try a support group first. Discussion groups or associations of people undergoing similar difficulties may help you to gain perspective and keep your chin up.

We have found that women are generally more comfortable with the idea of counseling than men. Since the conventional view of masculinity is not one of talking about problems or showing vulnerability, men don't readily search out therapy. However, there appears to be a move toward all-male groups where men do talk about what really worries them.

To locate support groups, you can check with pastoral counseling centers, women's and men's organizations, and friends. Additional sources of help might be:

- Community groups for single and divorced people.
- Therapy groups sponsored by individual therapists.
- Consciousness-raising organizations.

- The Parents Without Partners organization.
- Single-parent groups.

When you attend a group session, listen to what others have to say and judge what makes sense to you. Observe the people who seem to be learning the most about themselves. These are the people you want to meet.

You may find that group meetings are adequate for your current needs. If not, it's a short jump to private counseling.

RECOGNIZING THE NEED

What if the deeper fears and anxieties you are experiencing get worse, not better? Are you feeling:

- Stuck, overwhelmed?
- That you have no one to turn to?
- Tired, lifeless, run down?
- Unable to relate to others?
- Unable to come to conclusions or make decisions?
- Always depressed or anxious?
- More and more angry and hostile?
- Dependent upon friends beyond what is reasonable?
- Unable to function for long periods of time?
- That you can't handle the children?
- That life is over for you?
- Terrified of being alone?
- That you will never find anyone else?

These feelings should be giving you a strong message to *get help*. Treatment beats the alternatives.

There is nothing wrong or shameful about finding a therapist for yourself. Quite the opposite. It is a sign of strength. You are ready to take the courageous steps toward helping yourself.

ROLE OF A THERAPIST

A therapist or counselor will not make your problems go away. Therapy helps you to identify the most difficult issues that you face. It can help you to prioritize your needs and organize your thinking. It will en-

courage you to feel less overwhelmed and more competent in this new situation.

An additional function of a therapist is to get you to confront those areas of your marriage which may have led to its break up. It is tremendously beneficial to work out as many of those "divorce demons" as possible before you begin to negotiate a separation agreement.

Note By understanding and altering negative responses to the marital situation, you will be likely to confuse the opposition (who anticipates predictable past behaviors and reactions) and gain strategic advantage.

If you are worried about the expense, we assure you that with a small effort, you will most certainly be able to find the right professional at the right price. Many therapists will work within your budget, either through agreed-upon hourly rates or on a sliding scale basis. Social services frequently have low minimum rates.

FINDING THE RIGHT THERAPIST

Do you need short-term help just to see you through? Or, do you want to get into the kind of therapy that will help you to put all the pieces back together? Are you looking for a therapist who will work with you and family members or one who will work with you alone? Once you have made these decisions, you can begin your search.

You can ask for recommendations from other professionals such as clergy, doctors, and lawyers.

Additional assistance can be found through:

- Community mental-health agencies.
- Family service centers.
- College counseling centers.
- School counseling services.
- YWCA/YMCA.
- Hospital outpatient clinics.
- Professionals:

  Psychologists
  Psychotherapists
  Psychiatrists (MDs)
  Social workers (MSWs)

Making the Decision

Once you have compiled a list of people who meet your preliminary requirements, arrange for an initial interview with each. Be sure to find out ahead of time if there is a charge for this exploratory meeting.

There are any number of "feeling out" questions you can ask in the initial meeting. Don't be afraid to ask about such matters as the therapist's:

- Background and training.
- Marital state (past and present).
- Personal opinions regarding marriage.
- Preconceived ideas about gender.
- Religious and philosophical bias.
- Lifestyle.

Does the therapist have a sense of humor? Seem practical and down to earth? Have a realistic, but positive attitude? See problems as symptoms of illness or responses to a grim situation?

Do you feel you could open up comfortably and talk about anything you wanted to? Would you be given responsive and responsible feedback? (This is probably not the time to have a therapist who just listens.)

Finally, when you think you have the right person, trust your instinct. Let it be your own intuition that says, "Okay, this is the one."

FAMILY COUNSELING

When children need help, they can attend individual counseling sessions in which they have the opportunity to privately express their own feelings. There can also be family sessions during which everyone's feelings can be expressed in a safe and mediated surrounding.

The direction you choose can be strongly affected by what is or is not reasonable to expect from your children. Remember, they are not only going through their own normal growing pains, they are now additionally encumbered by some radical changes. They may need help from an unbiased professional.

It is an appropriate time to call in the help of a therapist or counselor when one or both spouses put pressure on children to make certain kinds of decisions or to make up their minds about important family issues.

Questions to Ask Yourself

Questions to ask yourself before deciding on family counseling include:

- Do you feel overwhelmed or in any way unable to cope with present parenting responsibilities, or parenting, in general?
- Do you think there are unresolved issues in your divorce that are adversely affecting you and your family?
- Do you feel that you or your children have special emotional or physical problems that stand in the way of moving forward as a family unit?
- Are you unable to communicate effectively with your children?
- Do you sense that you are emotionally or physically abusing yourself or your children?

Here are some questions to pose concerning your children. Are any of them:

- Acting abusively toward you?
- Having problems at school with peers, teachers, or the system?
- Associating with a group that could be dangerous to their well-being and development?
- Reacting in extremes by overreacting (for example, by consistently acting depressed or by constantly acting out) or appearing totally unaffected by the divorce?
- Talking about or threatening suicide? Do you have any reason to think it might be contemplated?

Few families are without some of the items listed. A divorcing family has a higher risk of being faced with more of them.

Catching dysfunctions early can be one of the few blessings of divorce. Without the divorce, you might never have thought about these things which would then have to be addressed at a much later date. As it is, you have a head start toward a much happier life if such problems can be addressed promptly with the proper professional help.

Chapter 13
BECOMING A SINGLE-PARENT HOUSEHOLD

Is there a family in the house? Even though divorce causes some major structural changes in the family system, the answer is a resounding "Yes!" Single parenting is a regular and more acceptable part of life these days making "single-with-kids" a recognized family unit. Look for the unique values that bind you together and make you a family.

PARENTING EXPECTATIONS

When you were parents together, you and your spouse had certain dreams and expectations for your children. Now that you are becoming a single parent, how will these change?

- Do you expect to provide all the tangible things of life?

- Will your life revolve around your children?

- Do you expect to compensate for the divorce by protecting your children from having any more "bad" things happen to them?

- Do you need to have your children always under your control?

- Will you feel responsible for the ways in which your children behave and react to others?

- Are you concerned with developing all of the special talents your children may have?

- Will you assume responsibility for your children's grades and overall intellectual development?

- Do you feel that you can resolve all of your children's problems?

- Do you accept responsibility for your children's mental health?

What Is Reasonable?

Are your expectations reasonable? What do you think your children expect now? Have you asked them? It is a good idea to clarify how you now want to lead your lives by discussing mutual expectations.

When parents have problems with their children, they often feel guilty and blame themselves. Divorced parents tend to lay an especially heavy trip on themselves. If you aren't careful, the children will continue to do your trip-laying for you as a way of avoiding their own growing self-responsibilities.

If unusually serious problems begin to occur with one or more of your children, either at home or in school, check with a professional. You don't necessarily have to take immediate action, but at least get a second opinion. Support groups are often the most helpful for quick, reasonable answers.

Truths About Parenting

Soothe yourself with a few truths about parenting, especially single parenting:

- It ain't easy!
- Kids don't come with operation manuals.
- Parents aren't trained. They learn by experience.
- In many ways, kids from two-parent families aren't very different.

Throw out preconceived notions about what divorce does to children. The good news is that your children *can:*

- Lead healthy, happy lives after divorce.
- Survive without life-long scars.
- Have solid, loving relationships with both parents.
- Grow up to be mature, tolerant individuals.
- Escape becoming antisocial, amoral, or destructive.

Naturally, none of this happens automatically. Your children will need your attentiveness to help heal their hurt and resentment.

When parenting is allowed to become only housekeeping and caretaking, without emotional commitment, children will begin to look elsewhere for the attention they need.

By working to make positive things happen in your own life, you become a role model for your children. As you triumph over your own adversities, you will demonstrate how they can handle the stress and pain in their own lives. You will give them an example of how to meet the disappointments and setbacks that are part of life.

HEALTHY RECOVERY FROM FAMILY SURGERY

There are constructive ways to work with your children during and after your divorce. Commitment turns the promise, "We're divorcing each other, not you," into a reality. It's making time for your children when there is none. It is coming through for them again and again, year after year.

Recognize that you have all been through "family surgery." Allow yourself and your children time to recover before emphasizing readjustment.

When a parent-child relationship is healthy, mutual love and caring will open new ways of being together. Here are some guidelines to follow to help keep your relationships healthy:

- Enable your children to express their feelings without fear of condemnation or retaliation.
- Leave lots of open space for communication to happen naturally and not be forced.
- Help your children make the transition between two single parents.
- Spend time with each child individually.
- If the creation of two households causes a financial problem for one or both parents, talk honestly about this with your children in terms of the practical ramifications. Don't try to shelter them from what they will have to learn to face.
- Let your children know that you have a life of your own. Don't feel guilty if you need to do things that do not involve them. (They just might be relieved to have their own free time because they have a life, too.)

Let go of the idea that you control your children's destiny. You know that you can never shape a child according to your image, wishes, or demands. Don't shirk your responsibilities just because your life is changing in ways you don't yet understand or may not want. Meet your financial support and other caretaking obligations. Remember, too, that children need consistent discipline and a sense of direction. Call their bluff when they make threats. Be parents, not peers.

Unrealistic Expectations

Be realistic in your expectations of your children. They should not have to succeed in all the ways that you think you may have failed. Nor should they have to live up to unreasonable standards just to make you look like the perfect parent.

The tendency to count on your children as you would another adult is always present with the single parent, especially when the child is an adolescent or young adult. It is wise to become familiar with your own dependencies. We cannot stress too much the dangers of turning your children into little adults who are expected to carry the extra loads of the absent parent.

Try not to put your children in the position of having to take sides in your divorce or to use them as spies and couriers for gaining information about the other parent.

Becoming unreasonably angry or bitter toward your ex-spouse serves to make your children feel insecure about their future. Whatever you say against your ex-spouse will eventually come full-circle. When children are not allowed to know both parents, they will build false dreams about the absent parent.

Children are going to grow up and leave. This is not to be reacted to in the same way as your divorce or separation. Perhaps the most difficult problem of the single parent is to respect a child's right to independence and privacy. Once you are a parent (either coupled or single), your job is to foster a strong, healthy, and individuated offspring.

Adult Vengeance

Experience and research has taught us that divorce can make devils out of us, if we let it. Vengeance usually arises from court battles, child-support payments, visitation, and the misuse of parental rights and responsibilities. When there is extended conflict in divorce, it is the children who are hurt the most.

Do the best you can to keep the issues with your spouse separate from issues involving children. Make it clear to your children that you have their best interests in mind. Do not try to explain the other parent's behavior, nor make excuses for it.

Resist the temptation to retaliate. Make your objectives clear and don't give way to threats; neither should you threaten others.

Also, make it clear that you have no intention of giving up or backing down on what you know to be fair and right.

NEW RESPONSIBILITIES

There will be new responsibilities for everyone in the household. You are not Superparent! You will need to make assignments. Remember to use **FORM-ula 14: Household Chores.**

In the light of your current budget, reevaluate the children's expenses for clothes, books, lunch money, lessons, musical instruments, and so on. Reduced allowances will probably be difficult for children who are accustomed to more, not less.

Suitable chores or part-time work give children a financial education and a sense of responsibility. Weigh these advantages against their needs for academic achievement and extracurricular opportunities. Also, consider their abilities to handle a heavier load.

Finding Helpers

If, in addition to your increased responsibilities, you try to do as much for your children as you did in predivorce days, you will soon become exhausted, overwhelmed, and resentful. You will have absolutely no time for yourself. There are many people who are willing and able to help you out. You just have to make the effort to find them.

Start a list of possible individuals who could contribute to your children's care and attention. In addition to your ex-spouse, consider:

- Family members.
- Teachers.
- Group leaders.
- Retired people.
- Counselors.
- Social workers.
- Sitters.
- Friends.
- Sunday or Hebrew school teachers.
- Neighbors.
- Other single parents.
- Parents of your children's friends.
- Volunteers from Big Brother/Sister programs.

Remember! God helps those who help themselves. Be creative.

Setting the Stage

The way you handle yourself during your divorce will set the stage for how your children approach their own growth and its ensuing problems. Compare these possible behaviors with their likely results:

Behavior	Result
Helpless wimp act	Increasingly "victimized"
Despairing doom-and-gloom	Defeatist attitude
Bitter complainer	Resentment collector

Everyone-is-out-to-get-me	Total mistrust
Artificial happiness mask	Will not face reality
Seek short-term gratification	Need constant excitement
User, exploiter, briber	Self-centered, friendless
Martyred, do-for-everyone else	Unhappy, self-destructive
Compulsive worker	Can't relate to others

Children will choose role models. Are you a good choice?

BEING A NON-CUSTODIAL PARENT

The role of each parent continues to be important whether or not she or he is still living in the family household.

There is always difficulty in retaining the subtleties of a relationship without the framework of being in daily contact. Non-custodial parents usually want to be good parents but often feel a lack of internal resources with which to span the emotional and geographic distances that separate them from their children.

It is easy to feel unimportant, unloved, and rejected when your children would rather be with their friends than with you. You must remember that this may be their way of escaping from their feelings of guilt, anger, and loss. It may also be their way of getting on with their lives.

If the non-custodial parent reduces visitation or withdraws completely from involvement with his or her offspring, it should not be assumed that the non-custodial parent is being neglectful; instead, the situation may simply be too painful to face. Be advised, however, that disappearing from the scene can promote animosity between parents and cause the children to feel neglected.

If, on the other hand, the custodial parent blocks communications and fills the children with negative propaganda, it is up to the non-custodial parent to try to resolve the problems, either through successful communication with the custodial parent or legal action.

Child's Wish List

Here is a list of things that children have asked us to tell non-custodial parents:

- Honor your visitation rights.
- Be consistent and dependable.
- If possible, live within a reasonable distance.
- Keep in touch regularly and frequently by phone.
- Don't get hung up trying to be the "other parent." Be yourself.
- Establish activities and hobbies that will provide continuity to our visits together.
- Remember that you are the parent and that we are not "guests."
- Maintain appropriate and consistent discipline.
- Keep us informed about how you can be reached.

The effort that you make to maintain a relationship with your children will affirm their confidence that both parents continue to love and care for them.

DIVORCE AND THE SCHOOL/PARENT RELATIONSHIP

A changed relationship with the school system can pose a major problem for the divorced single parent.

Divorce and single parenting has been going on for some time now. Yet, there has been relatively little training for school personnel to deal with divorce situations.

Designed for One Household

The 1974 Family Educational Rights and Privacy Act (also known as the "Buckley Amendment") makes a child's school records legally available to both parents. However, many principals choose to open them only to the primary custodial parent.

School forms and papers are designed for one home with two natural parents. For example, student emergency cards may only have room for one parents' identification information. Tickets for school activities are still issued in quantities for one family only. Materials necessary for presents to be made in school for Christmas or Hanukkah (and Mothers'/Fathers' Days, when families include step-parents) are often limited in quantity to one parent per holiday. Report cards and notices are routinely sent to one home only. (School offices frequently claim that "our computer can't handle two homes per child.")

If there is to be joint custody or you want both parents to receive all of the material, it is important to notify the school in writing, covering each and every instance of duplication. Check with your local school system since you may need to attach a letter from your spouse's attorney, or a copy of the section from your separation agreement with regard to education and visitation. (See **FORM-ula 52: Duplicate Information Request**.)

Custodial Fathers

Custodial fathers usually cause the system a lot of confusion because most schools are used to the mother being the family representative, particularly where daytime events are concerned. In order to be seen and heard, the custodial father may have to step forward assertively, particularly if he wants anything done differently.

Schools need a lot more father-participation before there will be any significant changes in their routines. We emphatically suggest that if fathers have any time or talent to offer their child's school they should, by all means, do so.

Parents and Teachers

Teachers are frequently unaware that a divorce is happening because no one has told them. It is critical for teachers, advisors and administrators to be informed of where you are in your divorce process and to know the status of custody and visitation schedules. This kind of information makes it easier to gauge the child's mood swings and daily responsiveness. A weekend with the other parent can leave a child nervous and restless. A missed or upsetting visit can render the same child virtually nonfunctional.

We've noticed that where children of divorce are concerned, parents and teachers can often seem to have unreasonable expectations. They somehow think that children will miraculously continue to function normally in school despite what may be going on at home! For instance, teachers become impatient when the student falls behind in homework.

Children who follow a "normal behavior pattern" are unquestioningly considered undisturbed by the divorce. On the other hand, children have been known to "play the system" to their own advantage. It takes careful watching on the part of parents and teachers to recognize when a child is truly upset.

The Function of Homework

The obvious purpose of homework is to provide a child with the opportunity to practice and strengthen academic skills. In addition, homework encourages responsibility, perseverance, improved time-management skills, initiative, self-reliance, and resourcefulness.

Single parents tend to become overly involved in a child's homework. This reinforces dependency, weakens tolerance for frustration, and diminishes the capacity for creativity and achieving individual success.

Parents, single or coupled, should function as "consultants" and be available to assist with any reasonable request. The child who is allowed to make mistakes and is encouraged to correct them by seeking information from other sources and authorities is the child who develops self-reliance and self-esteem.

BEATING THE HOLIDAY BLUES

Most of us will agree that holidays can be very *down* times. When you are in "divorce mode," holidays can make you particularly aware of your feelings of loss.

Are you one of those people who want things to go completely unchanged from the past? Do you have family members like this?

With a divorce, you have divided emotions: One side wishes for those truly wonderful holidays in which everything miraculously works out; the other side is scared and anxious about just getting through it. Who gets the children? For whom do I need to get presents? Who will be with me? Am I going to end up spending the holiday alone?

Expectations During Holidays

A major problem for all of us is that the American Dream about ideal holidays is way out of line with what is practical or reasonable to expect. So, start there. Temper your expectations with reality.

When you approach any holiday, make a conscious decision that this is *your* day as much as anyone else's and that the goal is to bring some joy to everyone, including yourself. Keep in mind that the coming event may be stressful to others, as well as to you. By some quirk of the gods, children get hyper and adults get depressed. It's an explosive combination.

Choices

You have choices. Give yourself ample time to think about them. Consider all of the options open to you that will make the best of family relationships, including your ex-family.

For Yourself

If you are going to be without your children for a holiday, plan alternatives in advance. Think about your comfort level and decide what you need to do for yourself. Do you want solitude or to be with other people? Perhaps this is the ideal time for a brief vacation or a change of scenery. The trip doesn't need to be expensive. Could you borrow an empty apartment or cabin, or visit a friend or relative? If you decide to stay home, how about inviting others who might also be alone?

For the Kids

If you have children who are old enough to participate in the decision-making, ask for their ideas and preferences. Be prepared to accept the idea that a child may choose to be with the other parent. This may not be a simple choice; it may be a way to express belonging to both parents. It may be in support of the spouse who has fewer family connections.

Leave room in your plans for compromise. Perhaps some up-front discussions with the other people in your family (and your ex-spouse's family) would be appropriate. Approach them with a plan and a couple of alternatives. Consider the possibility of creating new holiday rituals that will work better for everyone.

Here are some ideas for how to handle split celebrations:

- For Christmas or Hanukkah, have two celebrations: one on the eve and one on the holiday, alternating years.
- Alternate Thanksgiving and religious holidays.
- For other holidays such as July 4th, Labor Day, Easter, birthdays, and so forth, work out alternating systems that recognize children's ages and social needs.

Note If there is cooperation in co-parenting and you choose to celebrate together, recognize that it may rekindle hopes of a reconciliation which may not be in your best interests.

The issue of holiday visitation will come up in your separation agreement. Try to think long term. The least restrictive decisions may be best unless there are extenuating circumstances.

PLANNING AND RECORDING VISITATION

We suggest that you keep a schedule and record of visitation. It will allow for efficient planning and, if you add your own comments, will also be a useful record of how things work out for you, your ex-spouse, and the children.

FORM-ula 21: Visitation Schedule and Records is a record of the arrangements you are making and is helpful in establishing custodial guidelines.

HAVING THE LAST WORD

The last word is *kindness*. The next to the last word is *patience*.

Your children have a lot to swallow. They are not you. They may look like you and even act like you, but they are still not you. They are themselves; one of a kind. They are living and growing in various stages of formation: they are tender and bruiseable, trusting and resilient, problematical and lovable. Being a single parent is enough to overwhelm any normal person. Kindness and patience can help to bridge the gaps.

Section *IV*
FINANCIAL VALUE OF THE MARRIAGE

No one will take the same interest in your future welfare as you. Even though you will listen carefully to the suggestions of your lawyer and financial advisors, in the last analysis, you are the one who must consent to the final transactions of your divorce. Your decisions must be informed decisions. Otherwise, your divorce agreement will not reflect a fair evaluation of assets, liabilities, and extenuating circumstances.

Quality begins with an eye for detail. You cannot afford to be ignorant of your finances.

It is your job to gather accurate business and personal financial data. Estimates of assets, income, or expenses can be challenged. Lawyers and judges do not accept the words, "I can't find it." All of the material that you will need for a successful divorce should be in your possession as quickly as possible. Things have a way of disappearing. Even though there are appropriate legal methods for obtaining missing information, this adds to time and expense.

PUTTING THE FINANCIAL PUZZLE TOGETHER

Some of the biggest mistakes in financial decision making come from leaving out pieces of the puzzle. Your objective in this section is to determine:

- Where money goes.
- Where money comes from.
- What you currently have to show for your money.

You need this information to provide the financial analysis which will become the basis for your divorce sepa-

ration agreement. These figures will show the family lifestyle and the dollars spent to maintain it.

Both you and your spouse will have to consider how to divide your bills and accounts, and how you will manage your credit and creditors.

We have you start by compiling your marital expenditures for the past two years. By being aware of the previous operating expenses of your household, as well as your current situation, you will have a clearer picture of what you will need for the future.

In essence, what you are doing is gradually preparing all of the documentation you will need to negotiate the financial settlement of your separation agreement.

In order to make sure that you collect all of the correct material, we have developed a master list of documents you will need. You will find this information in Chapter 15. A legal process called *discovery* can be used by your attorney for assembling documentation not readily available to you. These legal resources are discussed in Chapter 18.

OPERATING EXPENSES BEFORE SEPARATION

At this point, it is necessary to reconstruct the financial history of your marriage. Your attorney will require a financial statement. If you do not already have a practical system of record keeping, use **FORM-ula 22: Expenses.** Use a separate FORM-ula 22 for each of the past two years.

Information to prepare this FORM-ula comes from the following sources:

- Paid bills and statements.
- Cancelled checks and bank statements.
- Credit card statements.
- Cash payment estimates.
- Tax statements.
- Cash receipts.
- Coupon payment stubs.

By using FORM-ula 22, you will be able to reconstruct your expenses by category, month, and year. The financial statement you will present to the court often requires that your expenses be broken down into weekly figures. When you have compiled an annual figure for each expense, you can then divide each category total by 52 (weeks).

Any special needs that you anticipate in the near future should also be itemized so that they can be worked into the budget. Items might be eyeglasses, orthodontia, or monthly payments on a new car, furnace, roof, and so forth.

The advantage to a long-term financial picture is that it will give you a much more accurate weekly average from which to fairly project future expenses. For example, your heat and electricity costs vary by season and could be skewed by using only high or low months. You will also be less likely to miss nonregular expenses such as property taxes, insurance premiums, and medical and dental costs.

CURRENT OPERATING EXPENSES

If you have not already done so, begin immediately to keep accurate financial records of your current expenditures. You already have an organized format for doing this. Use your accordion file and another copy of the **FORM-ula 22: Expenses**.

Keep records of all of your expenses. Paying by check is a good way to do this. In your small pocket notebook, list all items that you pay by cash so that you can later add them up against the checks or computerized withdrawals you have made. Be sure to add up checks made out during the month to cash in order to approximate spending on items such as magazines, gifts, meals out, and so forth. If you have been used to paying cash for food, switch to checks or be sure to save the register receipts.

It is important that you keep your records up-to-date and readily available as resources for meetings with your attorney and negotations with your spouse.

CURRENT INCOME

Income means all the funds that are paid to you, such as salaries (including payments for overtime work, and bonuses), trust money, interest and dividends, and payments on any loan notes you hold. Also, include any compensation you receive in lieu of cash, such as food, shelter, or transportation. Other examples include rent in exchange for maintenance duties and discounts in exchange for work. Public assistance grants (federal, state, and local) are not to be included as income.

At the moment, you need to compile a set of basic figures for your current income. This data will be needed to develop your "credit-ability." The **FORM-ula 23: Income** is a detailed form with which to record the financial information pertaining to all your sources of income. Income, as part of the overall financial picture in your divorce, will be covered in Chapter 15.

Note When you record numbers, it will save time if you round out cents to the nearest dollar and with larger figures, use the nearest ten dollars.

Chapter 14
THE CREDIT IN YOUR FINANCIAL SYSTEM: BECOMING A SEPARATE FINANCIAL ENTITY

In the business of divorce, the goal is to establish an independent credit and finance system. You need to have adequate money to meet current needs and a source of funds for major expenditures or unforeseen financial emergencies.

One thing that most of us take for granted is credit. In America, *credit* is a word that sometimes seems to go along with *Mom* and *apple pie*. We function on credit.

If you need to get your finance and credit situation squared away for your new life, start by understanding how credit bureaus operate.

CREDIT BUREAUS AND CREDIT REPORTS

Credit bureaus were established so that the people who lend money or give credit know whether or not you are a good risk. They function as paid services to collect and disseminate your credit history to banks, finance companies, department stores, and others legally entitled to have this information.

Credit bureaus act as clearing houses for your payment habits from the moment you establish your first account to the day you die or drop out of the credit world.

Each person has the right to be considered equal to all other credit applicants. When a business extends credit to you, they trust that you will pay, at some future time, for the goods and services you are receiving today.

How Credit Is Reported

The information collected by credit bureaus includes:

- Amount of credit extended.
- Terms of the account: 30/60/90 days and percentage of interest.

- Current account balance.
- Amount that is overdue.
- Promptness of payment.

This information is generally rated by the creditor or broken down by record of current annual activity.

A credit report will not necessarily be a complete record of your accounts. The only accounts that will be in the credit bureau's files are those that make regular reports to the bureaus. Most national credit card companies provide credit reports regularly while many local creditors do not. Also, some creditors only report delinquent accounts.

A credit profile may include data taken from public records, such as tax liens, civil suits and judgments, bankruptcy records, criminal convictions, or any other legal proceedings recorded by a court of law. Government information, such as student and small business loans, is also recorded. Unfortunately, these reports do not indicate the original amount due, only what you still owe or are in arrears on.

Investigating Your Own Credit

Most people don't think about their own credit report until they apply for new credit and are refused on the basis of a poor or nonexistent credit rating.

What does *your* credit report look like? Is it separate from your spouse's? The first thing to do is find out how your credit stands at the present time.

How to Get the Information

There are a number of federal laws that affect consumer credit information. The Federal Fair Credit Reporting Act, Equal Credit Opportunity Act, and Fair Credit Billing Act are all enforced by the Federal Trade Commission.

There are a few national credit reporting agencies: TRW, CBI, Trans Union, Chilton, Credit Bureau Inc., CSC Services (formerly Associated Credit Services). At the present time, TRW is the largest of the computerized reporting agencies. If you live in a small town, your credit history is probably kept by a local bureau, as well. You will find credit bureau listings in the *Yellow Pages*.

Contact a major credit reporting agency to obtain a copy of the files listed under both your name and your spouse's. Be sure to include full names on the account (Jr., Sr., etc.), social security numbers, previous addresses, and former names. If you are still married, you will not be required to have your spouse's signature on the request. The fee for this information is generally from $5 to $15 per copy.

What to Look For

When you receive this information, look for two things: (1) proof that there is a credit history recorded in your name, and (2) a confirmation that what is recorded is correct.

An authorized signature is not the same as joint credit. Your name embossed on a credit card, for an account opened by your spouse, does not necessarily mean that a credit report for that account is being reported in your name.

If you have been signing all the checks and paying the bills on a timely basis, you may think that you now have a marvelous financial credit record. "It ain't necessarily so." If you did not open the accounts jointly, and you are only a signee, you are a financial nonentity until you prove otherwise.

On the other hand, if yours is the primary or joint name listed on any account that is delinquent or in arrears, your credit will suffer no matter who has been signing the checks or taking the financial responsibility for paying bills.

In order to check the accuracy of your credit report, you can refer to the same documentation you used to complete your **FORM-ula 22: Expenses.** Your statements will show account numbers, expiration dates, and company addresses.

Using FORM-ula 24: Credit Card Inventory

There are two reasons for using **FORM-ula 24: Credit Card Inventory.** First, you need to have an up-to-date record of all family credit cards for your separation agreement. Second, you will quickly notice if there is a discrepancy between the information on your credit report and what you have on FORM-ula 24. Contact the accounts in question (through their customer service or billing departments) in order to:

- Verify the name listed for the account on the original application.
- Verify the name used on the account for credit reporting.
- Find out the primary and secondary credit reporting agency used.

Note Uncooperative creditors can be legally required to supply you with copies of all the account records you need. This legal request is called a *sub-poena duces tecum.*

Making Credit Corrections

The first reaction to trouble in the credit zones is almost always: "There has been some terrible mistake!"

How often do errors actually occur? Unfortunately, credit bureaus are notorious for keeping incorrect and out-of-date material in consumers' files. This happens because credit bureaus are not responsible for the accuracy of the information they receive. It is up to you, the consumer, to correct the errors that have to do with your account.

Consumer Rights

Under the Federal Fair Credit Report Act, as a consumer, you have the following rights:

- To know what credit information is held that relates to you (*without charge* if you have been denied credit within the past 30 days).

- To know who has received a report within the past six months.

- To know who has received a report for employment purposes within the past two years.

- To have information that you dispute reinvestigated and corrected (or removed if inaccurate or unverifiable), and to have an updated report sent to anyone who has requested a report within the last six months.

- To place a statement in the credit bureau's file if, after investigation, the dispute continues.

- To have adverse information removed after seven years (ten years for bankruptcy).

So it's a good idea, simply from a practical business standpoint, to check on your credit and your credit rating now. Start early and avoid the rush.

Common Questions About Divorce and Credit

Question: Can companies close your credit accounts because you have changed marital status?

Answer: No. A creditor cannot close an account or change the terms unless there is a proven inability or unwillingness to pay. However, the creditor can require you to submit a new application if the original application was based on only one spouse's financial statement. The creditor must allow you to use the account while reapplication is pending.

Question: When the divorce is final, will previous credit history be lost?

Answer: If the charge accounts you used with your spouse were contracted jointly, you will both have the same credit history. If you merely used the accounts as a signee, it may be necessary to confirm the fact that you were equally responsible for the payments with proof of canceled checks and a financial statement that shows your ability to pay. (This is why you are checking up on each of your charge accounts, so you can send out the proper notifications, fill in necessary papers, and begin to establish yourself as a separate financial entity.)

Question: How hard will it be to get separate credit?

Answer: If you have a good credit history and the necessary income, you should have little or no problem opening new accounts. If you are the spouse who was unemployed during the marriage and if you have never had a credit card, you may need a cosigner. If the account was in your name, a letter to the company can remove a previously authorized signature.

Question: After the divorce, are you still responsible for joint accounts?

Answer: Yes, which is why you should see to it that prior to the final decree, all joint accounts are paid off, closed, and new accounts started in the individual names. Be aware of running up charge account bills as part of divorce planning or retaliation. If it can later be proven that these expenditures were not agreed upon jointly (or were not for necessities such as food, housing, clothing, or health care) they may not be considered joint debt.

Note Creditors don't care how your separation agreement divides responsibility for debt. You are each liable for the full amount of debt on joint cards until the bill is paid.

BUILDING YOUR CREDIT FILE

If you already have credit, you will simply have to make sure that there are no errors or omissions on your credit report.

Joint accounts need to be separated so that the credit information is reported in both names. This process can be as simple as a phone call or complicated as the creditor's need for bureaucratic red tape.

Without a credit history, you might fall into a "Catch 22" situation: no one wants to give you credit until you have a record of paid accounts and you can't develop a record of paid accounts until someone gives you credit. There are ways to overcome this problem. Let's start with the Equal Opportunity Act.

Equal Opportunity Act

The Equal Opportunity Act acknowledges consumers' rights as:

- Being judged on an equal basis with all other credit applicants.
- Having joint accounts reported separately for each spouse after June 1977.
- Considering income without regard to sex or marital status.
- Recognizing child support and alimony payments (regularly received) as income, if so requested.
- Maintaining privacy from being asked questions about birth control or child-bearing plans.
- Permitting a married woman to apply for a credit card in her own name.
- Receiving information about the reasons why credit has been denied.

This act does not state that everyone has the right to credit. It simply asserts that everyone must be evaluated on the same basis.

The Equal Opportunity Act also gives all consumers the right to have their credit information sent to credit reporting agencies under their own names without the use of titles such as Mr., Mrs., Ms., or Miss. Most joint accounts opened after 1977 have been automatically reported in both names, but it doesn't hurt to check. If your accounts were opened before 1977, request that you now be reported separately.

In the event that you find certain creditors have not reported credit in both names (for an account that was opened jointly), notify the creditor by letter. Use the **FORM-ula 25: Requesting an Individual Credit Report.**

HOW BANKING AND CREDIT RELATE

When you get a divorce, it is a good idea to reconsider the bank you want to use. If you have a long-term relationship with your present bank, you may wish to continue it. If your spouse has been the major user, you may want to find a new bank. A fresh start may be to your advantage.

Choosing a Bank

Choosing a new bank brings up some considerations, regardless of the size of the account. Look for:

- A bank that has hours convenient to your lifestyle.
- Drive-up tellers and automated teller machines.
- High interest on savings.
- A MasterCard or Visa program.
- Linked savings and checking accounts with cash reserve and overdraft privileges.
- Safety deposit boxes.
- A Notary Public.
- Check information, such as
  service charges or costs per check.
  the cost of printed or personalized checks.
  procedures for bounced checks.
- Friendly and polite bank employees.
- A bank that cares about your account.
- Completely insured savings accounts.

If you are concerned about the financial soundness of a bank, call one of the following services to get a report (for a nominal fee) on the bank's current condition:

Veribank Inc.	(800) 442-2657
Weiss Research	(800) 289-9222
Bauer Group	(305) 441-2062

Working With Checks

In the introduction of Section II, "Getting Personally Organized," we suggest that you label specific categories in your accordion file for paid bills and canceled checks. We assume that you are now using this file as a safe and organized place to expedite the transfer of dollar amounts to the **FORM-ula 22: Expenses.**

Since divorce is a crazy time, here are a few reminders about checks:

- Never write a check in pencil.
- It's not a good idea to sign a blank check.
- Record the checks you write in your check register. (Try carboned checks if you tend to forget this task).
- Initial any changes you make on your checks.
- Endorse checks exactly as they are made out. (If the assignment is different from the name ap-

pearing on your account, re-sign the check correctly and write "for deposit only" and the account number.)

- If you transact a second party check, be sure to sign it first and then put "pay to the order of" and the person's name.

APPLYING FOR CREDIT

"Why is it called 'instant credit' when what it really means is 'instant debt'?"

Orben's Current Comedy

Do not try to apply for credit cards all at once.
A local supplier such as a drugstore, gift, or specialty clothing store will often approve your credit application if you have been a regular customer and your checks have always cleared. When you start to use these accounts, be sure to pay them promptly and in full. This will help you to quickly establish good credit.

Next time you go to your favorite department store, ask for a credit application. Apply for check-cashing cards at your regular grocery markets. It is also a good idea to have at least one major gasoline credit card. (This card may also be used for emergency auto repairs.)

Having a major credit card, such as MasterCard or Visa, will almost immediately qualify you for additional credit accounts. At the present time, business competition makes them relatively easy to get. Just be sure to read your contract for information on the:

- Rate of interest charged (if you are planning to make monthly payments), because percentages can be misleading.
- Amount of credit line.
- Limit of liability if card is lost or stolen.

Wisdom in Credit References

When asked on credit applications to give credit references, be sure to pick the accounts that have the best records. If you know of any former or current accounts that will not show up well through the credit reporting bureaus, explain the circumstances in advance so that the information does not come as a surprise. There is a good chance that the creditor will take into consideration the fact that the majority of your accounts are in good order. A creditor is looking for a number of things:

- Your ability to pay or repay.
- The kind of income you receive.
- The regularity of your income.

Establishing Credit

Some of the credit-application forms may require more financial information than you currently have available. Plan to complete them after you have done the work in Chapters 15 and 16. By then, you will then have organized the balance of your financial information.

Without a previous credit rating, verification of your ability to pay may be acquired through income tax returns, a letter from an attorney, a written court decree, canceled checks showing continuity of income, or a letter from your bank or investment firm.

If you are having an unusually prolonged or troublesome time establishing your credit, consider talking with relevant community services, a Legal Aid counselor, or a knowledgeable friend or relative. Your local bank officer may also be able to offer assistance.

Obtaining a "Secured" Card

A growing number of banks are offering *secured* Visa and MasterCards to borrowers who have never had credit or who are normally considered poor risks. To obtain a *secured* card, you will have to deposit money equal to the credit line you wish to receive. By maintaining this account properly you may qualify for a standard card and, incidentally, receive back your deposit. Just be sure that the bank issuing the card makes regular reports to a national credit bureau so that you really are developing a credit history.

Note Fraudulent *knock-offs* are appearing in the secured card industry. For information on legitimate institutions, write to:

RAM Research
College Estates, Box 1700
Frederick, MD 21701

or

Bankcard Holders of America
560 Herndon Parkway, Suite 120
Herndon, VA 22070

Short-Term Loan as Credit

Whether or not you presently have a need for the money, you can use a small, short-term loan to help establish good credit. Sources for this type of loan are banks, credit unions, and reputable financial organizations. If you don't need the money, put it in a savings account. Withdraw just enough each month to make the payment. It will cost you the slight difference in interest, but it will be a worthwhile investment toward future credit needs.

Make a secured loan from a financial institution for a major purchase: furniture, automobile, and so forth. Pay this loan off promptly.

Ask someone to cosign a loan with you. Select a person who can afford to be responsible for your debt in the event you cannot pay. A cosigner might be a family member or close friend. Once this loan is paid off, you will have established your own credit.

An unblemished payment record is the vital part of your credit rating, so be sure to borrow only what you can afford to pay back timely and in full.

Note As of January 1, 1991, interest on credit cards, car loans, and personal loans is no longer tax deductible.

Observation 1 Unfortunately, the bright mind that writes the bank advertising doesn't sign the loan agreement!

Observation 2 Banks loan billions to third world countries but, in their branches, they chain down the pens!

PROTECTING YOUR CREDIT CARDS

As you establish or reestablish credit, be sure to regularly update your **FORM-ula 24: Credit Card Inventory**.

To track your billings:

- Save your card receipts to compare with the billing statements.
- Reconcile these statements the same as you would your checking account.
- Report promptly, in writing, any questionable charges or discrepancies. (Check the back of your bill for the proper procedure.)

Credit card fraud is rampant. Never give your credit card number over the telephone unless you are placing an order with a reputable company that *you* have called, not one that has called you. (If you break this rule and get caught in a scam, your credit card company may be able to help you. Get in touch with the

company right away because time is of the essence.) When signing a charge slip, destroy the carbons.

There are credit card registration services designed to save you time, worry, and money in the event that your cards are lost or stolen. Most credit card companies offer this service, directly or through authorized contractors. Some have an annual fee and others require membership dues to qualify for "free" registration.

MANAGING YOUR CREDIT AND CREDITORS

Credit sounds great. A synonym is *debt*. Your consumer debt is the full amount of what you owe, not the total of your minimum monthly payments.

If you are having trouble paying bills, get in touch with your creditors immediately to set up a mutually satisfactory payment schedule. Try not to get so far behind in your payments that they are reported to a credit bureau. This is the kiss of death to your credit report because, once reported as delinquent, it stays on your report for seven years.

If you dispute a billing with a specific creditor (and you are afraid that your account will be sent to a collection agency), under the Fair Credit Billing Act, you have the right to:

- File a written complaint with the creditor within 60 days after the bill was mailed.
- Receive an acknowledgment from the creditor within 30 days of filing the complaint, and a settlement within 90 days.
- Forestall collection of the account until the dispute is resolved.
- Prohibit the creditor from reporting negative information regarding the disputed amount to credit reporting agencies until the dispute is cleared.

Credit Counseling

If you are in debt over your head and need help, consult with a consumer credit counseling service. This is a local nonprofit organization affiliated with the National Foundation for Consumer Credit, which provides debt counseling for you and your family. It is not a lending institution, charity, or government agency. It is supported by contributions from banks, consumer finance companies, credit unions, merchants and other community-minded firms and individuals. For the address of the service nearest to you, we suggest you write or call:

National Foundation for Consumer Credit Inc.
8701 Georgia Avenue, Suite 507
Silver Spring, Maryland 20910
(301) 589-5600

They will require a completed application and an appointment with a professional counselor. The counselor will review your financial problems and work out a satisfactory plan with your creditors for debt payment. (Be prepared to support your application form with copies of the proper documentation from your files.) There may be a small fee for administering your plan, but it is generally nominal.

The value of this kind of counseling is that most debts arise from lack of planning, miscalculation, or some kind of radical change in life style, such as a divorce. Consumer counseling helps because it:

- Provides a realistic program for dealing with the most immediate and pressing debts.
- Sets up a realistic budget and plan for the future.

If your debt amount is not serious enough to warrant a consumer credit service, other sources of counseling include your bank, family service agencies, and perhaps the human resources department where you work. Additionally, there are financial planners, bookkeepers, and accountants available to you for a fee.

Handling Debts by Yourself

When you are faced with serious debts, but are pretty much aware of what you must do and how to do it,

you will develop a pay-off plan that is within your current and foreseeable budget. Willingness to take charge of your debts and carry out such a plan will carry weight with most creditors, collection agencies, and judges (if your problem gets that far).

Notify your creditors that you are aware of the debt and are asserting your right under US Code 1692C (Fair Debt Collection Practices). Thereafter, the agency can only contact you to inform you of a specific legal step being taken against you, or to periodically inquire about your current financial situation.

Remember, if you are writing to accounts that have not been handed over to collection agencies, you will want to state your awareness of the debt, your intention to pay and what the repayment timing can be.

The Option of Last Resort

Bankruptcy is the option of last resort. Financial problems during a divorce can seem overwhelming but may have an eventual solution without seriously marring your credit. Do not file for bankruptcy without the advice and consent of your attorney.

Take heart. Dealing with dollars is similar to some of the other processes you are going through right now. By organizing your material, and going at it one step at a time, you will eventually end up with a clean financial slate and a set of operating procedures that will ultimately keep you within safe financial boundaries.

We are not saying that you won't have to go through some pretty rough terrain to get there. We're simply saying that you *will* get there.

Chapter 15
PULLING TOGETHER THE DOCUMENTATION

"There's your truth, my truth, and the real truth."

ANON

Redistribution of "the great estate" is something divorcing couples are generally not very good at. Dividing the assets and liabilities requires facts and their documentation. The more information you and your spouse share voluntarily, the less expensive the divorce is likely to be. Legal fees run proportional to the antagonism between spouses.

Don't worry if the facts and papers to which you presently have access do not add up to what you will need. It is as important to know what you *don't* have as what you *do* have. There are legal procedures your attorney can invoke to get the missing information. These procedures will be covered in Chapter 18.

The documentation process of your divorce consists of two parts:

- Gathering of information.
- Decision making.

Keep these two activities separate in your mind while you concentrate on the task at hand, the gathering of information to document the facts. Decision making will be covered in Chapters 23, 25, and 26.

Collecting information will empower you and your attorney to negotiate a satisfactory agreement.

CREATING YOUR DOCUMENTATION FILES

First of all, we will give you a master list and FORMulas for the documents you will need. The portable file box that you purchased provides the container for your divorce materials. It can be locked in a closet, stored in the trunk of your car, or placed with a trusted friend or relative.

Information to put in these files will come from:

- *The Divorce Decisions Workbook* file system.
- Your own personal files.
- Current and old family files.
- Your spouse.
- Friends and relatives.

- Business associates (yours or your spouse's).
- Letters and phone calls of inquiry.
- Monthly statements.
- Records held by outside institutions, professionals, government, and so forth.

As you collect the facts that you need, be sure to photocopy the more important documents for your files; it's cheaper and less time-consuming than having them reissued. Put the originals in a safe place.

In Section II, we suggest using Pendaflex files. If you haven't already made them, do so now for:

1. Personal papers
2. Children
3. Education
4. Credit card list
5. Household inventory and appraisal
6. Personal banking
7. Money loaned to others
8. Money borrowed from others
9. Investments
10. Applications and financial statements (prior to separation)
11. Titles and deeds
12. Medical insurance
13. Life insurance
14. Personal property insurance
15. Tax returns
16. Employment history and resumes
17. Employer policies and benefits
18. Proprietorship, partnership, professional corporation, family-owned business
19. Income records
20. Retirement dollars

There is frequently one FORM-ula (or more) for each category. You have already begun working on some of them. You can now store them in their appropriate file folders.

Personal Papers

This file will hold all of your profile FORM-ulas from Chapter 5, with the exception of the profile on children. The **FORM-ula 26: Personal Papers** is a checklist for important documents.

Children

Keep all FORM-ula records and papers relating to the children in this file.

Education

School transcripts, report cards, certifications, standardized test score reports (SAT, GRE, GMAT, etc.), and all other papers relevant to education go in this file.

Credit Card List

This file is for **FORM-ula 24: Credit Card Inventory**, **FORM-ula 25: Requesting an Individual Credit Report**, and copies of letters sent or received that relate to your credit picture.

Household Inventory and Appraisals

You have probably accumulated a lot of personal property during your marriage. Now that you are preparing for a divorce, it is important to take an inventory of it. As tedious and frustrating as the project may seem, you should make a tangible record of everything you own (be sure to date the record). The total value of your personal property, plus any special insurance policy riders you have, should agree with the figure you have the property insured for. (You will find this amount on your homeowner's or renter's insurance policy.) This figure is to be included on your current financial statement under the category "Household Furnishings." You will use the inventory during negotiations for your divorce agreement.

To make the process easier, use **FORM-ula 27: Household Inventory and Appraisal**. Start by going through the FORM-ula. Cross off items that you don't own. Add items that are not included on the list. If you have insurance photos or floor plans, use these as reminders.

Use **FORM-ula 28: Missing Items** to record items that you cannot find. This is information that you will want to give to your attorney.

Notice the columns provided on FORM-ula 27 to help you prioritize, record, and ultimately carry out the decisions made for the division of personal property.

The only columns you need to be concerned with at this time are:

- *How Acquired? Gift or inherited (by whom?), or purchased (when?)*. Consider items such as family heirlooms, items each brought to the marriage, personal collections.
- *Do You Want It, Yes or No?* Are you interested in having the item?
- *Appraisal, Value Date*. Does the item warrant a current appraisal?

Include in this file any existing appraisals or warranties. You will usually find indications of appraisals by riders that have been added to your homeowners' insurance policy. These riders provide special insurance for items such as art, jewelry, musical instruments, furs, and collectibles. If in doubt about current value, contact a qualified appraiser. You can refer to:

American Society of Appraisers
P.O. Box 17265
Washington, DC 20041

or

Appraisers Association of America
60 E. 42nd St.
New York, NY 10165

Personal Banking

FORM-ula 29: Personal Banking organizes bank and trust information. Whether or not you have been the major money manager in your family, you should be aware of what is happening to joint accounts. Unfortunately, it is common for divorcing couples to manipulate finances or to shelter money. So, you should take a closer look at the financial transactions of the previous year and keep close tabs on the family bank accounts.

- How many financial papers have you signed that you didn't read over carefully or keep copies of?
- Could it be that savings are being used for regular living expenses, while current income is being diverted to a new account?
- Has a joint checking or savings account been cleaned out recently?

- Have there been plans made to refinance the house or take out other kinds of loans?
- Could there be assets buried in safe deposit boxes or semi-invisible bank accounts (using other names)?

Money Loaned to Others

Information on FORM-ula 30: Money Loaned to Others is a family asset that is frequently forgotten about or overlooked. These loans could affect current and future income.

Money Borrowed From Others

Information on FORM-ula 31: Money Borrowed From Others is a family liability. These loans also could affect current and future income.

Investments

This file could be one of the most difficult ones to complete. In fact, you may want to use FORM-ula 32: Investments as a basic checklist. If you are the family investor or invest jointly with your spouse, this information is readily available through your own records or those of your financial advisors and/or stockbrokers. If not, you will have to search for it yourself, or go through legal channels to get the information.

Applications and Financial Statements (prior to separation)

"There are three kinds of lies—lies, damn lies, and statistics."

MARK TWAIN

In this file, you will keep copies of the financial statements that you and/or your spouse have completed in the past few years. Why? Because financial statements may reveal assets or liabilities that you have forgotten or overlooked.

If you are unsure of where to look to find it, a financial statement would probably have been required for any large loan or purchase. Check files that contain papers relating to these. If these papers are not in your possession, you should contact the lending institution. While all application information is officially considered their property, it may be possible to photocopy what you need.

Titles, Deeds, and Capital Improvements

To have a more complete picture of what you own and its current value, use **FORM-ula 33: Titles and Deeds**. Sometimes this project uncovers property that has been fraudulently conveyed in an attempt to remove it from the marital assets.

For homeowners, **FORM-ula 34: Real Estate Capital Improvements** will be important in determining the cost basis of the home whether or not it is to be sold as part of the divorce financial settlement.

Personal Health and Medical Insurance

Health conditions and medical insurance are topics for discussion in developing the separation agreement. Use **FORM-ula 35: Personal Health** and as many copies of **FORM-ula 36: Medical Insurance** as there are policies. This file can also be used for policy booklets and other medical records, including those for prescription medications and psychotherapy.

Life and Disability Insurance

Complete one copy of **FORM-ula 37: Life Insurance** and **FORM-ula 38: Disability Insurance** for each policy on any member of the family or other dependent. Whether or not you or your spouse are the present owners or beneficiaries, the future dispensation of these policies is negotiable. Policies have also been used as assurance and/or collateral for court-ordered support payments.

Personal Property Insurance

This file has three FORM-ulas for personal property insurance:

FORM-ula 39: Homeowner's/Renter's Insurance

FORM-ula 40: Automobile Insurance

FORM-ula 41: Recreational Vehicle Insurance

You will find the information for these FORM-ulas

on the individual policies or by calling your insurance agent.

Tax Returns

Keep copies of at least two prior years' tax returns in this file. If you cannot find them, **FORM-ula 42: Tax Returns** will tell you how to request copies of these returns from the government. When you complete the FORM-ula, it will provide the most pertinent tax data needed for your separation agreement.

Employment History and Résumés

This file is for employment information about you and your spouse. Use it to hold copies of résumés, lists, or notes on work history. If you do not have an existing résumé or curriculum vitae, use **FORM-ula 43: Employment and Education**. Armed service records, including military discharge papers (Form DD214 verifies separation from active duty) also belong here.

Note Military identification numbers *are not* the same as Social Security numbers.

Legally, minor children are not responsible for their own financial support. However, if minor children are gainfully employed, their income may be a factor in determining support amounts. For this reason, it might be a good idea to include their work information.

Employer Policies and Benefits

Financial negotiations will include information contained on **FORM-ula 44: Employer Policies and Benefits**. Many of these items affect lifestyle and they all have implications for the future financial status of one spouse or the other.

Proprietorships, Partnerships, Professional Corporations and Family-Owned Businesses

Private business information is not always readily available. Complete as much of **FORM-ula 45: Proprietorships, Partnerships, Professional Corporations, and Family-Owned Businesses** as possible. Recognize that private businesses require specialized accounting and legal knowledge. This fact will strongly affect the selection of the professional team you use for your divorce.

Income Records

FORM-ula 46: Income Records is a checklist of possible income sources, including those items on the FORM-ula 23: Income that you used in Section IV. Keep copies of both forms in this file. The originals stay in your accordion file.

Retirement Dollars

Organized retirement information is particularly important if:

- Either spouse is approaching retirement.
- The marriage is of some duration.
- The marriage was entered into late in life.

What belongs in this file is documentation of any personal, business, or corporate financial plans which you or your spouse have been using to accumulate funds for retirement. Any retirement information that you may have collected up to this point can now be put into this file.

As a result of the Federal Retirement Act of 1984 (REA), pension or retirement benefits are a properly divisable asset. They can be used as funds for spousal and child support. This is discussed in more detail in Chapter 21.

Retirement funds are often used as a bargaining tool. You will want to obtain a copy of the plan document or, the next best thing, a copy of the summary plan description. This easily understood version of your retirement plan is usually contained in an employee benefits booklet.

There are four basic types of employee retirement plans:

- Defined contribution plan. Each participant in the plan has one or more individual accounts into which the employee may make contributions as well as the employer. Value is based upon the amount of money contributed. You will want a Statement of Account.

- Defined benefit plan. There are no individual accounts. This type of plan promises to pay each retiring employee, for the rest of his or her life, a specified amount after the employee retires. Value is based upon average pay for a period of years prior to retirement and sometimes includes years of service. You will want a benefit statement and possibly a company affidavit of the employee's account.

- Excess nonqualified plan. These funds exceed the dollar amounts protected by law and are basically tax-deferred savings plans.

- Government plan. This type of plan includes the U.S. Civil Service, state employees, and the military. Each group has its own specialized plan and applicable law.

Social Security retirement benefits are benefits based upon earnings during the years worked. To find out what the records show for you and your spouse, complete a Personal Earnings Benefits Estimate Statement (PEBES), Form SSA-7004. The PEBES form indicates your Social Security earnings history; the amount of money you have paid in Social Security taxes; and an estimate of your future benefits. You can get this form by calling 1-800-234-5772, or your local Social Security office. You can mail a written request to:

Social Security Administration
PO Box 57
Baltimore, MD 21230

A marriage of at least 10 years prior to divorce is the key to eligibility for Social Security benefits under your spouse's earnings history. After that length of marriage, a nonmarried ex-spouse is usually eligible at age 62 for Social Security retirement and survivor's benefits. New spouses are also eligible. (Social Security pays double benefits; the ex- and current spouse do not split the available funds.)

Use FORM-ula 47: Retirement Dollars as a guideline for researching potential retirement funds.

Chapter 16
FINANCIAL SITUATION— AS IT STANDS RIGHT NOW

Now that you have a set of documentation files that put a financial value on the marriage, you are ready to create a usable financial statement. It will be a temporary "working" document until you and your attorney are both sure that the figures you have are complete and accurate. If you are the spouse who needs to establish new credit, it will also be your interim Asset and Liability Statement until by a court order, financial issues in the divorce are final.

To make the task easier, we have designed **FORM-ula 48: Assets** and **FORM-ula 49: Liabilities**. Refer to your documentation files for the appropriate figures.

Once you have completed these two FORM-ulas, you will have all of the information needed to fill out virtually any bank or credit statement. To ensure that you are familiar with the format, we have also included **FORM-ula 50: Generic Financial Statement**.

Later, when the divorce decree is granted, new blanks of these same FORM-ulas can be completed to reflect the terms of the separation agreement regarding changes in assets and liabilities.

In the meantime, as you prepare to work with an attorney, check the accuracy of your figures and look for missing information. It will be your attorney's responsibility to help you uncover hidden assets. We will discuss the assets that are most typi-

cally hidden and methods for confirming their existence.

Some issues in a marriage have an indirect financial value so we also include a list of the most common of these. One or more of these issues may be relevant to negotiating your separation agreement.

FLUSHING OUT HIDDEN ASSETS

Hiding assets is an ordinary occurrence during a divorce. It is usually begun by the spouse who is planning to divorce… long before the partner either suspects or is told about the proceedings to come.

Desperate times require desperate measures—or something like that. Unfortunately, this is the kind of cloak-and-dagger stuff that divorces are often made of.

Don't for a moment delude yourself into thinking that your spouse will go along with what you want or *be sensible*, and *do the right thing*.

Your spouse hasn't necessarily turned into a villain. Sometimes, though, when one partner in the marriage decides to divorce, energy is refocused toward walking away as financially comfortably as possible. In order to do this, the old adage, "What's mine is yours," frequently gets reversed.

Typical hidden assets are:

- Additional real estate, such as a house, condo, or piece of land.
- Boats or vehicles.
- Stocks, bonds, certificates of deposit, and annuities.
- Salary increases, commissions, and bonuses.
- Savings accounts and money-market funds.
- Custodial accounts for children.
- Phony debt to a friend or closely held business.

Look Before You Weep

Have there been any changes in the family finances over the last few years such as an increase in clothing and jewelry, travel, household furnishings, or heavy charging on credit cards?

Conversely, has there been any unreasonable belt-tightening? Is "for richer, for poorer" becoming unbalanced?

Pay attention to any red flags that may show up while you collect documents. This is the time to go back through the preceding documentation FORM-ulas and use a highlighting marker for missing or questionable information. Sneakiness is seldom blatant; small things count.

Revealing Statements

Look through old tax returns and checking and savings accounts for unexplained deposits or withdrawals. Sift through past financial statements made out for loans. Sometimes hidden assets will appear just long enough to give a more impressive borrowing picture to secure a particular loan.

Check securities and commodities statements to see if they tally with income tax reporting. At the same time, notice if there has been buying and selling you didn't know about. If so, where did the proceeds go? Where did the money come from to make the purchases in the first place?

Check the banks for accounts in your spouse's name. Until legal action is taken, you have a right to know that they exist and what is in them.

If you seriously suspect that your spouse is hiding assets in safe-deposit boxes or semi-invisible bank accounts (that use other names), make notes about the rationale for your feelings.

If your spouse is selling assets (such as a car that

has been paid for) or the reverse, accumulating liabilities (such as buying a new car), keep a dated record of these transactions.

Business Perks and Benefits

Money can be hidden through business dealings, including perks and benefits. Some methods are considered good financial planning under ordinary circumstances; others exist solely to deceive.

Through Employment

An employer will seldom risk a perjury charge to protect an employee, so it is possible to ask your spouse's company for information about:

- Voluntary reduction in income.
- Deferred compensation
- Senior executive life insurance (equity in split-dollar premium payment cash value).
- Stock plans.
- Pension fund.
- Deferred salary increases.
- Overtime or seasonal employment.
- Accumulated vacation pay.
- Uncollected bonuses or commissions.
- Loaded expense accounts.
- Trips.
- Company car.
- Club memberships.
- Vacation side trips.

Through Private Business

If you or your spouse are employed through a proprietorship, partnership, professional corporation, or family-owned business, you must realize that accounts may be manipulated to make income appear to be dwindling rapidly. Look into how the business is doing now compared with several years ago. (The overall economy and inflation will be factored in later if the issue is relevant to your separation agreement.) Consider the possibility of:

- Padded expenses.
- Nonexistent payments and payrolls.
- Recent increases or decreases of inventory.
- Retirement plan abuse.
- Debts by way of phony loans.

- Manipulations so income and value appear low.
- Temporary contractual agreements.
- Profit-sharing schemes.
- Cash payments.

HIDING ASSETS IS NOT SMART

If hidden assets exist, their documentation will probably require the legal discovery process, which will certainly prolong and complicate negotiations for the separation agreement. If hidden assets are discovered after a separation agreement is legally accepted, there could be a court order to increase or decrease support amounts. If discovery is made after the divorce is final, it is possible that a court will see this as perjury with intention to defraud.

Note Be careful that you have not concealed family assets. If you should need to close bank accounts, remove items from safe deposit boxes, sell stock, and so forth, make sure that the money or assets you remove are inventoried, dated, and labeled as to use. Accounting is *very* important. Be clear and specific about the use of funds and have documentary evidence to show that they were used for maintaining the previous family lifestyle. This may protect you from legal action if your spouse claims that you have deliberately hidden assets.

MAKING VALUE JUDGMENTS

There may be certain issues in your married life that are difficult to put dollar values on but that could be important items for negotiation.

Personal Issues

- The income-generating potential of surnames, celebrity status, and community or professional reputation.
- A serious health problem or psychological dysfunction.

- Some sexual difficulty or arrangement that has led to estrangement.
- Attempts to force the other spouse to divorce without regard to proper, fair, and organized settlement.
- The addictions of a spouse (alcohol, drugs, gambling, etc.) that have drained family funds.
- Previous suits for divorce or separate maintenance or consultations with attorneys regarding previous marital problems.

Financial Issues

- An unbalanced economic history during the marriage.
- Contribution made by one spouse to the education and training of the other.
- Educational credentials that make one spouse more employable than the other.
- Time one spouse has spent performing homemaking services.
- Gifts or inheritances anticipated by either spouse or children.
- Contingent rights to purchase or receive assets (property, stock, awards from lawsuits, etc.).
- A friend or relative who is holding assets.
- Benefits given up in order to marry (pension, social security).

Business Issues

- Excessive business travel that disrupted family life.
- Frequent relocations that caused financial losses on property or career interruptions of accompanying spouse.
- Share in increased value of family-owned business through labors of both spouses.
- Value of goodwill in business.

Any of these issues are appropriate to discuss during the negotiations for developing the separation agreement.

Section V

LEARNING ABOUT DIVORCE LAW

"Don't expect miracles."
Caption on a Product Advertisement

Before beginning this section, please reread the legal overview in Chapter 3.

As children, many of us were told that if we obeyed our mommies and daddies, believed in the democratic system, and ate our liver, we would be rewarded with liberty and justice for all. Too many of us have learned otherwise and to this day can't stand liver.

If your expectations are that the law will provide — the word is L-O-R-D, not L-A-W. You should, however, ask questions about how the system operates in your state. Research the divorce laws. Try to understand what you may be up against. Be clear that the law is not based upon all the nice things you did. Neither does it give you revenge for all the bad things that may have happened to you.

The law can be arbitrary, unreasonable, unwieldy, capricious, and outdated. It can also be surprisingly considerate. The law is limited by rules of evidence as to what it addresses and the amount of time it can set aside to hear your case. A case can drag on for months by delays, continuances, changes in the court docket, and untimely hearings. Frustration and misunderstanding on the part of both spouses about the court's actions often result in anger with both the court and each other.

Furthermore, the system allows for court decisions to be rendered without having had enough time or information and, too often, with an inadequate understanding of special circumstances. There is virtually no accountability for the consequences of the court's decisions.

WHOSE LAW IS IT, ANYWAY?

It is important to educate yourself on the legal realities of divorce in your state. This information is available from current books on divorce and attorneys. People employed by the court system are usually reluctant to give much information. There is a fine line between providing information and practicing law. They will usually encourage you to contact an attorney.

The problem with trying to read the actual state divorce law yourself is that it is written in "legalese," which might as well be Sanskrit to the average layperson. While there are individuals and organizations trying to rewrite the domestic relations laws so that they can be read and understood by anyone with a high school education, that job is far from completed.

Divorce law is essentially under state rule. The federal government has intervened in very few areas. Congress passed the Family Support Act of 1988 that created federal laws regarding:

- Interstate custody issues
- Medical coverage (COBRA)
- Taxation
- Bankruptcy

This same act requires each state to develop guidelines for the setting and enforcing of child-support orders that link payments to the quality of life that a child would have had if the parents were not divorcing.

If you or your spouse are presently covered under a group-employment medical insurance plan, a federal law (COBRA) enacted in 1986, provides for the right to continued coverage after you are divorced or legally separated. Since there have been legislative changes in the operational details of this law, be sure to check with your medical insurance carrier. You will want information about extended coverage, conversion options, cost, and eligibility requirements.

Where child support is concerned, all states must provide for automatic wage-withholding procedures against absent parents when the amount overdue equals one month's support payments. Overdue support can also be collected from a delinquent parent's tax refund, should there be one. Admittedly, collecting from an absent parent can be a difficult process, but the money does come through eventually, even when the absent parent lives in another state.

Chapter 17
GOING IT ALONE OR WITH PROFESSIONAL HELP

PRO SE DIVORCE

Pro se means that instead of having an attorney help you to draw up your separation agreement and represent you in court, you and your spouse will do it yourselves.

The legal procedures for obtaining a divorce are the same, with or without an attorney. In a pro se divorce you and your spouse will be responsible for filling out *and* filing all of the legal forms. You will also be obligated to arrange meetings, track court dates, and make sure that your decisions conform to legal requirements.

People in the best circumstances for a pro se divorce are those who:

- Have divided whatever property or money they have to each spouse's satisfaction.

- Do not want any settlement from each other.

- Have resolved emotional issues and can be cooperative.

- Have no children.

It is possible to do a pro se divorce when there are children involved, but we strongly suggest that you talk with an attorney before proceeding.

For a pro se divorce, your out-of-pocket expenses are limited to court costs and sheriff's fees for serving divorce papers. However, the cost of the divorce can be misleading if you forget to consider the value of your time and energy.

You can get written information about executing a pro se divorce from your state court system, the legal aid society, or your local library or bookstore.

FUNCTIONS OF THE DIVORCE ATTORNEY

The functions of a divorce attorney are to facilitate the client's decision-making processes and then to act on those decisions. The spouses structure the deal; the attorneys make it legal.

In order to work effectively, an attorney should be able to perform any (and preferably all) of the following services:

- Provide you with legally relevant facts of state codes.

- Tell you what the laws and procedures of your state allow.

- Determine the appropriate forum for you (for example, by advising a change in residence for more favorable treatment of your individual case).
- Stay current on new developments and fine points in the law.
- Maintain perspective and clear-headedness for you to be guided by.
- Prepare to litigate.
- Keep control over the case to protect you from willful violations of court orders or agreements.
- Frustrate attempts by your spouse to take advantage of you.
- Give you options to choose from rather than forcing results on you.
- Weigh advantages and disadvantages of alternatives.
- Prepare you to accept compromise where necessary or expedient.
- Help you get a fair settlement, not a punitive one.
- Advise you on the strong points of your spouse's case and the weak points of yours.
- Discourage arbitrary or vindictive demands.
- Support your discovery process of assets and expenses.
- Help you establish priorities that are workable for your postdivorce plans.
- Represent *you*, your knowledge, and your choices.

The method for hiring an appropriate attorney will be discussed in Chapter 24.

"No Can Dos"

Legal divorce is mainly about dollars. Your attorney can only handle the legal aspects of your divorce. The most an attorney can do is to arrange the best possible terms.

Very few of your personal problems will be addressed by your attorney. An attorney cannot bring back a spouse or reconstitute a family. Nor can this person make you happy. The attorney is not your confessor or your therapist. If you do use legal counsel for these purposes, remember that the time is not gratis. This money might be better spent with a counseling professional.

Specialized Divorce Attorneys

Among divorce attorneys, there are some who have created subspecialties of personal and financial issues dealing with:

- Corporations.
- Family-owned businesses.
- Sole proprietorships.
- International marriages.

Each category has distinct differences regarding salaries and benefits, perquisites, retirement arrangements, location transfers, and negotiable options.

To date, there is no legal certification in specific types of divorces. However, experience and a concentration of similar cases avoids the additional time and expense of a steep learning curve about typical details. If your divorce falls into one of these categories, you may want to consider using a specialized attorney. The value in knowledge and time saved could be worthwhile.

Chapter 18
THE LEGAL PROCESS AND HOW IT WORKS

"Ignorance of the law is no excuse."

Common Saying

The legal process is often a "hurry up and wait" proposition. You rush to get your case into the system and then you wait for it to go through the necessary channels. Any spousal conflict will extend the waiting time.

Who files for the divorce? The *plaintiff*. The plaintiff is the spouse who makes the first legal move. This can be a surprise attack or a negotiated choice made by the couple.

If you are the plaintiff and the divorce goes to trial, you get to present your side of the case first. The plaintiff also pays the initial court costs.

Since most cases do not go to trial, and since the initial court costs are minimal, the main issue of who files is primarily an emotional one. Ego, guilt, blame, family, and public opinion can all affect this decision.

THE SEQUENCE OF EVENTS

We have learned that most people heading toward divorce go immediately into the legal pipeline without understanding or having prepared for the inevitable process they have invoked. We are convinced that thorough preparation makes an enormous difference in the outcome.

However, whether or not you have prepared in advance, the legal procedure is the same. If you have been following the recommendations in this book, you are now prepared to move confidently into the legal process of your divorce.

Filing the Complaint/Summons

The plaintiff files a *Complaint* or *Summons* for divorce or legal separation with the court which states that the marriage is effectively over and indicates the basic claims and pleadings.

The format of this document varies from state to state. However, all initial divorce documents require certain basic information which must be presented to the court:

- Residence or domicile of both parties (place and length of time).
- Date and place of marriage.
- Names and birthdates of children (born or adopted).

- Reason for the divorce (irretrievable breakdown of the marriage, marital misconduct, or any other grounds recognized in your state).
- List of claims (dissolution of marriage, alimony, custody, child support, division of assets).

Serving Papers

Once the complaint or summons is filed, it is the duty of the sheriff to serve the papers to the *defendant* spouse.

In most states, papers can be served through the spouse's attorney. This is especially helpful when a divorcing couple is trying to avoid upsetting each other or the children.

Filing an Answer

There is a specified time period in each state for the defendant to *file an answer* which agrees with or disputes the allegations made in the complaint or summons.

A decision must now be made about the immediate financial and living arrangements as well as preparing to handle all of the details in the ultimate separation agreement. Sometimes, these immediate arrangements have been made prior to filing for a divorce.

Note to Military Personnel When one spouse is serving in the military, the marriage cannot be dissolved without the knowledge or consent given by a military affidavit unless the spouse in the military has *filed an appearance*.

Pretrial Orders

Pretrial orders and *written pleadings* are formal motions and hearings to get temporary court orders that apply to both spouses. Advance notice must be given to the defendant before such motions are brought to the court.

These orders usually concern interim arrangements about money, custody, and residence in the family home. They can also be *restraining orders* which place temporary restrictions on habitation, communication, and visitation as well as preventing the sale or waste of assets.

Preparation for pretrial orders will include the information that you have already put together. Depending upon the requirements of the pretrial orders, you will use information developed in Chapters 6, 13, and 15. Having this information already prepared and available may eliminate the possibility of a *motion to strike or dismiss* because the judge has insufficient information to make a decision.

Pretrial orders are binding until terminated or a new order is entered with the court. Usually pretrial orders include the phrase *without prejudice*, which simply means that the terms do not automatically (or even necessarily) become part of the final separation agreement.

If either party fails to comply with the temporary orders, a *Petition for Contempt* is the legal recourse.

When circumstances prevent negotiation of an acceptable temporary agreement, the court is able to provide emergency relief through an *ex parte motion*, based on one party's request without hearing from the other side.

This motion is granted by the judge to avoid irreparable physical or financial difficulties on the basis of acceptable legal testimony and/or evidence. For example, in documented claims of domestic violence, the court may issue an *ex parte order* for the offending spouse to stay away from the home. The court then arranges for a hearing to decide whether the order should be made permanent.

Discovery

Discovery is the legal process used to obtain information that is not voluntarily provided. If necessary, there are legal procedures an attorney can invoke to obtain most missing information:

- *Subpoenas* (ordering witnesses or others to appear).
- *Subpoena duces tecum* (court order for specific documents).
- Interrogatories (written questions answered under oath).
- Depositions (answering questions, under oath, before a court reporter).
- Notices to produce documents.
- Inspections of physical items.
- Requests for medical examinations.
- National credit reporting agencies (if ordered by a judge).

Your documentation files will show you what information is still missing. You and your attorney will decide which missing items are important to your case and how to get them.

Depositions

A *deposition* is the primary legal tool for getting information. It can be used in two ways.

- As evidence through testimony retained for a later court hearing when the testifying witness will not be available.
- For discovery of information that may be used any time during the divorce proceedings.

Depositions may be taken with regard to:

- Alleged misbehavior.
- Income.
- Assets.
- Financial need.
- Care and condition of children.
- Mental health.

Both spouses must be prepared to answer any notice of deposition from the opposing attorney. This could require presenting documentation such as:

- Bank records.
- Deeds and wills.
- Trust agreements.
- Insurance policies.
- Financial statements.

Procedures for a Deposition

Both spouses are entitled to be present at all depositions which are recorded by a court reporter.

Procedures for a deposition should be discussed with your attorney. You need to understand the kinds of questions that may be asked of you. You want to be prepared to answer difficult questions as well as know when to keep quiet.

If your attorney tells you not to answer a question during a deposition, follow those instructions, even though there may be a petition filed later requiring you to answer. At least you will have gained the time to prepare a statement.

If you are not questioned about information or documentation that you were asked to bring, *do not* volunteer answers on your own, even if it may seem to help your case. Let your attorney be your guide since information not brought forth earlier may hold an element of power or surprise later on.

Depositions can be ordeals but they often help to resolve some of the divorce issues. The apprehension and nervousness instilled by a deposition can cause one or both spouses to be more amenable to settlement rather than going to trial.

In any event, depositions can be a dress rehearsal of issues and problems to come. They can allow you and your attorney to assess the strengths and weaknesses of both sides.

Negotiation

The negotiation process begins when both spouses and their attorneys feel that they have all the pertinent facts.

The object of negotiation is to seek written agreement upon as many facts and issues as possible which will give the court the material it needs upon which to base a final dissolution decree. The subject of negotiation will be covered in greater detail in Chapters 23 and 25.

Mandatory Mediation

If you and your spouse are unable to come to an acceptable agreement about the custody and care of your children, you will probably be ordered by the court to see a court counselor. Your prepared documentation about the children will be invaluable.

The court may also require an investigation and written report on each of you. If this should happen, neither you, your spouse, nor either of the attorneys will have any further say in the matter. The final decision will be up to the judge after receiving report summaries.

Note If you foresee trouble in this area, seriously consider private mediation.

Pretrial Hearing

Attorneys and judges would like a divorce to be settled out of court and not have to go to trial. A pretrial hearing has two purposes:

- To focus the issues to be dealt with in a full-blown trial.
- To give information that may help the divorcing couple to settle out of court.

A pretrial hearing usually involves a judge (generally not the judge who will preside at the actual trial) who acts as a mediator. In some states, a panel of divorce attorneys is used instead of a judge.

The entire case, or just the unresolved issues (plus the accompanying personal and financial data), will be presented for advice and suggested resolutions. The spouses and attorneys will probably be interviewed, separately or together.

The pretrial judge or panel will advise both parties on how the actual trial judge is likely to rule giving a worst-case/best-case scenario.

The effects of this hearing, which include information about the probable outcome of a trial, can have a very sobering influence on both spouses, sometimes enough to bring about a settlement conference with the necessary compromises instead of going to trial.

A pretrial hearing has served its purpose when both spouses are able to see the risks, time, and expense involved in a full-blown court case and decide to work through their disputes in one or more settlement conferences.

Trial

A trial follows an orderly sequence of events:

1. *Opening statements.* Each attorney will present an opening statement of summary to the judge. In cases when the entire separation agreement is not at stake, but only a few remaining issues, the opening statements will be waived and the procedure will go directly to the next phase.

2. *The plaintiff's case.* (Plaintiff is the spouse who filed the original complaint.) The attorney for the plaintiff now presents evidence in support of the complaint, using witnesses, as necessary.

3. *Defendant's case.* The responding spouse's attorney now presents evidence to deny or counter the plaintiff's case, also using witnesses.

4. *Rebuttal by plaintiff.* The attorney for the plaintiff now denies or counters the new material presented on the defendant's behalf. (This step is not always necessary.)

5. *Surrebuttal by defendant.* Evidence is offered to deny or counter any new material brought up by the plaintiff. (This step is rarely necessary, but is available.)

6. *Closing arguments.* Each attorney (the plaintiff's first) summarizes the total evidence presented on her or his client's behalf. Since the judge has usually already heard what is needed to make a decision, this part is also generally waived.

7. *Judge's ruling.* A ruling is not necessarily given on the same day as the trial. This is to give the judge time to look over the material presented and think through the decisions to be made.

Note When a formal trial requires a closed setting for the protection of a spouse or minor children, an *in camera* (closed) hearing is usually held in the judge's chambers instead of a public courtroom.

Judgment and Court Orders

With or without a trial, the Judgment is a synopsis of the separation agreement and the court ruling. It will have a court docket number and appropriate legal signatures.

The separation agreement will now replace any temporary pretrial orders. This separation agreement, in its entirety, becomes a part of the final Judgment and is attached to the synopsis.

You will receive a copy of the signed separation agreement from your attorney at the time of the divorce. Since it takes time for the court to process the paperwork for the final judgment, be sure to request that a certified copy be sent to you.

Recording the Divorce

A record of the divorce (a Dissolution of Marriage form) will be filed with the vital records section of your state Department of Public Health Services.

FIELD TRIP TO A COURTROOM

There is no better way for you to prepare yourself for the courtroom than to visit one. You can watch divorce attorneys handle their cases and the reactions of the judge. Observe the procedures: how the judge calls witnesses; how the attorneys address the witnesses; the jargon and buzz words used; the customs and formalities.

OUTLINE OF A TRIAL

If it appears that your case will go to trial, you and your attorney will draw up a trial outline as a basic script for how your case will be presented. If your divorce is a relatively simple one, the outline will be uncomplicated and easy to follow. In all but the very simplest of divorces your attorney will want a pretrial interview of witnesses to go over the substance of their testimonies.

With a clear trial outline, you and your attorney will be able to point out to each witness which issues are most important for your objectives. You will also have a complete checklist of evidence and documentation to be presented, avoiding the last minute panic of running around hunting for certain papers.

Whether or not you actually go to trial, being fully prepared can serve to strengthen both you and your case.

Questions to Ask Your Attorney

In preparing for a trial, you will want to have a checklist of questions to ask your attorney *before* you get to court. The courtroom is your attorney's bailiwick, so don't be afraid to ask even the simplest of questions like, "Where's the rest room in the courthouse?"

- How should I dress?
- Can a friend or relative come along for moral support?
- Where do the witnesses wait? When do they come? Are they allowed to be in court before they testify and can they stay afterwards?
- Can I bring notes to the trial if I'm afraid I'll get nervous and forget something important on the witness stand? How will you let me know that I have missed something important?
- What kinds of questions will I be asked?
- What if the opposing attorney gets me rattled? Can I ask you to help me?
- Can I ask you questions while I'm on the witness stand?

In reality, if you have done the work needed to prepare for your trial, you know as much about the case as anyone else involved. You and your attorney need to narrow down the issues and select the strategies to be used in the courtroom.

Many of us have a tendency, particularly when under stress, to overstate our case, to talk too much, or the opposite, to freeze. If you and your attorney have discussed the case, or perhaps role-played the kinds of questions likely to be asked and your responses, you will have greater confidence when you go into court.

Rules of Evidence

In any trial or deposition, there are certain procedures which govern the conduct of hearings. While these may vary from state to state, they basically exist to ensure a fair and speedy trial. They also cut away extraneous material which one attorney or the other may try to force into a trial to throw focus away from the facts or to cast a questionable light on a witness.

Burden of Proof

The spouse making claims must give testimony and evidence to show why the pleadings should be granted. Failing to persuade the judge means not getting what is being asked for. In court language this process is called *seeking relief by pleading allegations*.

Documentation

When documentation is presented to the court, it is also open material for the opposing attorney to examine. This is why it is important for you and your attorney to decide what documents will be needed and list them on your pretrial outline.

Courtroom Terminology

In **FORM-ula 3: Divorce Business Supplies**, we suggest that you purchase the *Family Law Dictionary* written by Leonard and Elias and published by Nolo Press. That will be your resource for detailed explanations of legal jargon. In this section, we are only discussing the basic courtroom terminology.

- *Objection* means that the opposing attorney does not want the witness' statement to be admitted (recorded) as evidence.
- *Sustained* means that the testimony can continue but erase what the opposing attorney objected to.
- *Overruled* means that the judge allows the statement to be included in the records.

Another courtroom term to be aware of is *argumentative*, which refers to a series of statements or questions intended to start an argument between counsel and witness. The opposing attorney should object to argumentative statements.

Other kinds of objectionable questions are called *complex*, or *compound* questions. These are used to confuse or upset a witness, in order to try to get a different answer than the one first given. This courtroom tactic often involves badgering the witness. It is also referred to as *asked and answered*, meaning the question posed by an attorney has been asked and answered before and possibly in a number of different ways already.

If the witness is called upon by an attorney to state conclusions or opinions that constitute a *judgment*, the opposing attorney can object on the basis that the line of questioning was *calling for a conclusion* and should not be allowed.

Hearsay is evidence that comes from a third party

and not from the witness giving testimony; therefore, it is considered questionable.

Immaterial and irrelevant refer to testimony that does not relate to what is being asked or discussed or is not relevant to the procedure.

Other types of objections include testimony that could be self-incriminating by damaging credibility, particularly, in business or professional life. Since court records are open to the public, you and your attorney must discuss ahead of time any issues that might be incriminating. Find out the circumstances and procedures for making your own objections.

Privileged communication refers to communications between spouses while married or between spouses and their respective attorneys.

WITNESSES

It may be wisdom on the part of your attorney not to put your best friend on the witness stand, even though that person may know a great deal about your situation. This is because your best friend may be viewed as biased in your favor and, therefore, incapable of giving an objective opinion. This person would be called an *incompetent witness,* not because of a lack of knowledge, but because of the bias of the testimony.

Once again, we remind you that the court system is an adversarial one, *supposedly* based solely upon facts and objectivity. Paradoxically, in order to cross-examine or discredit a witness, attorneys frequently resort to all sorts of emotional trickery that may cause witnesses to lose objectivity and betray a truth that the attorney feels is being covered up.

Here are some tips on being an effective witness. These suggestions will apply both to yourself and to the other witnesses for your side of the case.

How to Dress

Dress the same way you would for an important business meeting, unless your attorney gives other instructions. First impressions count.

Protocol

You are not a member of the diplomatic corps, obviously, but good manners count in court. Being punctual, neat, organized, and objective will win you brownie points with the judge. This is probably one of the hardest times in your life to maintain your cool and to have your act together.

Preparation

Preparation will help you to maintain your cool. It is what we've been stressing since the beginning of *The Divorce Decisions Workbook*. This is also when your pretrial outline (and your dress rehearsal) will pay off. If your thoughts are in order and the documentation is ready, your attorney will be able to efficiently cover all of the important points in your testimony.

Be an Effective Witness

In responding to questions, listen carefully to all the questions you are asked. Attorneys can overstate or over-complicate a question. If you don't understand, ask that the question be repeated or rephrased.

Be direct and be truthful. If you need to quote, try to be exact or else say that you are paraphrasing. Don't be afraid to use the language used to you, when necessary, but refrain from using abusive or inappropriate language when it is not called for.

Try not to render opinions, that is the judge's job. Your attorney should give you the proper opportunity to say the most important things at the moments when they will count the most.

When it comes to being questioned by the opposing attorney, remember that this is simply the opposite side doing its job. Keep exactly the same professional attitude toward every person involved whether it is for depositions, conferences, hearings, or the trial itself.

It is very difficult not to be defensive when being cross-examined. It is normal human instinct to be defensive and it is an appropriate reaction in most offensive situations. Unfortunately, the courtroom is one place where being defensive can get you into trouble. Remember that it is the opposing attorney's job to present the best possible case.

A basic rule of thumb is that neither attorney will ask a question without being reasonably certain of the response. If there is a question you feel you have a valid reason for not answering, ask the judge's permission not to respond. You can be cited for contempt by simply refusing to answer. Be prepared to state your reason and to respond to a written petition about the issue.

When you are listening to the testimony of other witnesses, keep your reactions to yourself. Make notes. You will have opportunities to discuss the important issues with your attorney.

Chapter 19
TO HAVE AND TO HOLD

"The very rich are different from you and me."

F. SCOTT FITZGERALD

"Yes, they have more money."

ERNEST HEMINGWAY

The word *distribution* can be a touchy one in a divorce. Having to divide up what has been familiar to us during our lives can fan the flames of already explosive issues and emotions. Couples tend to become like scavengers in a war where ending up with the most stuff is considered a sign of having "won."

Based upon the concept of a marital partnership, the present trend is for the court to consider all of the financial issues in a marriage when determining distribution. Whereas alimony is essentially an award for support and maintenance, property division is related more directly to the relative contributions of the spouses to the increase, maintenance, or decrease of assets.

DIVIDING THE PROPERTY

If you think you will react strongly to the loss of property, work with a counselor/therapist. Deal with these emotions before they damage your ability to cope. The law does not concern itself with how you feel.

Your attorney will confirm information about the laws in your state regarding marital assets. Use the property and financial documentation from your Pendaflex files to organize this information.

These files will be particularly helpful because property settlements are not generally modifiable once the divorce becomes final. While it is always possible to re-open the property settlement section of a separation agreement if a mistake was made or if fraud is discovered, you will generally find that, once made, a deal is a deal. That's why it is to your advantage to be prepared!

THE TOUCHY ISSUE OF SPOUSAL SUPPORT

Both voluntary financial arrangements and *alimony pendente* (a pretrial order), are simply stop-gap measures for keeping the bills paid until a final divorce agreement is reached.

It is essential to look at the current economic factors of the family for a realistic approach to spousal support. Our legal system does not want divorced spouses on the public dole. However, putting too much pressure on the spouse who pays the bills (in an already toxic situation) can lead to an agreement that is never carried out. A spouse who is tired of fighting may agree to anything just to get out and then disappear.

We have compiled a list of the most common criteria for determining spousal support. You and your attorney will use your files and completed FORMulas to determine which of these issues apply to your particular case.

- Fixed obligations that either of you have undertaken.
- Sufficient property to provide for reasonable needs.
- Joint and individual assets and liabilities.
- Value of income-producing assets (once divided).
- Retirement and deferred-income plans held jointly or individually.
- Present and future earning capacity of each spouse.
- Time necessary for either spouse to acquire education, training, or experience to become self-supporting.
- Standard of living established during the marriage.
- Financial impact of maintaining two households.
- Duration of marriage.
- Age, physical, and emotional condition of each spouse.
- Special needs of either spouse, such as disabilities, medical conditions, institutionalization, and so forth.
- Needs of other dependents in your or your spouse's family.
- Needs of a subsequent or prior family.

In the final divorce agreement, there may be either no alimony or alimony that can be paid in a number of different ways.

We have observed that continuing alimony is much more likely to be given to an older woman who has never worked than to a younger person who is already a proven professional, especially when there will be joint custody of children.

Distribution Decisions

If spousal support seems appropriate, you have some decisions to make based upon the current laws regarding alimony distribution:

- The advantages and disadvantages of a lump-sum settlement.
- The amount of such a settlement and how it will be paid (transfer of paper, cash, property, etc.).
- Whether or not to make or receive payments on

an installment basis for a fixed or indefinite period.

- What those amounts should be and how they should be allocated.
- Conditions attached to paying or receiving regarding disability, death, remarriage, cohabitation, retirement, employment, or the radical change of financial condition through gain or loss.
- Security to be put up for unmade payments and the terms of its use.
- Conditions under which payments may be increased or decreased.
- The effect of wills and inheritances.
- Ownership and beneficiaries of life insurance policies.
- Tax effects of the proposed financial agreement (see Chapter 23 for more information regarding tax and divorce).
- Future medical insurance coverage, especially regarding policy extension, preexisting conditions, and the effects of counseling diagnoses and expenses.

What Are the Risks?

Even with the best of intentions, there is always some risk associated with actually getting all of the court-ordered alimony payments from the paying spouse:

- Additional expenses associated with remarriage and the start of a new family.
- Incapacitation through illness.
- Radical change in lifestyle.
- Payment withheld as "punishment."
- Refusal to pay.

To minimize these risks, there is the opportunity to waive extended alimony and work out a cash or lump-sum settlement. This alternative may also be a way to leave each spouse free to start over, particularly when there are no children and, therefore, little or no need for any further involvement.

Note Even when there is no desire or necessity for alimony, the courts often prefer to require a token annual sum to be established in the divorce decree. This may allow the issues of alimony and financial support to be reopened in the event of significant financial changes.

Chapter 20
CHILDREN: CUSTODY AND CHILD SUPPORT

The history of child custody is not a pleasant one. Children have been considered as "property" (usually belonging to the father) throughout recorded history and by most world cultures. In many countries, this is still the case.

In the United States, late in the nineteenth century, legal, social, and political authorities decided that mothers were biologically and emotionally better suited to raise children under seven years of age. Therefore, granting custody to the mother was deemed to be in the best interest of the young child.

CURRENT VIEWS ON CUSTODY

Our legal system still tends to deal with children in a divorcing family as "property," but changes are occurring. When it is the parental choice, the court currently tends to favor joint custody, especially when couples have a history of cooperating in matters concerning their child. This preference is in recognition of the studies indicating that when both parents remain actively involved with the children, there is a greater opportunity for the children to adjust to the divorce. Of course, the court will seriously question requests for joint custody when one parent is determined unfit by reason of aberrant behavior such as alcoholism or abusiveness.

Children are *not* property, however. Custody decisions should not be based upon one parent's emotional need or superior financial situation. Neither should children be used as emotional pawns in a win-or-lose game between the parents.

Since the most valued part of even the rockiest marriage is the children, neither parent is likely to want to give up total parenting.

The opposite can also be true when neither parent feels capable of taking on full responsibility for parenting, particularly if there is more than one child and they are all still quite young.

Both positions are understandable. This is where mediation can be helpful.

The danger of a custody battle is that it is usually not waged over what is best for the children. In most instances, it is a revenge, a financial strategy, or an attempt by one spouse to punish the other.

THE TERMINOLOGY OF CUSTODY

Children are in *temporary custody* while divorce proceedings are in progress. Residence is generally where the children were living at the time the summons was served. (This location *will* have a bearing on the permanent custody because most courts do not like to disturb the status quo.)

Permanent Custody refers to the primary home after the divorce. (The court will always consider change for a reasonable cause.)

Child custody has two basic components in the separation agreement, Legal and Physical:

1. **Legal custody,** or the parent's right to make legal decisions for the children.
   a. *Sole legal custody,* where only one parent is entitled to make decisions.
   b. *Joint legal custody,* where both parents will jointly decide vital questions and issues.
2. **Physical custody,** or the children's primary residence.
   a. *Sole physical custody,* where children live with one parent only and the other parent has visitation rights.
   b. *Joint physical custody,* where children continue to reside with both parents. They either alternate households or stay in the family home with the parents alternating households (this arrangement is also referred to as "Bird's Nest Custody"). Joint physical custody works if:
      (1) both parents can afford it.
      (2) parents live close enough to each other.
      (3) there is continuity in school and social contacts.
      (4) children do not feel confused and shunted.
   c. *Split custody,* where children live with each parent for a portion of the year or, one or more children live with each parent.

What the Custody Decision Means

In making custody decisions, a lot depends upon your children's ages and levels of maturity as well as consideration of their wishes, social lives, and educational continuity.

The sole custodial parent is given the legal right to determine the children's upbringing and general welfare including education, health care, and religion. This also means full responsibility for caretaking.

The joint custodial parents will have to form a co-operative relationship and set ground rules. All arrangements for household, support, education, upbringing, health, and religion will have to be established. (The details can be spelled out in your separation agreement.)

Under a joint arrangement, both parents will have equal rights and responsibilities for the children. This means giving each other first-class status as well

as access to both families when holidays and celebrations come along—not an easy task for two people who have agreed to disagree!

If parents are to have two residences and equal sharing of custody, it is probably best for each child to be able to attend school in one place.

Another typical arrangement for joint or equal custody is the "every other weekend, every other holiday and summers together" scenario.

There are so many conflicting emotions surrounding the subject of child custody that you need to take a look at all sides of the issue. You may want to keep in mind the information presented in Chapter 13 on becoming a single parent household while you are working on custody issues.

Be very practical about the realities of custody. You are tailoring your agreement to meet present and future needs. The court will look favorably on genuine efforts made by either parent on behalf of the children.

While it is more usual for the children to live with the mother, it is becoming less and less unusual for a father to have physical custody. This arrangement does not mean that the mother has deserted them, or is a "bad parent." Instead, it means that this arrangement may be the best for the child or, simply, that the child wants it that way.

This arrangement seems to work well when the mother needs to return to work or school. It may also mean that the father remains in the family home and the mother moves out. In this case, the mother will provide the second home or the place to go for visits, holidays, and summers.

Additional Custody Considerations

The most important feature of any parenting plan is the opportunity for periodic evaluations and changes. After all, there are a million reasons why circumstances can change after your divorce: remarriage, job relocations, illness, a special need of a child, a special need of a parent, and so on. Your decisions about custody should reflect your recognition of an on-going process rather than a once-in-a-lifetime event.

If a relative is responsible, in any way, for a child's care, housing, or financial support, we suggest that this person be included in custody discussions.

Any person claiming a meaningful relationship with your children may petition the court for visitation rights and/or custody. They may even intervene in a proceeding where custody is being argued.

Note Custody arrangements become legal agreements. You cannot promise children, "If you don't like it there, you can always live with me." Custody can be changed but it is not done arbitrarily.

Note If the wife is pregnant at the time of separation and divorce, the unborn child will be treated the same as any other natural or legally adopted child.

RESPECTING A CHILD'S RIGHTS AND FEELINGS

The most successful custodial agreements have usually come about because the children were included in the discussions.

Consider the Bill of Rights of Children in Divorce Actions, adapted by the Honorable Robert Hansen from decisions of the Wisconsin Supreme Court.

THE BILL OF RIGHTS
OF
CHILDREN IN DIVORCE ACTIONS

I. The right to be treated as an interested and affected person and not as a pawn, possession, or chattel of either or both parents.
II. The right to grow to maturity in that home environment which will best guarantee an opportunity for the child to grow to mature and responsible citizenship.
III. The right to the day by day love, care, discipline, and protection of the parent having custody of the child.
IV. The right to know the noncustodial parent and to have the benefit of such parent's love and guidance through adequate visitations.
V. The right to a positive and constructive relationship with both parents, with neither parent to be permitted to degrade or downgrade the other in the mind of the child.
VI. The right to have moral and ethical values developed by precept and practices and to have limits set for behavior so that the child early in life may develop self-discipline and self-control.
VII. The right to the most adequate level of economic support that can be provided by the best efforts of both parents.
VIII. The right to the same opportunities for education that the child would have had if the family unit had not been broken.
IX. The right to such periodic review of custodial arrangements and child support orders as the circumstances of the parents and those of the child may require.

X. The right to recognition that children involved in a divorce are always disadvantaged parties and that the law must take affirmative steps to protect their welfare, including, where indicated, a social investigation to determine, and the appointment of a *guardian ad litem* to protect their interests.

In addition, we would add that children be free to contact the absent parents when they wish to do so and to form close relationships with each parent's new friends.

CUSTODY AND THE ISSUE OF EMANCIPATION

For the purpose of developing custody and support arrangements in a separation agreement, *emancipation,* or the child's legal status of independence, has a different set of interpretations than those for determining freedom to marry or to drink alcohol.

In most states, children are considered emancipated when they:

- Reach the age of 18 (up to 21 in some states).
- Get married (even though the marriage may be void or voidable and despite any subsequent termination by annulment or divorce).
- Enter military service.
- Become self-supporting through full-time employment.
- Establish a permanent residence away from either parent or custodian (boarding school, college, or extended travel are not considered changes in permanent residence).

THE HEALTH, EDUCATION, AND WELFARE OF THE CHILD

What are the obligations of the custodial parent with regard to the child's health, welfare, education, religious training, trips, and special events of family life? How much authority and decision-making power does the custodial parent really have? What are the rights of the noncustodial parent? These are all issues that are easier to work out before the divorce is final, instead of afterwards.

Routine daily decisions are typically made by the

parent with physical custody. In an emergency situation, however, each parent is authorized to take every action necessary to protect the child and is expected to keep the other parent advised of procedures being followed. It is a good family business practice to complete and notarize **FORM-ula 51: Medical Permission to Treat Minor Child** whenever the child is in someone's care other than the parents'.

As parents, you will want to have a mutual understanding of each other's present value systems and methods of discipline. It is not helpful to the children if you override the objectives and routines that the other parent has set up.

Obtaining Duplicate Information

Cooperative parenting involves taking an interest in the children's church or temple, school, sports and community activities. This will require arranging for duplicate notices. Use **FORM-ula 52: Duplicate Information Request.**

VISITATION

When one parent has sole physical custody of the children, *reasonable rights of visitation* are authorized for the noncustodial parent. This right is automatic unless there are documented extenuating circumstances.

Visitation Protocol

Visitation is a new experience for children and parents. It helps for everyone to know what plans have been made, where the children will be, and for how long.

It's up to the custodial parent to see that the children are ready for their visit with the noncustodial parent. It is the responsibility of the noncustodial parent to follow visitation arrangements. Children can become tremendously upset when parents are unreliable. When a visitation appointment needs to be changed or broken, both the children and the other parent should be told as soon as possible.

Arranging Visitation

Visitation arrangements are based upon the schedules and wishes of parents and children. Once a schedule is established, it is not a good idea to make unilateral changes that can create conflict with each other's plans.

On the other hand, both children and adults will have times of pleasure or stress that warrant more shared time. You should also work out arrangements for telephone contact that is reasonable and unhampered.

Frequent visits in the home are good for toddlers (who have the shorter attention spans) while visits of longer duration, even at greater intervals, are usually better for older children. Preteen and teenage children need the greatest amount of flexibility.

When the custodial parent is going to be away, it would seem reasonable to make arrangements for the children to be under the care of the noncustodial parent. Details for this should be addressed in the separation agreement.

The children's special events (birthday parties, school and sports activities, and so on) are times to be shared by everyone, if at all possible. When parents cannot attend together, they can alternate events or arrange for one parent to be with the child before the event and the other parent to be with the child afterwards.

Trouble Signs

Children may refuse to visit the noncustodial parent for a variety of reasons. It is important to establish whether this is from an emotional trauma or a situation created by the parents. If parents and children aren't able to resolve the problem, it may require outside help.

Note In the event of illness or hospitalization, the other parent should be informed immediately so that both parents can provide emotional support to the child.

Legalities of Visitation

The legal assumption is that child visitation is appropriate. There are, however, justifiable circumstances in which other arrangements must be made.

When Can a Parent Be Legally Prevented From Visitation?

A parent can be legally blocked from visiting children when there is documented (and court-approved) evidence of:

- Extreme mental or emotional instability.
- Repeated violent behavior, especially toward children.

- Criminal activities.
- Drug usage (other than prescribed medication).
- Continuous influence of alcohol.
- Parental neglect.
- Explicit sexual behavior in front of children.

When Can Visitation With the Ex-Spouse Not Be Legally Prevented?

Generally unacceptable reasons for denying visitation include:

- When a child believes the other parent is "horrible" and refuses to visit (opinions change with moods, particularly in the early stages of divorce).
- When the other parent is "shacking up" (unless this behavior is disturbing to children).
- When support payments are late or in arrears.
- When the other parent is homosexual.

Traveling

There may be either state laws or stipulations in your divorce agreement that apply to divorced parents traveling with minor children (as protective measures against childnapping). In any event, it is a good idea to document your travels with the children. A copy of your itinerary, including photocopies of passports and visas, should always be given to the other parent as well as to a close friend or relative.

Travel agents often require a notarized letter which includes names, dates of travel, and destinations that has been signed by the nonaccompanying parent. Use **FORM-ula 53: Consent to Travel.**

When a child is traveling alone, both parents should have the specific travel information. Another copy goes with the child.

Moving

During or just after a divorce may not be the best time for a long-distance move, either with or without the children. If you move with the children you might be perceived as making it deliberately tough for your spouse to be with them. If you move without the children, it might look as though you don't care enough about them.

In developing your game plan, put yourself in your children's shoes and try to analyze what they would consider to be best for themselves, then discuss it with your attorney.

Parents with physical custody wishing to move

from the area are generally legally entitled to do so, unless specific state laws preclude it, or the separation agreement specifically prevents it. In any event, if a move is in the best interest of the custodial family, it would be both courteous and fair to get the other parent's approval and emotional support. The moving parent should be prepared to offer to:

- Pay transportation costs incidental to the other parent's visitation rights. (See the NOTE below.)
- Provide the other parent with longer periods of visitation to offset earlier, more frequent visits.
- Give legal assurance that the other parent will be kept up to date on pertinent data such as new location, schools, activities, and so on.
- Show the other parent how the move will benefit the children as well as custodial parent.
- Reassess physical custody and allow each child the option of remaining in the area with the other parent.

Note We have heard of cases where the non-custodial parent was allowed to deduct extraordinary costs of visitation (airfare, etc.) from the child support obligation.

PRESENTING YOUR CASE FOR CUSTODY

If you want sole custody of your children, you will want to demonstrate your ability to care for their needs. The documentation you may want to present is:

- A description of the home and neighborhood.
- A statement of the kind of care provided for each child when you are not available.
- A statement of the value system in the home.
- Evidence of the availability of enrichment opportunities and outside activities to support each child's abilities.
- A list of factors that favor you as the custodial parent, such as consistency, stability, background, and longevity as nurturing parent.

You will also want to develop a detailed and factual list of documented reasons why your spouse should not be awarded custody. This list may include such things as evidence of:

- Misconduct or abuses that affect the physical, emotional, or moral well-being of the children.

- Demonstrated or diagnosed emotional illness or instability.
- Inadequate parenting based on an inability to meet the daily needs of each child regarding:

  suitable living conditions.

  adequate supervision.

  proper nourishment, sleep, and clothing.

  reasonable discipline.

  genuine affection.
- Long work hours or frequent travel.
- Undue pressure on children to be involved in marital problems or to take on adult responsibilities in lieu of parent.
- Immoral conduct in front of or involving children.

Documenting Your Position

Documentation for your presentation as the most appropriate custodial parent will come from your Pendaflex file.

Use effective witnesses. Specifically, witnesses should be people who have no "axes to grind" and no prejudices about the case. For example, consider a respected teacher, religious leader, child psychologist, or even a regular babysitter who has consistently observed family patterns and behavior.

When Parents Are Equally Adequate

To this point we have been describing a situation wherein one parent is regarded as significantly superior to the other in child-rearing capabilities. What if both parents are equally adequate?

If the judge does not already have a bias (which is usually toward the mother, all things being equal) there is a distinct possibility that the parent with the most recent and comprehensive documentation of ability to care and provide will win the case.

A judge wants concrete evidence to support a difficult decision. This is where the work that you have done throughout the book, particularly Section III, "Pulling Yourself and Your Family Together," will be extremely helpful.

WHEN CUSTODY IS CONTESTED

If you and your spouse are unable to make custody decisions for your children, the judge will make them for you.

Frankly, how you present yourself to attorneys, a mediator, a pretrial judge, and to the trial judge will be crucial. (Reread Chapter 18.)

What constitutes the child's best interest and overall welfare is the basis for the judge's ruling. Determinations for these decisions are based upon the facts and circumstances of each particular case, including:

- The children's stated preferences.
- Where the children are currently living and the effects of a change in location.
- The nature of each parent's relationship with each child.
- The nature of each child's relationship to each parent.
- The amount of care, affection, and concern demonstrated by each parent.
- The stability of each parent's home.
- The mental and physical health of individual members of the family.
- The ability and availability of each parent to care for the children.
- The financial stability of each parent.
- The moral and ethical conduct of each parent, especially toward the other.
- Parental conduct that does or does not show concern for the best interest of each child.
- Each parent's history of compliance with personal agreements and existing court orders.

Court Appointed *Guardian Ad Litem*

In the event that you and your spouse are unable to come to a custody agreement, the court will appoint a *guardian ad litem,* usually an attorney, to protect the children's rights and to voice their interests and concerns at formal hearings.

The *guardian ad litem* will interview the children, the parents, and other potential custodians. Interviews may extend to teachers, neighbors, and other third parties who might be helpful. The attorney will also investigate the home neighborhood, school, and medical records.

Responsibilities of the Guardian Ad Litem

The responsibilities of the *guardian ad litem* are to:

- Make recommendations to the court or counsel for the parents with regard to custody, visitation, and further evaluations or therapies.

- Conduct or attend depositions and/or to file motions for the children involving health, abuse, or other problems that the parents have not communicated to their attorneys or to the court.

- Protect the children's financial interests with regard to support, visitation, health, education, and future needs. (This protection would include support payment assurance, even from the parents' estates, in the event of death.)

Fees for the Guardian Ad Litem

Fees for the *guardian ad litem* come from one or both parents, depending upon ability to pay. They could also come from the children's assets, should any exist.

CHILD SUPPORT OBLIGATIONS

Child support obligations begin on the day they are entered on the court registry. Money is not usually provided to either spouse retroactively unless by mutual agreement.

If support is not voluntarily provided by both parents, the most immediate and pressing issue of a separation will be to obtain a temporary court order for child support.

A separated parent who does not have physical custody of the children will still have a legal responsibility to help provide for each child's needs.

In 1988, the federal government mandated the establishment of child support guidelines for determining the minimum amount of child support to be paid. The government also stipulated that the states periodically review the guidelines. Nonpayment of court-ordered child support is now considered economic abuse of a child.

The primary ingredients of a child-support order are:

- Social Security number of each child.
- Amount to be paid for each child.
- Frequency of payments (weekly, monthly, etc.).
- Manner of payment (to parent or state agency by check, direct deposit, cash, or wage withholding).

The dollar amount of payment will be determined either by agreement between the parents or by an independent decision of the presiding judge. This agreement will remain in effect until the child reaches majority (usually at age 18), becomes emancipated, or dies.

How Support Is Calculated

In most states, the amount of support to be given each child depends upon the particular circumstances of the case, including:

- Financial resources of each parent.
- Income and earning capacity of each parent.
- Financial resources of each child.
- Financial needs of each parent and child.
- Parents' prior standard of living.
- Standard of living to which each child is accustomed.
- Ages of each child.
- Impact of maintaining two households, rather than one.
- Best interests of each child regarding physical, educational, or vocational needs.
- Tax consequences, where practical and relevant.

It is *your* responsibility to bring the specific circumstances of *your situation* to the attention of both your attorney and the judge. It is also *your* responsibility to document special needs and show why you should be given special consideration.

Examples of such situations are:

- A very large disparity in the income levels of parents.
- Constant medical attention for you or a child.
- Disability of you or a child.
- Special education or vocational training for a child.

Money for Education

Written into any divorce agreement should be provisions for fair and reasonable educational opportunities for each child, and how the ensuing financial obligation will be met.

From nursery school through high school, there will be extra costs of special lessons, tutoring, summer camp, religious training, and so on. Attendant to these expenses may be fees and money for uniforms, equipment, supplies, and transportation. You and your spouse will want to clarify how these kinds of costs will be covered.

Parents who can come to terms about almost every

other kind of expense for children often have difficulties in determining how to pay the costs of higher education. A college education is now so costly that trying to agree on terms for what may happen years down the road seems almost impossible. But, if you don't make some arrangements for helping them, these young adults may feel emotionally and financially abandoned.

Medical Expenses

The parent with corporate medical coverage usually accepts the responsibility for maintaining the health coverage for the children. There is minimal difference in cost between single and family rates relative to the insurance value. We strongly suggest that you have a contingency plan in your agreement to ensure uninterrupted coverage.

The sticky wicket is the myriad expenses that are not covered by medical insurance. For instance, who pays the deductible and other unreimbursed amounts? Who pays the dentist, orthodontist, ophthalmologist, or optometrist? What about the continuous outpouring of medical expenses for such items as eyeglasses, nonprescription medications, and emergency and first-aid supplies?

Note Decide what form of authorization will be used for family medical insurance forms after the divorce.

Providing for Life Insurance

Divorcing parents may elect (or be required) to insure themselves for the benefit of their children. If this is the case, you will need to decide on:

- Beneficiaries.
- Amounts.

- Duration of coverage.
- A trustee or custodian for the proceeds.
- A policy owner.
- Premium payment assurance.
- Whether the owner has a right to borrow or switch policies.

Making New Wills

Since a divorce automatically nullifies all existing bequests to a former spouse and also removes the former spouse as an executor, wills should be reexecuted as quickly as possible.

If a new will contains provisions for the minor children, you will want to notify the other parent by letter detailing that particular information. If you should die *intestate,* that is, without a will, distribution of your property will be determined by the laws of your state.

Covering Your Bases

Have you thought about

- Cost of living increases?
- Escalating expenses as children grow up?
- A slush fund for family emergencies?

What kinds of financial resources do you have to use in a pinch? Is there a family member who can step in and help? If your children have their own money, how much should be used toward their own support?

Note A stepparent is not legally responsible for the financial support of a stepchild unless the child has been legally adopted.

Chapter 21
PAYMENT "ACCOUNT-ABILITY"

The subject of this chapter is how funds can be made available and alimony or child support payments assured. Once a separation agreement is finalized, the usual methods for making payments are:

- Personal check.
- Direct bank deposit.
- Automatic withdrawal.
- Contingent or automatic wage withholding.

The payment method selected depends upon a number of factors such as geographic distance between spouses, convenience of payment, and urgent financial need for prompt and regular payment.

GETTING PAYMENT ASSURANCE

Where sufficient property is involved, it is often written into the divorce agreement that a bond be posted or money placed in trust to ensure the full and timely payment of support funds.

If funds are available for investment, money can be put into custodial accounts, conservative investments, or tax-free bonds in order to meet future support obligations. To satisfy support and alimony obligations, some spouses will transfer property into a trust, with the income going to support each member of the family. This is a useful tool when divorcing couples have considerable assets. An income-producing trust ensures timely payments while also protecting the assets. Life and disability insurance are also ways of making it possible to carry out financial intentions and obligations. Length of life does not always turn out as planned.

It is also possible to transfer any or all IRA assets from one spouse to the other without incurring tax liability as part of the financial arrangements in a divorce.

Social Security benefits may be available to satisfy valid support claims. Under federal law, those funds are subject to being available but it is on a first-come-first-serve basis. The social security system does not give priority to a previous or current family. It simply recognizes the family that makes the first application.

Increasingly, payments are made through the court system. This way, the court maintains the payment records and is free to take action for delinquencies. This is particularly useful if the paying spouse has a history of unreliability.

Federal bankruptcy laws have priority over state divorce orders. With a few exceptions, such as child or spousal support, all debts owed by a person who files for bankruptcy are cancelled. That means that obligations intended to carry out terms of a property settlement (for example, payment of bills, balance of payments to buy out share of home ownership, and so on) may be canceled!

Since obligations in the nature of a support obligation are not canceled, careful wording in the separation agreement to describe specific payments as an additional form of support may avoid future problems. Court orders for payment of a spouse's attorney fees are also considered in the nature of support.

A Chapter 13 Bankruptcy can actually be used to benefit the recipients of support dollars. This type of bankruptcy provides a method of adjusting debts by extending repayments up to five years, thereby freeing up present income that can then be used to meet support obligations.

It is common to back up promises of future payments with collateral. State law determines whether or not particular types of collateral are exempt from the bankruptcy process.

The impact of bankruptcy on pension payments depends upon where you live. Some courts rule that pension-payment obligations can be discharged in bankruptcy, while others rule that such obligations survive bankruptcy. A possible way to avoid confusion is to arrange for a *qualified domestic relations order* (QDRO, pronounced *quadro*). This order makes the pension-plan administrator responsible for making the payments directly to the ex-spouse.

A QDRO assigns a portion of the retirement benefit of the employee spouse to the other spouse, called the *alternate payee,* and sets up a separate account and benefit under the plan. Negotiations will include discussions about whether to divide the employee's accrued benefit at the time of the divorce or the marital portion of the employee's ultimate benefit at the time of retirement. Decisions need to be made for providing protection in the event that the employee should die prior to retiring, building in an early retirement subsidy for the alternate payee's benefit and confirming a "surviving spouse" benefit.

QDROs can only be applied to retirement plans subject to the Employee Retirement Income Security Act (ERISA). Retirement plans that do not fall into these categories are government plans such as the US Civil Service Retirement System, state retirement systems (public employee pensions), and military pensions. Each of these government pensions requires its own specialized type of order to divide the retirement benefit.

Recourse When Support Payments Lag

What recourse is there when support doesn't come?

A California entrepreneur has developed a workable alternative to yelling and hair-pulling: a pre-printed invoice and bookkeeping system called BYX (for "Bill Your Ex"). Billing has proven to be an effective way to collect. In addition to providing child- and spousal-support "bills" (just fill in names and amounts), the BYX system includes a payment ledger for record keeping that is strong documentation if you need to go back to court. Call (800) 828-2BYX for current information about availability and cost.

Professional resources are available. Consider attempting to resolve the problem through hiring a mediator. Another option is to get in touch with the original divorce attorney.

The ex-spouse should be notified that all necessary steps will be taken to collect what is due.

When the Support Payer Is Missing

When the support payer cannot be found, start a search by checking with the parents and relatives of the missing ex-spouse and with past or present employers and friends.

Certain agencies are able to perform a computerized search of federal, state, and private records to locate absentee parents. Their databases include the IRS, Social Security Administration, national personal records centers, Department of Defense, Veterans Administration, Selective Service, state revenue departments, registries of departments of motor vehicles, Department of Employment and Training (unemployment records), private credit reporting agencies, U.S. Postal Service, and other state parent-locator organizations.

Besides executing a computer search, these agencies can publish the name of the delinquent absentee parent in the local newspapers. They may also give the information to credit-reporting agencies or hire a collection group to go after the money. Telephone or write your local state representative to determine the names and phone numbers of the appropriate organizations. Be prepared to wait because these agencies are inundated with requests.

Help Through the Courts

If the separation agreement does not spell out the remedy for nonpayment or consistently late payments and you have exhausted all other options, it's time to go back to court. The court has additional ways to help you.

Motion for Contempt

When an ex-spouse or parent does not receive support payments, he or she can file a *motion for con-*

tempt. This procedure is valid when there has been a legal court order for support and the delinquent spouse had the ability to pay at the time of default.

In most states, the judge has the power to order payment of arrears within a set period of time. This payment is in addition to continuing the regular payment. The judge can also punish the offender by levying a fine or ordering a jail sentence.

Recording a Lien

A *lien,* or an attachment upon real or personal property, may be executed (real estate, bank accounts, cars, etc.) in order to settle past or current support debts. The court will require documentation to verify the amount.

Wage Withholding

Wage withholding is used to legally attach a portion of the delinquent spouse's income. This includes any regular source through which the person deposits or receives money; these sources include employers, retirement plans, unemployment payments, annuities, Social Security payments, and bank accounts.

There are limits to what can be taken under wage withholding. Typically, no more than 50 percent of a person's weekly income can be withheld to a maximum of $200. Wage withholding can be applied to all earnings except federal employee disability income. It can be applied to up to 60 percent of military pay. For further information on the rights of military spouses and former spouses, contact:

EXPOSE
P.O. Box 11191
Alexandria, VA 22312
703-941-5844

CHILD SUPPORT ENFORCEMENT

Child support delinquency has become a national epidemic. The usefulness of any law is in its enforcement. Unfortunately, it appears that divorce law can be manipulated by technicalities so that even contempt of court citations do not insure that support payments are made in full and on schedule.

Information on current laws and practical strategies for collecting child-support payments can be obtained from an action group such as the Organization for the Enforcement of Child Support. That organization studies federal, state, and local child support laws and procedures, monitors changes, and makes this information available to the public through newsletters, telephone contacts, workshops, and the news media. The OECS is a grassroots organization that has branches throughout the US. The main headquarters are at:

119 Nicodemus Rd.
Reisterstown, MD 21136
301-833-2458

FOCUS (For Our Children and Us) is a nonprofit group consisting of lawyers, paralegals, and community leaders. Its telephone number in New York City is 212-693-1655.

In addition, most states have child support administration agencies. You will find a list in the Resource section of this book under "State Child Support Enforcement Offices."

The Family Support Act of 1988

The *Family Support Act of 1988* (Title IV, Part D of the Social Security Act) emphasizes the enforcement of child-support orders. Under the act, all states have until 1994 to include automatic wage attachments in new or modified child-support orders. It also requires the use of financial guidelines in making support awards. By 1995, states must develop automatic tracking and monitoring systems for parents who have defaulted on court-ordered support payments.

This law also provides interaction between the states so that a court order filed in one state may be carried out in another. If state court efforts are exhausted, the law allows a child-support case to be moved into federal courts.

Prior to this act state and federal collection resources were only available to a parent receiving public assistance, referred to as a "IV.D." case. Today, a nonpublic assistance parent (non "IV.D.") can pay a nominal fee to her or his state child-support enforcement program and receive help.

Joseph X. Dumond, an attorney and supervisor of the Connecticut unit of attorneys for child support enforcement in that state's Attorney General's office, provided the information for Figure 21.1. The figure is a graphic representation of the procedures used throughout the U.S. when child support payments require court enforcement.

Attaching IRS Refunds

Believe it or not, there is child support help available through the Internal Revenue Service. Federal and

This is a graphic representation of procedures for recovering delinquent child-support payments after they have been ordered by a court.

Contingent Wage Withholding: Support payments will not be withheld from wages unless the payments are 30+ days in arrears.
Immediate Wage Withholding: By court order or by choice, all support payments begin immediately to be withheld from wages.
"IV. D.": Recipient of public assistance (Aid for Families of Dependent Children-AFDC) or have applied for child-support enforcement.
Non "IV. D.": Not receiving public assistance and have not applied for child-support enforcement.
NCP: Noncustodial parent
CP: Custodial parent

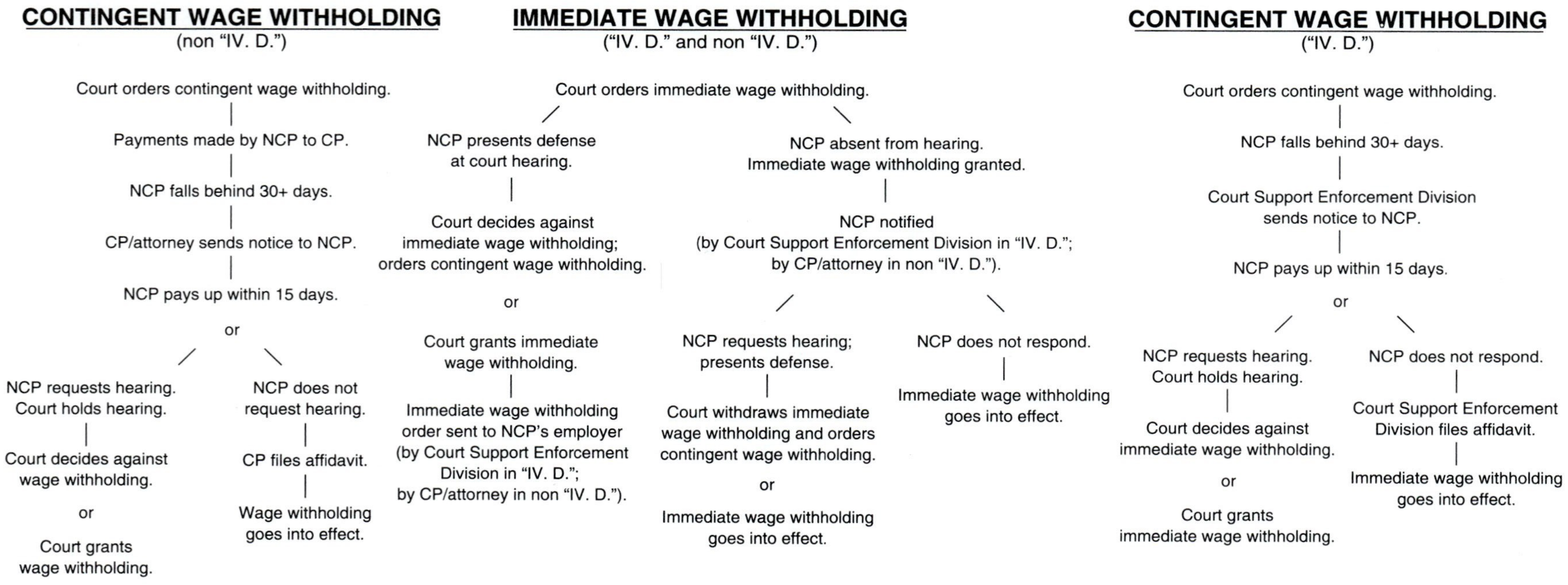

CONTINGENT WAGE WITHHOLDING (non "IV. D.")

Court orders contingent wage withholding.

Payments made by NCP to CP.

NCP falls behind 30+ days.

CP/attorney sends notice to NCP.

NCP pays up within 15 days.

or

NCP requests hearing. Court holds hearing.

Court decides against wage withholding.

or

Court grants wage withholding.

NCP does not request hearing. CP files affidavit. Wage withholding goes into effect.

IMMEDIATE WAGE WITHHOLDING ("IV. D." and non "IV. D.")

Court orders immediate wage withholding.

NCP presents defense at court hearing.

Court decides against immediate wage withholding; orders contingent wage withholding.

or

Court grants immediate wage withholding.

Immediate wage withholding order sent to NCP's employer (by Court Support Enforcement Division in "IV. D."; by CP/attorney in non "IV. D.").

NCP absent from hearing. Immediate wage withholding granted.

NCP notified (by Court Support Enforcement Division in "IV. D."; by CP/attorney in non "IV. D.").

NCP requests hearing; presents defense.

Court withdraws immediate wage withholding and orders contingent wage withholding.

or

Immediate wage withholding goes into effect.

NCP does not respond. Immediate wage withholding goes into effect.

CONTINGENT WAGE WITHHOLDING ("IV. D.")

Court orders contingent wage withholding.

NCP falls behind 30+ days.

Court Support Enforcement Division sends notice to NCP.

NCP pays up within 15 days.

or

NCP requests hearing. Court holds hearing.

Court decides against immediate wage withholding.

or

Court grants immediate wage withholding.

NCP does not respond. Court Support Enforcement Division files affidavit. Immediate wage withholding goes into effect.

Figure 21.1. *Court-Ordered Child Support*

state income tax refunds can be intercepted to pay past or current child support. The past due amount must be $500 or more and that amount *cannot* include spousal support. (Be aware of this rule in the event that your separation agreement lumps the two payments together for tax purposes.)

To be eligible:

- You must apply through the Child Support Enforcement Administration in your state. For information, call 1-800-424-1040.

- The amount in arrears must be at least $150 or 3 months of child support payments.

Petitioning an Order to Remain

If there is an indication that the parent who is delinquent in payments is preparing to leave the state, it is possible to petition the court for an *order to remain*. This order requires the delinquent parent to post a bond in the amount of the arrears which would be forfeited in the event that he or she leaves the state without paying. The money would then be turned over to the appropriate child support agency for distribution.

Section *VI*
"BIG PICTURE" PLANNING

"Only the supremely wise and the abysmally ignorant refuse to change."

CONFUCIUS

For the first time since you started reading *The Divorce Decisions Workbook*, we are going to ask you to pause. Take a break. Step back and get emotional and intellectual distance. Take a look a what you have already accomplished. If you have followed the book, you now have a better understanding of the divorce process, have gotten yourself personally organized, pulled yourself and your family together, documented the financial value of the marriage, and learned about divorce law.

Now it's time to think about how you want to use all this information to form the basis for your separation agreement. You should start deciding how you feel about:

- Your willingness to negotiate.
- The continuity of parental roles.
- The division of assets and liabilities.
- Financial support.

Give these subjects serious consideration so that, later on, you won't look at the final agreement and wonder, "What in the world was I thinking?"

The basic business of divorce is to leave the marriage with your self-esteem intact, suitable housing, and some financial wherewithal.

THE CASE AGAINST FIGHTING

"War at best is barbarism...War is hell."

WILLIAM TECUMSEH SHERMAN

Other than giving in, you have only two ways to go: fight or work it out.

A fight will leave behind a lot of emotional and financial waste. It can create bitterness and an impossible situation for co-parenting. Fighting in court is predictably unsatisfactory.

Early in a separation, anger, disappointment, stress, and anxiety—all the bad feelings left over from the marriage—become externalized. If you get hung up in these feelings, then you're going to battle over egg timers.

A lot of people let their frustrations lead them to making bad judgments. There is a point of no return when anger and revenge use up more time and energy than they are worth. Even for those who never wanted a divorce in the first place, there comes a time to end resistance, accept the facts as they are, and begin to plan for the future.

The pattern for many divorcing couples is to fight for as long as they can stand it, racking up huge bills for professional services rendered, and then end up with some kind of an agreement just before the case goes to trial.

As Aristotle said, "It is easy to fly into a passion—anybody can do that. But to be angry with the right person to the right extent and at the right time and with the right object and the right way—that is not easy, and it is not everyone who can do it."

During the divorce proceedings, keep in mind the following:

DIVORCE CANONS

I will act in my own best interests.

I will do my best to express my own ideas.

I will ask for what I want and give what I can.

I will demand respect and consideration for myself and return the same to my spouse.

I will try to forgive any harm done.

I will take responsibility for my own actions and reactions.

The Authors

Chapter 22
YOUR PERSONAL OBJECTIVES

You and your spouse need to come to your own separate decisions about what you want from your divorce and how you want it. If it was acquired during marriage and produces income, it can be divided!

When a marriage goes down the tubes, the strong-minded will go to extraordinary lengths to protect what they feel belongs to them. Frequently, the underlying issue is one of power or control.

Dividing up personal possessions can be negotiated depending upon how much items are worth to you and your spouse. Everything has a dollar value as well as a sentimental or emotional value.

Recognize these feelings and examine how strong they are. Think about what you will need in the future and what you won't need anymore. Analyze how far you are willing to go to get what you want. What kinds of trade-offs are you willing to make?

Where the children are concerned, you must consider past history, current feelings, and future realities before you meet at the negotiating table.

FINANCIAL SUPPORT: THINK ABOUT THE FUTURE

"It's no disgrace to be poor, but it might as well be."
From the Sayings of Abe Martin

This section is being brought to you by the color *red*. It is wise to have figures on hand about what the future will cost. Whether you are on the paying or receiving end of the divorce dollar, this information will be required as part of the written preparation for your separation agreement. Include in your thinking the amount of money you need, when you need it, and the form in which it will be useful to you.

Defining Your Needs

This is the time to define what it is you *really* want and how you can shift your priorities to get it.

If you have done your documentation homework, you know what is available for division. Pull out your documentation files on:

- Credit cards.
- Household inventory and appraisals.
- Finance—banking, personal, institutional, and brokerage.
- Titles and deeds.
- Employer policies and benefits.
- Proprietorship, partnership, professional corporation, and family-owned business.
- Income records.
- Retirement dollars.

Use this information to create a list of needs and desires in some order of importance or necessity to you.

Start with the family residence. Will the house be kept or sold? How will a value be established? If the house is not sold, will there be sole or joint ownership? If joint, for how long and how will the expenses be paid?

The division of personal possessions (in humorous legal jargon, called "pots 'n' pans") can be done in any number of ways.

Some couples, using a combined list of mutual possessions (**FORM-ula 27: Household Inventory and Appraisal**), have taken turns picking out what they wanted. Whatever is left can be sold or given away.

That is one way to do it. At the other extreme is letting the court handle the division of property. There are many ways in between and they all involve negotiation. When you have determined your short- and long-term objectives, you will have the two components necessary for deciding whether what you want is realistic.

Analyze how to utilize future dollars to their best advantage. Study the subject, attend workshops, talk to your accountant or a financial planner.

In creating a budget, remember that it is a blue print of what you are trying to accomplish. Nothing is fixed in stone. All plans are firm…until changed. There are always so many "what ifs."

What if:

- I continue to live where I am?
- I move? Should I buy or rent?
- I have physical custody of the children?
- My spouse has physical custody?
- We have joint physical custody?
- I go back to school for some kind of training?
- I change jobs?
- I remarry?
- The financial agreement is not honored?

Warning: Don't go by what others spend! Or even by what you have been in the habit of spending. Look at *where you are going and what you need to do to get there.*

WILLINGNESS TO NEGOTIATE

Good negotiating is based on information, psychological advantage, leverage, and timing. It also requires a large dose of common sense. You must be ready to deal realistically with the facts at hand and make them work *for* you, not *against* you.

To negotiate from strength means being adequately prepared. Your record-keeping and present knowledge of the facts will dictate how you set the priorities for your separation agreement. They will also give you a reasonably good idea about the important issues as well as the ones that may give you the most trouble.

A credible negotiating position is one that is clear and documented. Your position cannot be arbitrary, untruthful, or unrealistic. Unreasonable expectations are the chief obstacle to an equitable divorce.

Note Details about the negotiating process will be found in Chapter 25.

Proposals and Counterproposals

The spouse who served the papers (the plaintiff) will usually be the person to present the first separation agreement proposal. The other spouse (the defendant) will decide to accept or refuse the proposal or offer a counterproposal.

These proposals go back and forth until, slowly but surely, negotiations and compromises begin to form into something resembling a workable separation agreement.

There are certain elements that work to each spouse's advantage in the divorce process. One of them is money:

- Money to work with.
- Money to buy any and all of the professional services needed.
- Money for the wherewithal to be financially secure in the interim.

The other is emotional balance, providing you with:

- The ability to stay flexible.
- The imagination to look for options.
- The commitment to decision-making by setting time limits.

Some Observations by Those Who Have Gone Before

"If at first you don't succeed, try again. Then stop. No sense in making a damn fool of yourself."

W. C. FIELDS

There seems to be a consensus of opinion among the already divorced about the kinds of behaviors and attitudes that get you through the quagmire.

Many of the comments we have collected are simple "one-liners" that are easy to remember and take a long time to think about. These are food for thought while you are stuck in traffic, doing the chores, or lying awake in the middle of the night:

- Do not expect to go through a divorce with everyone being fair and acting agreeably.

- Information is power.

- Future peace of mind depends upon the kind of financial decisions you make right now.

- Blatant confrontation alienates.

- Trust your instincts. Listen to them over the din of outside opinion.

- It's a small mind that cannot hold two opposing viewpoints at one time.

- Make an agreement that works for both of you—even if it isn't "the way things are done." It's *your* agreement.

- Find creative solutions, not pat answers.

- Unreasonable expectations are the chief obstacles to a fair settlement.

- You can say what you think without thinking, but it's not a good idea.

- If you keep on trying long enough and hard enough, all of a sudden some large pieces begin to fall into place.

- Stick with it. Don't give up. Hold to your end of the responsibilities. Hang in there. Trust yourself. Trust your hunches. Have respect for your own needs and feelings. *Illigitimae non carborundum* (Don't let the b_ _ _ _ _ _ s get you down.)

NAME TO USE AS A SINGLE PERSON

A change in name is both a psychological and a business decision. Sometimes, it gives an important feeling of independence and individuality. In any event, it is one more decision you may need to make.

Not so long ago, whether to retain or change your name after a divorce applied solely to women. With the increased use of hyphenated surnames, some men also have this decision to make.

For instance, an artist we know had signed many paintings with the combined surnames of himself and his spouse. He chose to retain the name that was professionally recognized.

The length of marriage and the age of children are often the determining factors in the choice of name that a woman makes.

The point is that, in most states, a divorce gives you the opportunity to legally change a name. Your options are a birth name, a name from a previous marriage, or even a name that you create.

While you can choose to change your name at a later date, either through common law or a formal name-changing procedure, there may be advantages to having the legal document now. It will cut through red tape when you start changing all of your other documents. Making the change as part of the divorce also means that you can make all document changes (name, address, ownership) at the same time. Another side benefit of making the change at the time of the divorce is that there is no extra charge for the legal and filing services.

Chapter 23
TAX FACTS IN DIVORCE

It is time to consider that great pain in the neck, *taxes*. Divorces involve money and money *always* involves taxes.

A divorce creates tax changes for both spouses, generally offering benefits to one and burdens to the other. The spouse with the best tax advice usually gets the best deal.

When figuring out the distribution of assets, you need to know how the proposed financial agreement will be affected by future taxes. The court is not obliged to consider the tax effects if you do not provide adequate evidence of potentially negative tax consequences.

In order to understand the taxes involved in your divorce agreement you can:

- Ask your attorney to figure out the income tax angles of your agreement.
- Consult an accountant or tax expert.
- Read the paperback guides on tax preparation that are published each year.

TAX PUBLICATIONS

You can request the following IRS publications by calling 1-800-424-3676:

- *503 — Child and Dependent Care Credit*
- *504 — Tax Information for Divorced or Separated Individuals*
- *508 — Educational Expenses*
- *521 — Moving Expenses*
- *523 — Tax Information on Selling Your Home*
- *525 — Taxable and Non-Taxable Income*
- *551 — Basis of Assets*
- *552 — Record Keeping for Individuals and a List of Tax Publications*
- *561 — Valuation of Donated Property*
- *929 — Tax Rules for Children and Dependents*

DEDUCTIBLE FEES

Ask your attorney what part of the legal fees are deductible. For example, you can deduct attorney fees which are paid to obtain taxable income such as alimony or an increase in alimony. Bills for legal advice incidental to the separation or divorce are subject to limitations; they currently are considered a miscellaneous itemized deduction subject to exceeding 2 percent of the tax payer's adjusted gross income. Tax advice to defend property is not generally deductible but currently may be added to the cost basis (original purchase price plus cost of capital improvements) of the property.

Be sure that you receive itemized statements of accounting for services received and costs incurred during your divorce. This will help you and your accountant analyze deductibles.

SPOUSAL SUPPORT

Alimony and maintenance payments are generally taxable income for the receiving spouse and tax deductible for the paying spouse. In order for the deduction to qualify, your separation must be legal either by written agreement or by court order. The separation agreement must contain a clause that states that alimony payments stop in the event that the recipient spouse dies.

Since these payments may also include medical expenses, life insurance premiums, mortgage payments, and so forth, be sure that the financial package is structured to take advantage of tax credits.

Under the Tax Reform Act of 1984, alimony is considered earned income for purposes of making annual contributions to an IRA fund. This means that the recipient spouse can choose to contribute up to $2,000 each year to this retirement plan.

RETIREMENT EQUITY

Included in the Tax Reform Act of 1984 is the Retirement Equity Act. This act permits all qualified tax-deferred employee pension and retirement benefits to be shared between divorcing spouses without penalty to the vested party or loss of any tax advantages of the plan. There are some restrictions such as the need to keep the funds in the same plan or in a similar tax-favored retirement plan, for example, an IRA.

HEAD OF HOUSEHOLD

An unmarried or legally separated person who furnishes over half of the household maintenance for at least one relative (child or parent) during the tax year will be entitled to head of household status with the IRS and pay lower taxes than other single persons.

PROPERTY TRANSFERS AND CAPITAL GAINS TAXES

Part of a divorce settlement may be a transfer of partial or total residence ownership from one spouse to the other. Such transfers are tax-free at the time of the divorce settlement. However, under the Internal Revenue Code, Section 1041, the spouse who becomes the owner will be subject to a capital gains tax based upon the *original* purchase price (adjusted for capital improvements) when the house is sold. To fully understand what this means to your situation, discuss the financial implications with your accountant.

Other property such as automobiles and household effects do not have tax consequences when they are redistributed as part of a divorce settlement.

ADULT EDUCATION EXPENSES

Expenses for adult continuing education may qualify for certain tax deductions. Since the regulations governing these deductions are fairly complicated, we suggest you read IRS Publication 508, *Educational Expenses,* and talk with your attorney to learn if this expense could be a factor in your financial arrangements.

TAXES AND ANNULMENTS

When a marriage is legally annulled, the IRS takes the position that the marriage never existed. This means that if a couple has been filing joint returns during the period of marriage, they must *file corrected returns* for the prior three years—even if one of the spouses had no separate income to declare.

TAXES AND CHILDREN AS DEPENDENTS

The federal government does not consider child support as taxable income to the receiving parent nor a tax deduction for the paying parent. You should check with your attorney regarding state income taxes.

There are a number of advantages and disadvantages for separating or combining alimony and child-support payments. It is a topic that needs careful consideration. If the decision is to combine them, be sure to keep accurate records of the separation agreement distribution.

One Child/One Exemption

A child can be an exemption to only one parent in a given year. (The IRS uses the children's Social Security numbers to check for duplication.) Unless otherwise specified, the exemption usually goes to the parent with physical custody.

The exception to this is when the noncustodial parent has contributed over half of the child's support. In this case, if the parents agree that the noncustodial parent is to have the deduction, the custodial parent must complete and sign IRS Form 8332 acknowledging the right of the noncustodial parent to claim the exemption. This form must be completed and submitted for each year that the noncustodial parent claims the exemption.

Should both parents claim the children as dependents in the same year, they will each be required to document their claim of majority support, and the IRS will make the decision on eligibility.

If the child-support deduction is being negotiated, figure out the tax advantages for each parent and then use these figures in your negotiations.

A child is treated as a dependent of both parents for purposes of their individual contributions toward medical expenses and reimbursements.

Tax Implications of Child Care

You will need accurate records to claim deductions for child support when you employ a housekeeper, nanny, or babysitter. Be sure to have each caretaker fill out a Form W-10 which includes name, address, and Social Security number.

If you pay $50.00 or more in a calendar quarter to any one individual, you must pay Social Security tax. You may also be liable for employee federal, state, and city withholding taxes. Be sure to check with local tax officials or your accountant.

The exception to your tax liability is when the person providing services is an independent contractor and, therefore, responsible for paying her or his own taxes. In this instance, you file a Form 1099 at the end of the year to report the total dollars paid to this individual for services.

The child care credit (for children under the age of 13) can only be used by the parent eligible for the dependency deduction. The amount is subject to limitations. Ask your attorney or accountant for information on the current IRS rulings.

Chapter 24
CHOOSING AND WORKING WITH YOUR PROFESSIONAL TEAM

"The winds and waves are always on the side of the ablest navigators."

GIBBON
Decline and Fall of the Roman Empire

In any divorce, there are storms and there are calms. You can ride out the storms if you have knowledgeable and compassionate people with you in your lifeboat.

You find the help you need by asking the right questions and hearing the answers that are right for your circumstances. How do you know the questions to ask? How can you be sure you are getting the right answers?

In this chapter on assembling your professional team, you will be using your spiral notebook labeled Attorney/Accountant, the Rolodex cards for Divorce Professionals (whichever color you chose), and your Personal Files: Family Profiles, Operating Expenses, Financial Statement, and Documentation for the Financial Value of the Marriage.

The work that you have done thus far in documenting, filing, and thinking has prepared you to talk intelligently and confidently about your divorce. Now is the time to complete your professional team and begin actively working with all of them.

DIVORCE TEAM MEMBERS

The members of your divorce team include:

- Attorney
- Accountant
- Mediator
- Therapist

To obtain your legal divorce, a vital member of your team is your divorce attorney—who may or may not be assisted by your accountant.

On the practical side, you may decide to use a mediator for negotiating the separation agreement. If so, refer back to the section on mediation in Chapter 3.

A therapist (or other trained counselor) may already be helping you to cope with the emotional part of your divorce. If you are not currently working with this kind of professional and think you might want to, refer back to Chapter 12.

This chapter is primarily concerned with finding and working with the attorney who can most effectively deal with the particular issues of your divorce.

FINDING AN ATTORNEY

Before you begin your search, here are a few time-tested, generally proven truths and facts about attorneys:

- *An attorney is your employee.*
- An attorney has additional team members, including paralegals, secretaries, and other firm personnel.
- An attorney only provides legal advice (not therapy).
- Each spouse should have her or his own advocate.
- Once you have discussed the details of your case with an attorney, that attorney has privileged information and should not subsequently represent your spouse.

Hire an attorney who can do the job—not one to be your best friend. Be aware, though, that the attorney's technical abilities and style must suit your personal needs and comfort level.

Compiling a Master List of Candidates

Finding an attorney is not something you want to do quickly or without researching thoroughly. Start by making a list of potential attorneys from:

- Your Rolodex, files, and notebooks for names and suggestions of professionals you have already made notes about (or cut clippings about from newspapers and magazines).
- Attorneys you have known in the past.
- Recommendations from divorced friends and acquaintances.
- American Academy of Matrimonial Lawyers (312-263-6477).
- Bar Associations (state and local attorney referral services).
- Public interest law firms.
- Law school alumni chapters.
- Law school clinics.
- Divorce decrees. (These are a matter of public record, so they can be read to find the names of the attorneys involved. If possible, you may want to talk with the ex-spouses about their respective attorneys.)
- *Yellow Pages,* under "Attorneys" and "Matrimonial Law."

- Counselors, doctors, clergy, rabbis, and other members of the helping professions.
- Recommendations from friends and relatives.
- Self-help organizations.

Selecting Your Attorney "Type"

Think about the kind of an attorney you want to represent you. In Chapter 22, you began to visualize the impending divorce proceedings and their outcome. With that outcome in mind, how do you picture your attorney?

- Do you want a fighter, because you know you will have an adversarial situation?
- Do you want a communicator who will help you to keep the lines of communication open?
- Will the sex of the attorney have a positive or negative effect on you or your spouse?
- Do you have substantial business to conduct with your spouse and therefore need a more corporate-oriented tax or real estate attorney?
- Have you and your spouse already reached an amicable agreement so that you need an attorney primarily for legal compliance and format?

Pre-Screening the Candidates

We've created a list of questions for you to ask of other people to help pre-screen a potentially enormous list of attorneys.

- What made you decide to choose your attorney?
- Were you satisfied with the handling of your case?
- What did your attorney do best? Least well?
- Do you feel your attorney helped you to negotiate the fairest deal possible? Explain.
- Since your divorce, have you discovered anything important that your attorney overlooked?
- What was your fee arrangement, and did it work out as originally estimated? If not, why?
- Was your attorney sensitive to your needs?
- Was your attorney available to you when you needed to be called back quickly, or when you needed prompt consultation?
- Did your attorney help or hinder communication with your spouse?
- Would you use the same attorney again?

Making the First Contact

There are some clear-cut steps in making the attorney selection:

1. *Make your first cut by phone.* Use the telephone to weed out attorneys who are unavailable by reason of case load, office accessibility, or conflict of interest. Be open to suggestions of new names.

2. *Cull your list down to about six attorneys.* One by one, as you speak with each of the attorneys on your list, trust your own gut response and first impression to tell you whether or not to set up a meeting. Have a second phone conversation if you are indecisive.

3. *Determine if there is any professional or personal relationship with your spouse's attorney.* If you know the name of your spouse's attorney, be sure to ask about any professional or personal relationship between the two parties. Have they dealt with each other before? How do they get along and work together? Are they cooperative or has there been bad blood between them? It is important that the attorney you choose is professionally concerned with your separation agreement and has no positive or negative personal issues with the opposing attorney.

4. *Schedule appointments.* The next step will be to schedule appointments. Make sure they occur during your emotionally "up" hours. Generally, there will be no charge for this first meeting because the attorney wants an opportunity to check *you* out, too. However, confirm in advance the attorney's policy for any preliminary consultation fees.

5. *Prepare carefully for each appointment.* Be ready to make maximum use of your allotted hour. In addition to the basic facts, be able to state your personal divorce objectives. This will give the attorney an overview of your divorce situation and an opportunity to observe you as the client.

The Final Selection

To help make an educated choice, use FORM-ula 54: Attorney Selection. Use a separate FORM-ula 54 for each attorney you interview.

FORM-ula 54: Attorney Selection helps you to choose your legal counsel based upon four main issues:

- Competence
- Personality
- Price
- Gut Reaction

When you formally ask an attorney to represent you, and the attorney accepts, the selection is made.

If acceptance of the case is conditional upon payment of a retainer, the attorney's responsibility does not begin until this fee is paid. (We have seen retainer fees ranging from $500 to $20,000.) This money may be refundable if your spouse becomes responsible for divorce expenses. In any event, if you pay in cash, be sure to ask for a receipt.

Setting the Fee and Working Terms

Clarifying the financial arrangements should be done up front. For some unknown reason, attorneys are seldom the ones to initiate this piece of business, so it is your responsibility to do so.

Because of an antitrust ruling by the Supreme Court, there are no recommended fee schedules. An hourly fee or a flat fee (which covers all services needed to complete the divorce) are the typical fee arrangements. While the fee is somewhat negotiable, the attorney will base the fee upon the nature of services to be provided. Issues usually considered are:

- Time and labor required (difficulty of issues and special skills needed).
- Potential conflicts of interest with current or potential business.
- Local fee standards for similar legal services.
- Time limitations.
- Former professional relationship with you or person who recommended the attorney to you.
- Experience and reputation of attorney.

When you and an attorney have agreed on the functional details of working together, it is a good idea to have a formal letter or written contract.

BEGINNING THE LEGAL PROCESS WITH YOUR ATTORNEY

The first few meetings with your attorney will be basically question-and-answer sessions. The attorney will need information and so will you.

Your relationship with your attorney will, of necessity, be about very private matters. It is important that you are able to talk about "anything and everything" to do with both your marriage and your divorce. These conferences are considered privileged and confidential information.

Unless this is not your first divorce, the whole experience will be new to you. When you don't understand, say so. When something bothers you or does not seem right, say so. No one knows your situation as well as you do. Your attorney cannot read your mind.

The Initial Business Meeting

It is important that you take the FORM-ulas from *The Divorce Decisions Workbook* with you to the first appointment with your attorney. They will provide you with the information you need when asked for:

- Your full name, age, and Social Security number.

- Your spouse's name, age, and Social security number.

- The same data for each of your children.

- Date of marriage and the number of years married.

- How long you have resided in your state and county.

- A clear, written summary of your marital problems (taken from the chronological family history).

- Copy of marriage certificate (also of earlier marriages).

- Copies of earlier divorce papers.

- Copies of birth certificates or adoption papers of children (if the court requires it, you may later have to show the document originals).

- Copies of financial statements, income taxes, and annual bookkeeping statements for the past several years.

- Current financial statements and copies of quarterly taxes filed.

- Present monthly bookkeeping (from the first of the year to the present).

- Budget for future needs, based on current living expenses and future projections.

- Employment records for yourself and your spouse.

- Estimate of annual income and projections for both yourself and your spouse.

- Inventory lists of current assets including stocks, bonds, bank accounts, retirement plans, real estate, joint personal property, individual property, and insurance policies.

Once your attorney has the facts, there can be an evaluation of what is involved in completing the divorce relative to the laws of your state, including the potential for winning a litigated case.

It will also be possible to give you an estimate of time and costs for the various scenarios.

Your files will assist in the preparation of your case. Your attorney will ask for items as they are needed. It will be either your job or your attorney's to obtain the missing information.

Tracking the Process

Be sure that your attorney has your phone numbers and mailing address (the location to which you want your mail sent). If your spouse is in the same residence and you want to protect your privacy, consider using a post office box or another address.

Keep a running list of questions and ideas for your attorney so that both your phone calls and your appointments will be time and money well spent.

Make notes (use your attorney notebook) of meetings and phone conversations; include the date, time, and subject matter. For quick reference, highlight tasks to completed by you and your attorney.

Request periodic fee statements of billing-to-date, including time sheets and a report of people contacted. At the same time, ask that copies of all incoming and out-going correspondence be sent to you.

Mark your calendar with the dates and times of meetings about your divorce. This will serve as your reminder and also be a permanent record.

THE ATTORNEY-CLIENT RELATIONSHIP

Studies show that clients who are actively involved in the planning and negotiation of their separation agreement end up with the most satisfactory divorces. This, in turn, results in the greatest amount of postdivorce cooperation with your ex-spouse.

If you do not relinquish responsibility and control by expecting the attorneys to battle it out, you will have a greater chance of avoiding litigation, more opportunity to work out compromises, and a much better attitude toward your agreements after the divorce becomes final.

As with any relationship, you can do all the checking you want beforehand but it isn't until you begin to work with someone that you get down to the nitty gritty of how it is likely to go. Working with your attorney is no exception.

Evaluation is an on-going process. There will be days when you and your attorney are working in harmony. There will also be days when you seriously question the choice of attorney that you made. Keep a rational perspective by periodically answering the following questions:

What Kind of a Client Are You?

- Do you provide your attorney with accurate and complete information on a timely basis?
- Are you clear on the objectives of your divorce agreement or do you waffle in making decisions or compromises?
- Have you neglected to cover matters that you later blame your attorney for forgetting?
- Do you discuss your disagreements with your attorney until you have resolved them?
- Where are you on the continuum of being a pest or unavailable?
- Do you insist on clarification of legal issues you do not understand?

Is Your Attorney Meeting Your Legal Needs?

- Are you treated as a valued client?
- Are you kept regularly informed, or are there long gaps between appointments, telephone calls, and agreed-upon projects?
- Are you comfortable with the working relationship between the opposing attorneys?
- Is your attorney making decisions or taking steps that you have not discussed or preapproved?
- Is there a clearly defined strategy for your divorce?
- Do you feel time is being wasted? Do you know the reason for delays?
- Do you feel pressured into accepting a settlement instead of working out a proper deal?

COMPLAINTS AND GRIEVANCES

If there appears to be a conflict of interest or a confirmed indication of malpractice (something unethi-

cal or improper in conduct), you may have a valid legal reason to find another attorney.

Examples of malpractice include:

- Charging improper fees.
- Failing to follow through on judgments to secure money owed.
- Unwarranted procrastination on a case.
- Failing to inform you of a hearing or trial date.
- Failing to appear on specific court dates.
- Omitting to advise you of your rights.
- Omitting to discover or include assets to which you are entitled.

Contact the Clerk's Office of the Superior Court in your judicial district to discuss the matter. Representatives will advise you of any steps to be taken and, if necessary, will provide you with an attorney complaint form and a copy of the *attorney grievance procedures*.

Changing Attorneys

If you have doubts about your attorney, don't mess around. Get a second opinion right away from another attorney on your list. Present what has occurred to date and state your concerns. What you need is a another professional viewpoint. You, however, will have to be the ultimate decision maker.

Before you change attorneys, discuss your grievances with the attorney you originally hired. You had a lot of information to work with when you hired your attorney and presumably you did it for some very sound reasons.

If you restate those reasons and present the difficulties you are having, your attorney may see what needs to be done to get the client-attorney relationship back on track. After all, a change of attorneys means loss of time and money to you both and the problems may not be insurmountable.

Do not be without legal representation if your divorce has already been filed. When you do decide to retain another attorney, be sure that you have copies of all correspondence and documents.

Once you have set up a new fee agreement and are satisfied that the second attorney can meet your needs, you can let go of your first attorney by "making a change for personal reasons." You need say no more than that. You may have to file a *substitution of attorney form* with the court.

Even though your original attorney has the ethical obligation to cooperate during the transition, you will be paying for time and expenses already incurred on your behalf.

FINDING AN ACCOUNTANT

When your divorce involves a straightforward division of assets and liabilities, an accountant should review the financial arrangements to make sure that the outcome (after expenses, taxes, and so forth) matches the intent of a proposed separation agreement.

If your financial security is at stake (particularly with children in the picture), it is smart business to use an accountant from the very beginning of the divorce process. The separation agreement should be reasonable for each spouse and reflect the divergent needs of each former partner.

Answer the following questions to help you decide whether or not you need an accountant:

- Are there different kinds of assets and liabilities involved?

- How complicated will the taxes be in this divorce?

- Do you feel there are assets and liabilities that cannot or should not be divided in half?

- Do you feel that assets and liabilities will be unfairly dealt with unless you add the clout of an accountant to your team?

- Does your attorney's firm have enough accounting experience for your particular situation, or do you need additional accounting expertise?

- Do you suspect your spouse of hiding assets or earnings? (A reputable accounting firm will add some weight to a contested case.)

If you feel that an accountant would help you to clarify your financial options (bearing in mind that emotions do get a bit stretched during divorce), the possibility of hiring one certainly warrants investigation.

Selecting an Accountant

There are two primary considerations in selecting an accountant. The first is suitable experience in all of the ramifications of dividing assets in a divorce and familiarity with the accounting procedures used for your family's particular type of income. There are significant variations between the income sources from sole proprietorships, family-owned businesses, trust funds, investments and large corporations. The specialized expertise of the accountant you choose may make a substantial difference in the financial outcome of your separation agreement.

The second issue is to select an accountant who will work cooperatively with your attorney.

GETTING YOUR LEGAL DECREE AND A SUCCESSFUL DIVORCE

"This above all, to thine own self be true,
  And it must follow, as the night the day,
  Thou canst not then be false to any man."

Hamlet
WILLIAM SHAKESPEARE

Throughout *The Divorce Decisions Workbook,* you have taken a good look at yourself, your marriage, and the resources you have to work with. You have done research, selected an attorney, and clarified your goals and strategies.

You and your attorney will have used material from your entire file system (and possibly additional information acquired through legal discovery) to prepare your version of the separation agreement.

A successful divorce is not one where one partner gets substantially (and unfairly) more than the other. A successful divorce is one where good faith and good communication allow both spouses to move away from each other and to move forward separately.

Now is the time to be clear and straightforward about the value system and priorities that you have already established.

Review what is most and least important to you. Issues may be as small as who keeps a vacation souvenir or as large as visitation rights. Before you go to the bargaining table, evaluate acceptable trade-offs.

It is not likely that you will be able to have it all your way nor will you be able to turn all of your negatives into positives. Creative negotiating will allow each of you to find solutions to the weightiest issues and problems.

You want to create an agreement that can "grow," meaning that it can deal with changes in circumstance.

You and your spouse will be forced to state your differences in legalistic terms and allow each other to speak. You need to be able to state your position clearly and rationally.

If all else fails, litigation will literally become your court of last resort.

Chapter 25
NEGOTIATING WHAT IS ACCEPTABLE AND AFFORDABLE

"You don't get what you deserve—you get what you negotiate."

Advertisement for Karrass Negotiation Seminars

There is a common pattern to all negotiations. It is a cycle of initial contact, planning (research, goals, strategies, and tactics), and one or more negotiating sessions that lead to a signed agreement, complete with provisions to ensure its implementation.

There are two basic components to any divorce negotiation: what is affordable and what is personally acceptable. The objective is to find a reasonable and legally acceptable balance between them.

Your first experience in negotiating starts with your own attorney. The two of you must work together until you achieve a meeting of the minds so that what you want can be spelled out in the first draft of the separation agreement.

When you are ready for the first negotiating session with your spouse and the other attorney, how will you approach it?

THINKING LOGICALLY

"Most of our so-called reasoning consists in finding arguments for going on believing as we already do."

The Mind in the Making
JAMES HARVEY ROBINSON

When women use accepted business logic in preparing for a divorce, they will perhaps be perceived as ruthless, calculating, and manipulative. When men use accepted business logic in preparing for a divorce, they are usually perceived as being practical, logical, and direct. Regardless of clichés and biases, the reality is that organized and rational thinking is a must for both men and women if spouses are going to create a mutually satisfactory separation agreement in our family court system.

Be concrete in your ideas and remain open to reason. Ask questions until you are satisfied about your spouse's basis for reasoning. Be prepared to answer questions that clarify the integrity of your position. Be as tough as you want where a problem needs resolution but be soft on the people involved.

Since the beginning of *The Divorce Decisions Workbook,* you have been asked over and again to analyze and formulate your objectives. You have been requested to actively participate in your own future. You have been challenged to gather together the facts about what you have, what you want now, and what you wish to accomplish by the time you have changed the marriage vow "I do" to the divorce disclaimer "I don't anymore."

The sooner you learn to put yourself into your spouse's shoes and ask, "What would I do if I were you?" the sooner you will be ready to arrive at a mutually acceptable separation agreement.

ENTERING NEGOTIATIONS

Bargaining for the future welfare of yourself and your family is no picnic. Here is a collection of tips offered by some of our clients that will walk you through the process. They refer to both the personal and the practical sides of negotiating.

- Request that negotiations be held where the atmosphere is quiet and professional.
- Be prompt in attendance.
- Dress the way you will feel the most comfortable for the setting of the meeting.
- Make sure you have a written agenda from your attorney.
- Be prepared to take notes and check off each item as it is completed.
- Be sure to have copies of whatever documents you have been asked to bring.
- Sit tall and use direct eye contact as much as you can since body language "speaks loudly."
- Speak in your normal tone of voice. (You're not on stage, even though you may feel like it.)
- Listen quietly and patiently to what is being said.
- Make sure that you have equal opportunity to voice your opinions or disagreement.
- Try to stay in the first person when you speak. (Don't be afraid of the word "I." In fact, present all of your feelings, facts, and observations in the "I" mode, for example, "I think we ought to...," and "I defend this issue on the basis that...")

- Try not to be defensive about your ideas and be open to advice, even constructive criticism.
- Refuse to discuss business and personal matters in the same conversation.
- Don't succumb to pressure for an immediate response. (Request a minute to think, or time out to discuss the matter with your attorney.)
- Never be forced into a decision—even if it is one that your attorney approves. (If you are not sure, table the issue so that you have time to review your material and to think.)
- When you need to release the tension/frustration/ irritation that builds up during negotiating sessions, take a couple of deep breaths from the diaphragm and let them out slowly.
- Don't use alcohol or drugs to calm your nerves during these times.

THE BARGAINING TABLE

Everything is negotiable and anything can be used as a tool for negotiations. Go to the bargaining table prepared for promises to be exchanged and deals to be closed.

It is not a matter of simply putting a value on everything when you are working out what you want or what you are willing to give in a separation agreement. The bargaining process requires setting three different basic values:

- The least you would be willing to give or give up.
- The most you would be willing to give or give up.
- The bottom line you would be willing to agree upon.

Divorcing couples tend to think in terms of things they want (assets) and frequently forget about what they don't want (liabilities). Remember, ownership of items such as debts, a bad piece of property, and attorney's fees must also be negotiated.

When you reach a stalemate, the attorneys should be able to provide information about how a similar situation has been previously handled within the judicial community where your case is being processed.

The bargaining table is only used to resolve previously undecided issues. As you reach agreement on each issue, consider that topic closed. Agreements never come together if you keep rehashing what was supposedly already settled (in fact, they are more likely to fall apart). Whereas every agreement must adapt to new circumstances or information, too many new issues late in the game cast doubt on the good faith of what was previously settled.

Avoiding a Free-for-All

Divorce negotiations can be traumatic. In addition to the business at hand, it is very easy to get trapped into old emotional patterns when your spouse begins to act in predictable ways. Either one of you can become overly defensive or hostile.

How do you respond to threats or defuse anger? What happens if the meeting starts to get ugly?

When you and your attorney discussed your divorce files, especially the profiles and information on extenuating circumstances, you anticipated the danger points and prepared suitable ways of coping. However, when both spouses are wound up, something totally innocuous can trigger an outrageous response. How can it be dealt with right then and there?

First of all, there should be time-out to cool down the emotions before returning to the facts. Then, allow your attorneys to summarize the situation.

If new issues come to light through an emotional outburst, they will require discussion and verification. Then a decision can be made about how this new information will affect the developing agreement.

When to Be Reasonable

Not all divorces are adversarial. Not all agreements are structured from long and bitter disagreements over who gets what. Just because you are getting a divorce doesn't mean you cannot continue to work together.

Be open to brainstorming. If you are at an impasse or seem to be totally deadlocked, you can always flip a coin. Seriously, the very idea that you have only a 50-50 chance of "winning" usually revives the interest in negotiating.

If the other side will not negotiate, do not attack the position—look behind it.

Helpful Phrases and Questions

Here are some useful model statements to use if the proceedings stall or if you encounter other difficulties.

- "Please correct me if I'm wrong…"
- "I appreciate what we've done thus far…"
- "My basic concern is fairness…"
- "I'd like to settle this on a basis of principle, not power."
- "Could we go over this once more to make sure that I understand clearly?"

- "What is the principle behind your request?"
- "Let me show you where I'm having trouble with that."
- "A more equitable solution might be…"

SIX DEADLY OBSTACLES TO NEGOTIATION

The deadly sins can never be seen or imagined more clearly than in the process of divorce. When any of the negative patterns of a marriage are brought to the negotiating table, the battle will be long and bloody.

Greed will make any reasonable financial negotiation impossible.

Anger will waste time and energy.

Lust will fire up old memories that might get in the way.

Jealousy will get you nowhere—it's not your relationship anymore.

Pride causes stalemates.

Fear—perhaps the greatest sin of all.

Fear

Fear is perhaps the worst enemy of good negotiation—fear of rejection and loss of position, property, or place in the community. There are also the fears of loneliness and of having to start all over again; of personal and financial hardship, and of not being able to handle all that is ahead. The more dependent you have been upon your spouse—financially, personally, or emotionally—the deeper the roots of fear.

The fear of negotiating with a spouse who is more powerful, more prestigious, or more "important" than you creates problems, particularly if the spouse is well-connected or has a prominent family.

Under any of these circumstances, sitting down at a bargaining table seems like risky business. When there are significant emotional or practical inequities, you must do whatever you can to change the expected patterns of your position. Use all available resources: *The Divorce Decisions Workbook*, counseling, and so forth. If you can avoid succumbing to predictable old ways and if you have an attorney who is not impressed or easily intimidated, you will be able to balance the pressures against you by using strategies that are different from those expected from you.

Whatever the obstacles, the basic rule in negotiating is to understand what options exist for both of you. Insist upon realistic objectives. Focus on the problems, not the person. Try to find a different approach to the same problem. Reframing a seemingly insoluble problem may solve it.

It is not necessarily all the things you know that will help you during negotiations, it is what you can think of at the right moment to back your issues and arguments. This is where your files of prepared information can be invaluable.

RECOGNIZING COERCIVE TACTICS

What's fair and what's not fair in the arena of divorce? What does it mean to step over the bounds of common decency? Just what kind of tactics are allowable? What is considered good strategy to one spouse might be seen as deceptive to the other, depending upon the motives of negotiation.

An early step in understanding what your negotiations will be like is to try to recognize the tactics being used. If your divorce is adversarial, you are likely to face some tactics designed to wear you down such as:

Deliberate deceptions

Misrepresentation of facts.

Less than full disclosure.

Building in complicated compliance features.

Psychological warfare

Stressful situations.

Personal attacks.

Silent treatment.

Withholding money or children.

Playing on spouse's sense of guilt.

Body language.

Black hat-white hat designations.

Threats.

Dependency and helplessness.

Positional pressures

Refusal to negotiate.

Unreasonable demands.

Escalating demands.

Hardheartedness.

Calculating delays.

Hiring a "barracuda" attorney.

Control versus dependency.

SPOUSE BLINDNESS

A spouse who wants to remain in a difficult marriage even after the relationship has become so untenable is usually suffering from what we call *spouse blindness*; that is, a condition whereby that spouse is unable to see the marriage as being anything other than perfectly acceptable. This delusion can continue up to the very day of, and remain long after, being served with divorce papers.

Getting over spouse blindness requires time to see the issues clearly and to heal some of the hurt. Only then will it be possible to develop a balanced separation agreement. Unfortunately, having finally made the decision to divorce, the departing spouse is usually in a hurry to get it over with. The blind spouse will often try to drag the divorce out interminably in the hope of a change of heart. The departing spouse and attorney must be prepared to set compassionate limits for a reasonable transition period.

Chapter 26
STRUCTURING THE SEPARATION AGREEMENT

"If we continue in the direction we are going, we are likely to end up where we are headed."

Old Chinese Proverb

A well-structured, mutually acceptable separation agreement brings about a satisfactory dissolution of the marriage. This final document is the legal signification of closure. The separation agreement should also include the methods for dealing with future changes of circumstance.

A separation agreement is a piece of writing created by both spouses and their attorneys (see Figure 26.1). All of the unique features of your divorce will have to be incorporated within the structure and guidelines of your particular state. The actual language of the separation agreement will vary from state to state.

From the beginning of *The Divorce Decisions Workbook*, we have helped you develop your own special package of divorce information relating to the four legal areas of divorce:

- Peace.
- Property.
- Spousal support.

- Responsibility to children.

There are also the words and items that make the document official, which we call "legalese."

Arriving at this point in the book means you have completed your documentation, worked with your attorney, met at the bargaining table, and are probably ready to complete the business of your divorce. As you prepare the final separation agreement, you and your attorney should make sure that you have covered each item that is important to you.

We are going to review each of the above areas separately. The first paragraph of each topic heading extrapolates from actual legal terminology and jargon. After that, we list all of the issues that we feel come under that specific category. We hope that every topic mentioned will look familiar. Each of them has been discussed in the preceding chapters and much of the information developed through a FORM-ula.

Once you and your spouse have agreed upon the primary objectives of the separation agreement, it is the responsibility of each of your attorneys to make sure that the legal language of the document

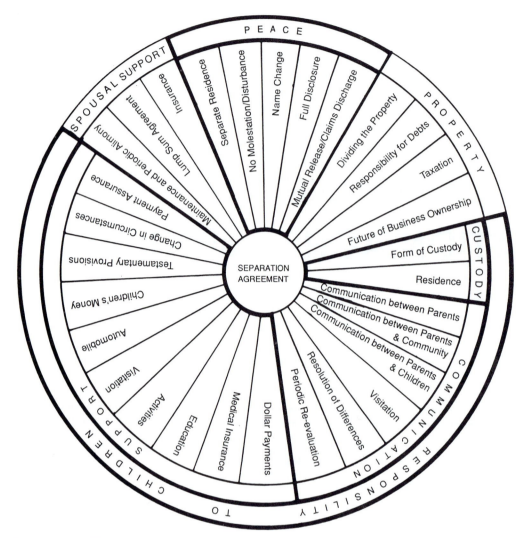

Figure 26.1. *Wheel of Future*

reflects the spirit and intent of what you want to achieve.

Unfortunately, the legal system has not yet developed a readily available master checklist so it is up to you to make sure that nothing falls through the cracks.

PEACE

Separate Residence

This section of your separation agreement establishes your legal right to live apart from your former spouse and to be free from any form of control or interference by that spouse.

Living in a new residence (or the old residence without your former spouse) poses some new issues:

- Changing locks.
- Forwarding mail.
- Filling out change of address cards.
- Making agreements about maintenance.
- Deciding on right of entry (if joint ownership continues).
- Determining final residence (that is, family burial plots).

No Molestation/Disturbance

Neither ex-spouse is to deliberately bother or interfere with the peace or comfort of the other. (This requirement includes trying to force a renewed association or sexual relationship.)

Further items to discuss include:

- Bad-mouthing each other.
- Spousal abuse, if relevant.
- Former in-law family celebrations (or funerals).

Name Change

Remember that a spousal name change can be included in the terms of the divorce agreement, as permitted by laws of your particular state.

Full Disclosure

Each spouse, aided by her/his respective attorney, has done the necessary homework to be fully informed about the assets, liabilities, income, and future financial prospects of the other. Both spouses acknowledge that their separation agreement has been formulated after full disclosure and with competent legal representation.

We suggest that you use your documentation files to make sure that important items are not overlooked:

- Finances (banking, personal, institutional, and brokerage).
- Titles and deeds.
- Insurance (medical, life, and personal property).
- Employment (history, policies, benefits).
- Income.
- Retirement dollars.
- Household inventory and appraisals.
- Credit and credit cards.
- Liabilities.

Verify that your separation agreement includes a statement that provides an automatic remedy to deal with fraud if it is discovered in the future. The statement should include how related legal expenses will be paid.

Mutual Release and Discharge of Claims

You and your spouse will never again have the right to make a claim against each other for anything except what is specifically stated in your separation agreement. This includes estates and inheritances.

This small but very important part of your divorce decree has very large teeth in it. So, whatever claims you think you should make, make them now or forever hold your peace, because once this document goes on record in the courthouse, you have very limited further recourse.

Include in your discussions the issue of executors and beneficiaries of wills.

PROPERTY

Once the divorce is final, the ownership of distributed property is free of any claim, no matter what the circumstance. The owner has full power to administer the property, including the disposal of it.

Dividing the Property

The spouses agree that all items of real estate, securities, finances, vehicles, and household inventory have been divided to their satisfaction.

We suggest that all personal property (automobiles, household furnishings, jewelry, collections, income from various sources) divided between you and your spouse (or awarded separately because it is not properly divisible) be specifically listed in the separation agreement, including the property's agreed-upon value, if relevant.

In addition, you will want to discuss land and buildings:

- Continuing co-ownership of real property, including

    Physical possession
    Departure terms for nonresident spouse
    Right of nonresident spouse to enter/inspect premises
    Restrictions as to tenants, visitors, roommates
    Payment of mortgage, taxes, insurance, liens
    Funding maintenance and improvements
    Property as collateral for additional indebtedness
    Restriction of conveying interest to third party
    Agreement not to force sale
    Provision in event of death of either party
    Methods to handle noncompliance.

- Agreement to sell property, including

    Documentation of capital improvements.
    Payment of liens and other encumbrances.
    Payment of necessary expenses until sale.
    Responsibility/cooperation in marketing property.
    Determining fair market value and asking/selling price.

Tax consequences and capital gains obligations.
Distribution of sale expenses and proceeds.
Provision in event of death of either party prior to completion of sale.
Methods to handle noncompliance.

- Waivers of interests in property, including

Release from mortgages, liens, or encumbrances.
Consideration for conveyance, sale, or transfer.
Date for transfer of property.
Party responsible for document preparation.
Waivers to right, title, and interest.
Methods to handle noncompliance.

Consider how you prefer to divide what are frequently "emotional assets," including

Future pension income.
Future income from past, present, and future academic degrees.
Miscellaneous items, including club memberships and entertainment subscriptions.

Be sure that your attorney includes a statement that you and your spouse have revealed all property owned.

Responsibility for Debts

Both spouses make the statement that they will not create future financial liabilities for which the other can be held responsible. All current liabilities need to be dealt with in the separation agreement, including a legal remedy for default.

Some guidelines for agreement on debts would be to:

- Establish a schedule of creditors, balances due, and due dates.
- Decide who will pay what and when.
- Determine security for the payment of debts.
- Agree on which spouse will pay taxes (past and current), assessments, and/or penalties.
- Insert a clause of indemnification, or hold harmless, for debts to be paid by the other spouse. Creditors will continue to hold both spouses responsible for debts incurred during the marriage, so it's best if all joint accounts are paid off, closed and re-opened individually. An alternative is to transfer account ownership, including balance due, to one spouse only.
- Determine legal fees for the divorce and all other matters arising in direct relationship to divorce ar-

rangements, such as noncompliance, nonsupport, and the like. (The separation agreement might include the date by which fees are to be paid in full as well as a hold harmless clause and a penalty for nonpayment.)

- Establish ownership of cosigned loans.
- Agree to or not to repay loans on cash value of life insurance.
- Determine items designated to one spouse with other spouse responsible for debt payments. (For example, what happens if your spouse stops making the car payments without your knowing it and the car is claimed by the finance company?)

Use your FORM-ulas for property and finance to be sure that your attorney is aware of who owns what and who is making the payments.

You and your spouse may want to consider selling assets to reduce or eliminate debts contracted during the marriage. This would allow each of you to either clean the slate or renegotiate a manageable debt payment plan with the remaining creditors.

If your financial picture is difficult or complicated, we suggest the use of a financial advisor. One or two sessions might help you to work out a feasible plan to incorporate into the separation agreement. There are a number of ways to handle debts that you may not be aware of, such as taking secured loans or using the cash value of a life insurance policy.

Taxation

Will you be filing a joint income tax for the last year you were married? If so:

- What taxes are owed?
- Who owes them?
- Will there be a refund, and if so, who will get it?
- Who prepares supporting income and deduction documentation?
- Be sure that each spouse is indemnified from liability for errors and omissions of the other.

Will you be filing a separate income tax return for the last year you were married? If so:

- Who will claim the children as deductions?
- Who will receive credit for mortgage interest and real estate taxes?
- How will capital gains be handled if your home was or is to be sold during the year?

- Who will be responsible for any delayed liability of tax payment on tax-shelter assets?
- How will you handle possible tax ramifications of transfers of assets such as cars, life insurance policies, and so forth.
- Who is responsible for taxes in arrears on any items of property to be transferred per the separation agreement? (You will need a form from the town or city where personal property is taxed stating that no tax is due before the transfer can be completed.)

Additional tax reminders:

- Alimony payments are taxable to the recipient.
- Child support payments are taxable to the payer.
- Unallocated payments are taxable to the recipient.
- Lump-sum payments, within a specified number of years, are not taxable to the recipient.

Include a clause stating that financial decisions and payment amounts have been based upon tax laws existing on the date of your separation agreement. This escape clause allows renegotiation if future tax laws significantly alter the *intent* of the agreement.

Future of Business Ownership

If you and your spouse now own or have recently owned a joint business, you must settle the question of how profits, losses, and business expenses will be divided. Be sure to include relevant capital contributions to the business. Also, determine how tax filing will be handled. Use your documentation file **FORMula 45: Proprietorships, Partnerships, Professional Corporations, and Family-Owned Businesses.**

SPOUSAL SUPPORT

Maintenance and Periodic Alimony

In the separation agreement, support and maintenance for the spouse should include the following:

- Amount to be paid.
- Payment intervals (weekly, monthly, etc.).
- The location where money is to be paid: name and address, bank account number, and address.
- Social Security number of recipient.

- A method of payment in case of death or emergency.
- Insurance policies ownership, name and address.
- Medical coverage: who pays, the amount, and due dates.
- Information on how cohabitation, remarriage, or shared housing affect spousal support and maintenance.
- A statement on whether you want a cost of living adjustment.
- Payment assurance, to include:
    Insurance policies (owned by support recipient with fully paid premiums by spouse making support payments).
    Liens against real property.
    Trust instruments.
    Promissory notes.
    Restraining orders prohibiting alteration of documents designated for compliance in separation agreement.
- Recourse for noncompliance, including attorney fees (who pays and under what circumstances), recognition of how expenses will be paid in the interim, and interest charges on default payments.

In some cases, alimony can be paid for a specified period to pay for training, work start-up expenses, educational costs, and so forth. The amount and duration of these payments should be stated.

There might also be a provision for alimony to be paid at a later date based upon need, for example when a spouse starts to work later in life and there is no pension plan available.

If there is to be no spousal support at all, it is suggested that instead of removing this subject entirely from the court's power, some spousal support should be set, perhaps at $1.00 per year, to allow modification, should substantial changes occur.

For tax purposes, financial arrangements for spousal support should be clearly defined in the separation agreement. You may want them separated from the arrangements made for child support.

Lump-Sum Agreement

Where it is agreed that alimony is not desired or appropriate, one spouse may agree to pay the other a lump sum which is the same as a final payment.

This distribution is made in addition to the division of property. At the present time, lump-sum payments are nontaxable whereas periodic alimony is taxable.

Insurance

Unless it is specifically stated otherwise, the divorce decree automatically removes an ex-spouse as beneficiary to any existing life insurance policies of the other ex-spouse. This includes all policies that are owned by the insured person personally or through business and pension plans.

Life insurance policies can provide a guarantee of good faith and support to divorcing spouses and their children. In any event, all life insurance policies owned by either spouse should be specifically identified. Policy numbers should be shown along with the name of the insured and the issuing company. The disposition of each policy should be clearly set out in the agreement or judgement.

Northwestern Mutual Life Insurance Company provide the information for **FORM-ula 55: Divorce Settlements: Life Insurance Checklist**. These are negotiable issues that should be discussed with your attorney.

Liability insurance is also a good idea for working spouses in case of illness or accident.

If new policies are going to be issued as payment assurance, the person to be covered must agree to cooperate if medical exams are needed.

RESPONSIBILITY TO CHILDREN

Before making decisions in this section of your separation agreement, we suggest that you reread Chapters 20 and 21 and refer to the corresponding FORM-ulas.

1. Establishing Custody

Form of Custody
- Parenting plan.
- Legal custody: sole or joint.
- Physical custody: sole, joint, or split.
- Guardianship provisions in wills.

Residence
- Relocation changes: procedures and consequences

2. Support

Dollar Payments to Custodial Parent
- Amount to be paid for each child.

- Payments:
  weekly, monthly, etc.
  length of time.
- Form of payment.
- How paid: check, direct bank deposit, salary deduction (wage assignment), to court.
- Payment arrangements when one or more children visit noncustodial parent for extended period.
- Payment arrangements when one or more children are away from home for extended periods, such as to attend summer camp.
- Reserve for emergencies.

Payment Assurance
- Insurance policies (owned by custodial parent with fully paid premiums by parent making support payments).
- Liens against real property.
- Trust instruments.
- Promissory notes.
- Restraining orders prohibiting alteration of documents designated for compliance in separation agreement.
- Recourse for noncompliance:
  Attorney fees: who pays and under what circumstances.
  How expenses will be paid in the interim.
  Interest charges on default payments.
  Penalties.

Medical Insurance
- Parent responsible and when obligation ends.
- Authorized signatures.
- Type of coverage: routine, major medical, pharmaceutical, dental.
- Proof of coverage documentation.
- Payments, reimbursement, deductible procedures.
- Who fills out insurance forms?
- Unreimbursable expenses:
  out-of-pocket costs.
  elective procedures.
  preexisting conditions.
- Conditions not covered by insurance (plastic surgery, orthodontia, etc.)
- Care exceeding covered limits.
- Therapies: physical or emotional.

- Arrangements for continued coverage in the event of death, disability, or change of current employment coverage.
- Provision for parent not providing basic medical coverage to be able to buy "catastrophic coverage" for the children.
- Compliance assurance for coverage and procedures.

Education (including method of payment: direct or through parent with physical custody)

Minors

- Tuition and supplies.
- Tutoring.
- Special education.
- School trips.
- Fees for applications and tests.
- Religious training.

Emancipated children

- Tuition for college, graduate school, or trade school.
- Related expenses: room and board, books, transportation to and from school, incidental expenses.
- Clothing.

Activities (including method of payment: direct or through parent with physical custody)

- Special lessons and related equipment and supplies.
- Camps.
- Group or class trips.

Visitation

- Telephone bills.
- Transportation for visits.
- Special clothing and supplies needed for visit (bathing suits, ski boots, etc.).

Automobile Expenses (for minor and emancipated children enrolled in school)

- Cost of vehicle.
- Fuel.

- Insurance.
- Upkeep: repairs, maintenance, registration, and emissions.

Responsibility for Children's Money

- Allowance.
- Stocks.
- Trusts.
- Custodial accounts.
- Inherited assets for minors.

Testamentary Provisions

- Life insurance beneficiaries.
- Irrevocable beneficiaries.
- Trusts.
- Provisions for child support payments from the noncustodian's estate in the event of her or his death.

Changes in Circumstance

- Emancipation of minor children.
- Shared housing, cohabitation, remarriage of either parent.
- Cost-of-living increases.
- Increase or decrease of parent's income.
- Financial aids, grants, loans, scholarships.
- Catastrophic illness and related family changes.

Post-Divorce Communication

Spelling out the details of communication in changed family circumstances lays the groundwork for meeting the obligations of the separation agreement. How you agree to divide and handle the details of your new responsibilities can provide structure and reasonable expectations for the future relationship of your entire family. Specifically, how will contact be made and who will be physically responsible at what times for the following situations.

Communication Between Parents

- Health.
- Education.
- General welfare.
- Discipline and daily procedures.

- Emergencies:

    medical authorizations.
    visitation during.

Communication Between Parents and Community

- Medical professionals.

- Schools.

- Social organizations and activities.

- Authorized signatures for report cards, permission slips, etc.

- Notarized letters of consent for travel, permissions, etc.

Communication Between Parents and Children

- Telephone.

- Visitation:

    transportation.
    related expenses.

- Procedure for changes of plans.

Visitation

- Basic schedule.

- Holidays and special events.

- Rights of relatives.

- Care of children when custodial parent is traveling (paid sitter, noncustodial parent, etc.).

- Reciprocal visitations when noncustodial parent has children for extended period.

- Expenses and effect upon support.

Resolution of Differences

- Methods for handling noncompliance:

    mediation.
    legal.

- Terms:

    time frame.
    payment responsibilities.

Periodic Reevaluation

- Method.

- Terms.

LEGALESE

Separation agreements usually have sections that use the following words and phrases.

Implementation

Both spouses agree to cooperate in the implementation of this agreement. They will do it promptly and without further cost to each other.

Modification and Waiver

Both spouses agree that there will be no changes in the agreement unless automatic changes have been built into the agreement, or changes are made through the court system. If both spouses agree to waive any condition of the agreement for one or more times, this does not constitute a precedent that voids the terms of the original agreement.

Legal Representation

Unless it is a prose divorce, each spouse declares that she and he has legal representation and names the attorney. Each spouse also declares that there is no other attorney involved who will come forward to claim fees.

Legal Interpretation

This section of the separation agreement ensures that the agreement is in compliance with the laws of your state and that the agreement is to be carried out in that state. It also indicates whether you intend for the separation agreement to be merged within the divorce judgment or incorporated within the judgment but also surviving as an independent contract.

Possible Invalidity

If any state, country, or jurisdiction considers any portion of your separation agreement invalid or illegal, it will not affect the rest of your agreement. In the United States, however, most states have separation agreement reciprocity (under the Uniform Enforcement of Judgements Act).

Entire Understanding

Last, but by no means least, we come to the grand finale of what you have been struggling to achieve over all this time: the statement that says that both you and your spouse have read the agreement and understand it (no other kinds of agreements or understandings will be honored except this one) as your lawful separation agreement. It is then signed, witnessed, and dated.

Reconciliation

This says that once your separation agreement is signed, sealed, and delivered, it is a "done deal." Reconciliation or resumption of marital relations does not change the fact that you are divorced and must continue to operate under the conditions and obligations of your agreement.

If you and your ex-spouse decide that the divorce was a mistake, you can start all over and get married again.

Chapter 27
SHOULD YOU SETTLE OR GO TO TRIAL?

To settle, or not to settle: that is the question! Let's say that you have reached a stalemate and there is just no way you are going to be able to settle amicably on the major issues of your separation agreement. You feel that your spouse is:

- Attacking your every weak spot.

- "Making you pay."

- Stretching your patience to the limit.

- Trying to force you into a corner.

- Playing every legal dirty trick in the book.

You have done your work in *The Divorce Decisions Workbook*, and you know the strengths and weaknesses of your position. Do you sign the agreement now and fight over it later? What are your alternatives? What if your case is too good to sign the kind of agreement your spouse is proposing or counterproposing.

Every case is completely different, so there are no pat answers to your individual dilemma. You and your attorney have more thinking and talking to do.

ABOUT GOING TO TRIAL

Once your case is in court, the judge and the attorneys become the principal players in the drama. These three people will determine the outcome of all unresolved issues. Will this arrangement be to your advantage?

There may be good reasons for going to trial, also called *litigation*, such as proof of fraud or a situation of child, drug, or alcohol abuse.

The thing to remember about going to trial, though, is that it almost always takes a long time for the case to be heard by a judge. This may or may not be worth the additional financial and emotional cost, plus the delay in getting on with your life.

On the other hand, just the willingness to go to trial may force a reopening of negotiations and result in a satisfactory pretrial separation agreement.

When talking with your attorney about the merits of your position, you should:

- Ask for an evaluation of the pros and cons of your case.

- Think about the merits of the various proposals made by your spouse.

- Review financial advice and tax ramifications of the options.

- Find out what precedents have already been set in cases like yours.

- Ask which judge is likely to preside over your trial and the personal biases and typical rulings likely to be made on your kind of unresolved issues.

- Consider alternative strategies.

- Reconsider the advantages of making a settlement now, thereby eliminating additional legal fees, court costs, and the possibility of losing anyway.

- Recognize the fear, guilt, or desire to have it done with that may affect your decision to accept a less than wise or fair separation agreement.

By going to trial, you may be trying to assert the fact that you will not be pushed around. This is not the proper arena for assertiveness training because a trial actually takes away your control and makes you more vulnerable.

If you are going to trial to counterattack an aggressive and hostile spouse or attorney, you and your attorney should have strongly documented facts, credible witnesses, and legal precedents on your side.

The main thing is to be realistic and, at the same time, fair to yourself. Reread the material on the legal process presented in Chapter 18.

IF YOU LOSE AND WANT TO APPEAL

Appealing a court decision is costly and time-consuming and doesn't usually change the original ruling.

Every trial has to have a loser. If you are the one, you will have to decide quickly whether or not you wish to appeal as you have a limited amount of time in which to file.

Before making this decision, find out why you lost the case. There may be good reasons that would not increase your chances of winning an appeal. This may require additional legal opinions.

The next decision is whether to rehire the same attorney or go for a specialist in appeals. The attorney who represents you for an appeal will write the *briefs*, or reasons on your behalf, and then cogently argue them.

If you do decide to file an appeal, a judge will read the trial transcripts and the briefs to determine whether or not the original trial judge erred in the decision. A new trial begins if the new judge determines that it is warranted.

Be sure to ask your attorney if the financial obligations (spousal and child support) of the original court support orders are in force while the appeal is pending. The answer to this question may affect your desire for an appeal.

AFTER WORDS

"Every experience is worthwhile. What I learned in this marriage I'll put to use somewhere else."

THE AUTHORS

It is likely that during the separation, most of your personal contacts with your spouse have been for the purpose of dissolving your marriage. Now that the formalities are over, there is one last covenant you and your spouse may want to create that has nothing to do with courts or legalities. It has to do with the kind of personal and business relationship that the two of you want to establish and maintain now that you are divorced.

A divorce is a visit to court in which the facts of an agreement are disclosed, discussed, and finalized. A few friends may come along for support. But when it is over, there is an emptiness. You might say to yourself, "Well, that's done." Anticlimactic. No rites and no blessings.

Rituals give public support to life's passages and the letting-go process. If you are in a frame of mind to put closure on your marriage, there is a way to do it that has proven to be healthy, cleansing, and very sane.

A DIVORCE CEREMONY

Divorce mediators and family counselors sometimes use a *divorce ceremony* to give respect and recogni-

tion to the parting couple. A ceremony provides acknowledgement to each other and to the children that an old chapter is finished and a new one is beginning.

A ceremony can be conducted in any manner or place you both wish. To lead it, choose a person who is special to both of you and include your children and others who are particularly close to each or both of you. How you structure the ceremony will depend upon your own personal needs.

The most effective ceremonies come from the leader asking the ex-spouses to address one another. The ex-wife and ex-husband express gratitude for the best parts of the marriage and tell what they each remember about the other with pride or joy.

If there are children and they are present, inviting them to speak is one of the most important parts of the ceremony. They can tell their parents how they feel about the divorce and about their expectations for the future.

Others attending will have the opportunity to express their feelings and openly offer friendship and support to either spouse or both of them.

This is not an easy ceremony. Yet, if it comes from the heart, as it usually does, some important truths will surface. Things that need to be said will get said in a safe and secure surrounding. Often, there will be tears but there is also healing.

A divorce ceremony validates the past and honors the future.

Appendix A
DOCUMENT CHANGES

Information about changes of names and addresses needs to be given to almost everyone who has been in your life up to the moment of your divorce decree. Once again, your Rolodex serves as a major resource.

Contacts should be in writing because a copy of your signature is usually required. Written correspondence will also give you a record of notification in the event of problems.

Your correspondence breaks down into four main categories:

- Personal.
- Legal and public documents.
- Business.
- Children.

Note If you have always wanted to use a variation of your name such as Sandy instead of Sandra or Robert instead of Bob, this is a perfect time to do it and to give people official notification.

PERSONAL

The following list suggests a variety of individuals and groups from one's personal life who need to be informed of changes of name and address.

- Friends.
- Neighbors.
- Religious affiliations.
- Medical records: doctors, dentists, pharmacies, etc.
- Alumni associations.
- Memberships: social, community, and professional.
- Community organizations: charities and special interests.
- Theaters and cultural subscriptions.
- Sports and exercise groups.
- Book, record, and video clubs.
- Personal publications: magazines and newspapers.
- Insurance agents.
- Home appliance service contracts.
- Charitable organizations

LEGAL/PUBLIC DOCUMENTS

Here are some suggested legal and public organizations to inform:

- Social Security.
- Passport.

- IRS.
- Registrar of voters.
- Pet registration.
- Property ownership (there is usually a charge for name changes on land records).
- Department of Motor Vehicles for driver's license and automobile registration.
- Pleasure craft registration (You will need: a completed application for registration, certificate of title designating sale or transfer, current registration, proof of insurance, and proof of current tax payment.
- Will.

BUSINESS

Some business organizations to inform of changes of name and address include:

- Professional licensing agencies.
- Employer personnel department.
- Professional membership organizations.
- Professional publications: magazines and newspapers.
- Post office box.
- Credit bureaus.
- Insurance agents.
- Professionals such as attorneys and accountants.
- Office equipment service contracts.

- Charitable organizations.
- Frequent-flyer programs.
- Financial accounts.

CHILDREN

Institutions and organizations in which your children participate also need to be informed of changes in name and address.

- Schools.
- Medical records.
- Friends and neighbors.
- Membership groups.
- Special activities, such as sports and clubs.

STATUS OF PRE-EXISTING APPOINTMENTS

Clarify the status of pre-existing appointments for your now ex-spouse:

- Power of attorney.
- Health care proxy.
- Beneficiary.
  Will.
  IRA.
  Retirement funds.

Appendix B
BIBLIOGRAPHY

Abrahms, Sally. 1983. *Children in the crossfire: The tragedy of parental kidnapping.* Atheneum, N.Y.

Anderson-Khleif, Susan. 1982. *Divorced but not disastrous: How to improve the ties between single-parent mothers, divorced fathers, and the children.* Prentice-Hall, Englewood Cliffs, N.J.

Berke, M., and J. Grant. 1981. *Games divorced people play.* Prentice-Hall, N.Y.

Bernard, Janine, and Harold Hackney. 1983. *Untying the knot: A guide to civilized divorce.* Winston Press, Minneapolis, Minn.

Cassety, Judith. 1983. *The parental child-support obligation.* Lexington Books, Lexington, Mass.

Cromie, Richard M. 1987. *Now you have custody of you (In favor of the divorced).* Desert Ministries, Pittsburgh, Pa.

Diamond, Susan Arnsberg. 1985. *Helping Children of Divorce: A handbook for parents and teachers.* Schocken Books, N.Y.

Fisher, Roger, and William Ury. 1981. *Getting to yes: Negotiating agreement without giving in.* Houghton Mifflin Company, Boston: Mass.

Folberg, J. and A. Milne (eds.). 1985. *Divorce mediation: Theory and practice.* Guilford Press, N.Y.

Francke, L. B. 1983. *Growing up divorced.* Linden Press/ Simon & Schuster, N.Y.

Fritz, Robert. 1989. *The path of least resistance: Learning to become a creative force in your own life.* Fawcett Columbine, N.Y.

Gardner, Richard A. 1986. *Child custody litigation: A guide for parents and mental health professionals.* Creative Therapeutics, Cresskill, N.J.

Gill, H. 1981. *Stolen Children: How and why parents kidnap their children.* Seaview, N.Y.

Goldstein, Sonja, and Albert J. Solnik. 1985. *Divorce and your child: Practical suggestions for parents.* Yale University Press, New Haven, Conn.

Goldzband, Melvin. 1985. *Quality time: Easing the children through divorce.* McGraw-Hill, N.Y.

Gottlieb, Dorothy Weiss, Inez Gottlieb, and Marjorie Slavin. 1988. *What to do when your son or daughter divorces.* Bantam Books, N.Y.

Haynes, John M., and Gretchen Haynes. 1989. *Mediating divorce: Casebook of strategies for successful family negotiations.* Jossey-Bass, N.Y.

Jacob, Herbert. 1988. *Silent revolution: The law transformation of divorce law in the United States.* University of Chicago Press, Chicago, Ill.

Johnson, Colleen L. 1988. *Ex-families: Grandparents, parents and children adjust to divorce.* Rutgers University Press, N.J.

Kalter, Neil. 1990. *Growing Up with Divorce, Helping Your Child Avoid Immediate and Later Emotional Problems.* The Free Press.

Kaslow, Florence W., and Lita Schwartz. 1987. *The dynamics of divorce: A life cycle perspective.* Brunner/Mazel, N.Y.

Kranitz, Martin. 1987. *Getting apart together: The couple's guide to a fair divorce or separation.* Impact Pubs, San Luis Obispo, Calif.

Kressel, Kenneth. 1985. *The process of divorce: How professionals and couples negotiate settlements.* Basic Books, N.Y.

Lannan, Paul A., and LeRoy Spaniol. 1984. *Getting unstuck: Moving on after divorce.* Paulist Press, Mahwah, N.J.

Luepnitz, Deborah Anna. 1982. *Child custody: A study of families after divorce.* Lexington Books, Lexington, Mass.

Mahoney, Dennis C., Allan Koritzinsky, and Thomas Forkin. 1987. *Tax strategies in divorce.* Professional Education Systems, Eau Claire, Wis.

Morawetz, A., and G. Walker. 1984. *Brief therapy with single-parent families.* Brunner/Mazel, N.Y.

Neumann, Diane. 1989. *Divorce Mediation: How to Cut the Cost and Stress of Divorce*. H. Holt.

Paylor, Neil, and Barry Head. 1983. *Scenes from a divorce: A book for friends and relatives of a divorcing family*. Harper Row, N.Y.

Rosenstock, Harvey A. 1988. *Journey through divorce: Five stages toward recovery*. Human Science Press, N.Y.

Sheehy, Gail. 1976. *Passages: Predictable crises of adult life*. E. P. Dutton, N.Y.

Sheehy, Gail. 1981. *Pathfinders*. William Morrow, N.Y.

Stearns, Ann K. 1988. *Coming back: Rebuilding lives after crisis and loss*. Random House, N.Y.

Straus, Murray, R. Gelles, and S. Steinmetz. 1980. *Behind closed doors: Violence in the American family*. Anchor Books, N.Y.

Teyber, E. 1985. *Helping your children with divorce*. Simon & Schuster, N.Y.

Townley, Roderick. 1985. *Safe and sound: A parent's guide to child protection*. Simon and Schuster, N.Y.

Trafford, Abigail. 1984. *Crazy time: Surviving divorce*. Bantam Books, N.Y.

Triere, Lynette and Richard Peacock. 1982. *Learning to leave*. Contemporary Books, Winston Press, Chicago, Ill.

Vaughan, Diane. 1987. *Uncoupling: Turning points in intimate relationships*. Oxford University Press, N.Y.

Walker, Glynnis. 1986. *Solomon's children: Exploding the myths of divorce*. Arbor House, N.Y.

Wallerstein, Judith S., and Sandra Blakeslee. 1989. *Second chances: Men, women and children a decade after divorce*. Houghton Mifflin Company, Boston, Mass.

Wallman, Lester, and Lawrence Schwarz. 1989. *Handbook of family law*. Prentice-Hall, Englewood Cliffs, N.J.

Ware, Ciji. 1982. *Sharing parenthood after divorce: An enlightened custody guide for mothers, fathers, and kids*. The Viking Press, N.Y.

Weiss, R. S. 1982. Attachment in adult life. In C. M. Parkes & J. Stevenson-Hinde (eds.). *The place of attachment in human behavior*. Basic Books, N.Y.

Weitzman, Lenore J. 1981. *The marriage contract: Spouses, lovers, and the law*. The Free Press, N.Y.

Weitzman, Lenore J. 1985. *The divorce revolution: The unexpected social and economic consequences for women and children in America*. Free Press, N.Y.

Wittlin, William, and Robert Hinds (eds.). 1989. *Custody and the courts: Mental health and the law*. Irvington Pubs., N.Y.

Wren, Harold G., et al. 1987. *Tax aspects of marital dissolution*. Callaghan, Deerfield, Ill.

Note A comprehensive listing of divorce reference books and numerous articles found in periodicals and professional publications, is available at a nominal charge by writing to:

Margorie L. Engel, President
Hamilton-Forbes Associates
Exchange Place, 33rd Floor
Boston, MA 02109

Appendix C
RESOURCES

CHILDREN'S LEGAL RIGHTS

Children's Defense Fund
122 C Street, NW
Washington, DC 20001
(202) 628-8787

Children's Legal Rights Information and Training
2008 Hillyer Place, NW
Washington, DC 20009
(202) 332-6575

Children's Rights Group
693 Mission Street
San Francisco, CA 20009
(415) 495-7283

CHILD SUPPORT ENFORCEMENT

Association for Children for Enforcement Support
Suite 204
1018 Jefferson Avenue
Toledo, OH 43624
(419) 242-6130

EXPOSE (for military spouses)
P.O. Box 11191
Alexandria, VA 22312
(703) 941-5844 (day)
(703) 255-2917 (evening)

Federal Parent Locator Service
Department of Health and Human Services
Family Support Administration
Office of Child Support Enforcement
4th Floor
370 L'Enfant Promenade, SW
Washington, DC 20447
(202) 252-5443 (Federal Parent Locator Service)
(202) 252-5343 (Family Support Administration)
(202) 475-0257 (Dept. of Health and Human Services)

For Our Children and US Inc. (FOCUS)
60 Lafayette Street
New York, NY 10013
(212) 693-1655

National Child Support Advocacy Coalition
P.O. Box 4629
Alexandria, VA 22303

National Child Support Enforcement Association
Hall of the States
Suite 613
444 North Capitol Street, NW
Washington, DC 20001
(202) 624-8180

National Institute for Child Support Enforcement
 (NICSE)
Suite 500
7200 Wisconsin Avenue
Bethesda, MD 20814
(301) 654-8338

National Organization to Insure Survival Economics
12 West 72d Street
New York, NY 10023
(212) 787-1070

Office of National Child Support
National Child Support Enforcement Reference
  Center
370 L'Enfant Promenade SW
Washington, DC 20447

Organization for the Enforcement of Child Support
  (OECS)
119 Nicodemus Road
Reisterstown, MD 21136
(301) 833-2458

Single Parents United 'N' Kids (SPUNK)
1133 Rhea Street
Long Beach, CA 90806

DOMESTIC VIOLENCE

AMEND (Abusive Men Exploring New Directions)
8000 East Prentice Avenue, #C3
Englewood, CO 80111
(303) 220-1707

American Association for Protecting Children
c/o American Humane Association
9725 East Hampden Avenue
Denver, CO 80231
(303) 695-0811

American Bar Association National Legal Resource
  Center for Child Advocacy and Protection
2d Floor
1800 M Street, NW
Washington, DC
(202) 331-2250

Batterers Anonymous
1269 North East Street
San Bernadino, CA 92405
(714) 355-1100

Child Abuse Institute of Research (CAIR)
P.O. Box 1217
Cincinnati, OH 45201
(606) 441-7409

Child Abuse Listening Mediation (CALM)
P.O. Box 90754
Santa Barbara, CA 93190
(805) 965-2376

Child Welfare League of America
Suite 310
440 First Street, NW
Washington, DC 20001-2085
(202) 638-2952

Clearinghouse on Child Abuse and Neglect
  Information (CCANI)
P.O. Box 1182
Washington, DC 20013
(703) 821-2086

Defense for Children International-USA (DCI-USA)
210 Forsyth Street
New York, NY 10002
(212) 353-0951

EMERGE (A men's counseling service on domestic
  violence)
2d Floor
280 Green Street
Cambridge, MA 02139
(617) 547-9870

Institute for the Community as Extended Family
(Including Parents United, Sons and Daughters
  United, and Adults Molested as Children)
P.O.Box 952
San Jose, CA 95108
(408) 280-5055

International Society for Prevention of Child Abuse
  and Neglect (ISPCAN)
1205 Oneida Street
Denver, CO 80220
(303) 321-3963

National Center for the Prosecution of Child Abuse
  (NCPCA)
Suite 200
1033 North Fairfax Street
Alexandria, VA 22314
(707) 739-0321

National Child Abuse Hotline
(800) 422-4453

National Coalition Against Domestic Violence
  (NCADV)
P.O. Box 15127
Washington, DC 20003
(202) 293-8860

National Committee for Prevention of Child Abuse
Suite 950
332 South Michigan Avenue
Chicago, IL 60604
(312) 663-3520

National Council on Child Abuse and Family Violence
 (NCCAFV)
Suite 400
1155 Connecticut Avenue, NW
Washington, DC 20036
(202) 429-6695

National Court Appointed Special Advocate
 Association
Suite 202
909 NE 43d Street
Seattle, WA 98105-6020
(206) 547-1059

National Domestic Violence Hotline
(800) 333-SAFE (7233)
(800) 873-3636 (equipped with TDD for hearing
 impaired)

National Exchange Club Foundation for the
 Prevention of Child Abuse (NECF)
3050 Central Avenue
Toledo, OH 43606
(419) 535-3232

National Woman Abuse Prevention Project (NWAPP)
Suite 508
2000 P Street, NW
Washington, DC 20036
(202) 857-0216

Parents Anonymous
6733 South Sepulveda Boulevard
Los Angeles, CA 90045
(213) 410-9732

Sexual Assault Center
Harbor View Medical Center
325 9th Avenue
Seattle, WA 98104
(206) 223-3047

Task Force on Families in Crisis (TFFC)
Suite 223B
4004 Hillsboro Road
Nashville, TN 37215
(615) 383-4575

MISSING CHILDREN

Adam Walsh Child Resource Center
Suite 244
3111 South Dixie Highway
West Palm Beach, FL 33405
(407) 833-9080

Child Find of America
P.O. Box 277
New Paltz, NY 12561
(914) 255-1848
(800) I-AM-LOST (Hotline for runaway or abducted
 children)
(800) A-WAY-OUT (Mediation hotline for parental
 abduction cases)

Children's Rights of America (CRA)
Suite 9
12551 Indian Rocks Road
Largo, FL 34644
(813) 593-0090

Citizen's Committee to Amend Title 18, Section 1201A
 (Exempts parents of minors on kidnapping charges)
P.O. Box 936
Newhall, CA 91321
(805) 259-4435

Find the Children
11811 West Olympic Boulevard
Los Angeles, CA 90064
(213) 477-6721

Medical Network for Missing Children (MNMC)
67 Pleasant Ridge Road
Harrison, NY 10528
(914) 967-6854

Missing Children of America (MCA)
P.O. Box 670-949
Chugiak, AK 99567
(907) 248-7300

Missing Children...Help Center
Suite 400
410 Ware Boulevard
Tampa, FL 33619
(813) 623-KIDS (5437)
(800) USA-KIDS (5437)

National Center for Missing and Exploited Children
Suite 600
1835 K Street, NW
Washington, DC 20006
(202) 634-9821
(800) 843-5678 (Hotline)

Nationwide Patrol
P.O. Box 2629
Wilkes-Barre, PA 18703
(717) 825-7250

PARENTING

Fathers Are Forever (FAF)
P.O. Box 4804
Panorama City, CA 91412
(818) 846-2219

Fathers for Equal Rights
P.O. Box 010847, Flagler Station
Miami, FL 33101
(305) 895-6351

Foundation for Grandparenting (FG)
P.O. Box 31
Lake Placid, NY 12946

Grandparents Anonymous (GPA)
1924 Beverly
Sylvan Lake, MI 48053

Grandparents'/Children's Rights (GCR)
5728 Bayonne Avenue
Haslett, MI 48840
(517) 339-8663

Joint Custody Association
10606 Wilkins Avenue
Los Angeles, CA 90024
(213) 475-5352

Mothers Without Custody (MWOC)
P.O. Box 56762
Houston, TX 77256
(713) 840-1622

Parents Without Partners
Suite 1000
7910 Woodmont Avenue
Washington, DC 20014
(202) 654-8850

Parents Without Partners
8807 Colesville Rd.
Silver Spring, MD 20910
(301) 588-9354
(800) 638-8078

Single Parent Resource Center
Room 504
1165 Broadway
New York, NY 10001
(212) 213-0047

Sisterhood of Black Single Mothers (SBSM)
1360 Fulton Street
Brooklyn, NY 11216
(718) 638-0413

Toughlove, International
P.O. Box 1069
Doylestown, PA 18901
(215) 348-7090

PROFESSIONAL SERVICES

American Academy of Matrimonial Lawyers
Suite 540
20 North Michigan Avenue
Chicago, IL 60602
(312) 263-6477

American Bar Association, Family Law Section,
   Mediation and Arbitration Committee
750 North Lake Shore Drive
Chicago, IL 60611
(312) 988-5584

American Bar Association Standing Committee on
   Dispute Resolution
Suite 200
1800 M Street
Washington, DC 20036
(202) 331-2258

Center for Dispute Settlement
Suite 501
1666 Connecticut Avenue, NW
Washington, DC 20009
(202) 265-9572

Institute for the Study of Matrimonial Laws
Suite 1116
11 Park Place
New York, NY 10007
(212) 766-4030

National Academy of Conciliators
Suite 1130
2530 Wisconsin Avenue
Chevy Chase, MD 20815
(301) 654-6515

National Association of Counsel for Children
1205 Oneida
Denver, CO 80220
(303) 321-3963

National Center on Women and Family Law
Room 402
799 Broadway
New York, NY 10003
(212) 674-8200

National Committee for Fair Divorce and Alimony
 Laws
Suite 1116
11 Park Place
New York, NY 10007
(212) 766-4030

National Council for Children's Rights
2001 O Street, NW
Washington, DC 20036
(202) 223-NCCR (6227)

National Court Appointed Special Advocates
 Association
Suite 202
909 Northeast 43d Street
Seattle, WA 98102
(206) 547-1059

National Legal Resource Center for Child Advocacy
 and Protection
1800 M Street, NW
Washington, DC 20036
(202) 331-2250

United States Divorce Reform
P.O. Box 243
Kentwood, CA 95452
(707) 833-2550

Women's Legal Defense Fund
Suite 400
122 C Street, NW
Washington, DC 20001
(202) 887-0364

STATE CHILD SUPPORT ENFORCEMENT OFFICES

Alabama

Division of Child Support Activities
Bureau of Public Assistance
State Department of Pensions and Security
64 N. Union Street
Montgomery, AL 36130
(205) 261-2872

Alaska

Child Support Enforcement Agency
Department of Revenue
201 E. 9th Ave., Room 302
Anchorage, AK 99501
(907) 276-3441

Arizona

Child Support Enforcement Administration
Department of Economic Security
P.O. Box 6123, Site Code 966C
Phoenix, AZ 85005
(602) 255-3465

Arkansas

Office of Child Support Enforcement
Arkansas Social Services
P.O. Box 3358
Little Rock, AR 72203
(501) 371-2464

California

Child Support, Program Management Branch
Department of Social Services
744 P Street
Sacramento, CA 95814
(916) 323-8994

Colorado

Division of Child Support Enforcement
Department of Social Services
1575 Sherman Street, Room 423
Denver, CO 80203
(303) 866-2442

Connecticut

Bureau of Child Support
1049 Asylum Avenue Resources
Hartford, CT 06105
(203) 566-3053
(800) 228-KIDS (5437)

Delaware

Services for Children, Youth and Their Families
Program Support Division
1825 Faulkland Road
Wilmington, DE 19805
(302) 633-2670

District of Columbia

Bureau of Child Support Enforcement
Department of Human Services
3d Floor
425 I Street, NW
Washington, DC 20001
(202) 724-5610

Florida

Office of Child Support Enforcement
Department of Health and Rehabilitative Services
1317 Winewood Boulevard
Tallahassee, FL 32301
(904) 488-9900

Georgia

Office of Child Support Enforcement
State Department of Human Resources
P.O. Box 80000
Atlanta, GA 30357
(404) 894-5087

Guam

Child Support Enforcement Unit
Department of Public Health and Social Services
Government of Guam
P.O. Box 2816
Agana, GU 96910
(671) 734-2947

Hawaii

Child Support Enforcement Agency
Suite 606
770 Dapiolani Boulevard
Honolulu, HI 96813
(808) 548-5779

Idaho

Bureau of Child Support Enforcement
Department of Health and Welfare
Statehouse Mail
Boise, ID 83720
(208) 334-4422

Illinois

Bureau of Child Support
Department of Public Aid
316 South Second Street
Springfield, IL 62762
(217) 782-1366

Indiana

Child Support Enforcement Division
State Department of Public Welfare
4th Floor
141 South Merridian Street
Indianapolis, IN 46224
(317) 232-4894

Iowa

Child Support Recovery Unit
Iowa Department of Social Services
1st Floor
Hoover Building
Des Moines, IA 50319
(515) 281-5580

Kansas

Child Support Enforcement Program
Department of Social and Rehabilitation Services
Perry Building, 1st Floor
2700 West Sixth
Topeka, KS 66606
(913) 296-3237

Kentucky

Human Resources Cabinet
Family Services Division
275 East Main Street
Frankfort, KY 40621
(502) 564-6852

Louisiana

Support Enforcement Services
Department of Health and Human Services
P.O. Box 44276
Baton Rouge, LA 70804
(504) 342-4780

Maine

Support Enforcement and Location Unit
Bureau of Social Welfare
Department of Human Services
State House Station 11
Augusta, ME 04333
(207) 289-2886

Maryland

Child Support Enforcement Administration
Department of Human Resources
5th Floor
300 West Preston Street
Baltimore, MD 21201
(301) 383-4773

Massachusetts

Child Support Enforcement Unit
Massachusetts Department of Revenue
215 First Street
Cambridge, MA 02142
(617) 621-4750

Michigan

Office of Child Support
Department of Social Services
P.O. Box 30037
Lansing, MI 48909
(517) 373-7570

Minnesota

Office of Child Support
Department of Human Services
Space Center Building
444 Lafayette Road
St. Paul, MN 55101
(612) 296-2499

Mississippi

Child Support Division
State Department of Public Welfare
P.O. Box 352
515 East Amite Street
Jackson, MS 39205
(601) 354-0341

Missouri

Child Support Enforcement Unit
Division of Family Services
Department of Social Services
P.O. Box 88
Jefferson City, MO 65103
(314) 751-4301

Montana

Child Support Enforcement Bureau
P.O. Box 5955
Helena, MT 59604
(406) 444-3347

Nebraska

Child Support Enforcement Office
Department of Social Services
P.O. Box 95026
Lincoln, NE 68509
(402) 471-3121

Nevada

Child Support Enforcement Program
Welfare Division
2527 North Carson Street
Carson City, NV 89710
(702) 885-4744

New Hampshire

Office of Child Support Enforcement Services
Division of Welfare
Health and Welfare Building
Hazen Drive
Concord, NH 03301
(603) 271-4426

New Jersey

Child Support and Paternity Unit
Department of Human Services
CN 716
Trenton, NJ 08625
(609) 633-6268

New Mexico

Child Support Enforcement Bureau
Department of Human Services
P.O. Box 2348–PERA Building
Santa Fe, NM 85793
(505) 827-4230

New York

Office of Child Support Enforcement
New York Department of Social Services
Albany, NY 12260
(518) 474-9081

North Carolina

Child Support Enforcement Section
Division of Social Services
Department of Human Resources
433 North Harrington Street
Raleigh, NC 27603
(919) 733-4120

North Dakota

Child Support Enforcement Agency
North Dakota Department of Human Services
State Capitol
Bismarck, ND 58505
(701) 224-3582

Ohio

Bureau of Child Support
Ohio Department of Human Services
State Office Tower
31st Floor
30 East Broad Street
Columbus, OH 43215
(614) 466-3233

Oklahoma

Division of Child Support
Department of Human Services
P.O. Box 25352
Oklahoma City, OK 73125
(405) 424-5871

Oregon

Child Support Program
Department of Human Resources
Adult and Family Services Division
P.O. Box 14506
Salem, OR 97309
(503) 378-6093

Pennsylvania

Child Support Programs
Bureau of Claim Settlement
Department of Public Welfare
P.O. Box 8018
Harrisburg, PA 17105
(717) 783-1779

Puerto Rico

Child Support Enforcement Program
Department of Social Services
Fernandez Juncos Station
P.O. Box 11398
Santurce, PR 00910
(809) 722-4731

Rhode Island

Bureau of Family Support
Department of Social and Rehabilitative Services
77 Dorance Street
Providence, RI 02903
(401) 277-2409

South Carolina

Division of Child Support
Public Assistance Division
Bureau of Public Assistance and Field Operations
Department of Social Services
P.O. Box 1520
Columbia, SC 29202
(803) 758-8860

South Dakota

Office of Child Support Enforcement
Department of Social Services
700 Illinois Street
Pierre, SD 57501
(605) 773-3641

Tennessee

Child Support Services
Department of Human Services
5th Floor
111-19 Seventh Avenue
Nashville, TN 37203
(615) 741-1820

Texas

Child Support Enforcement Branch
Texas Department of Human Resources
P.O. Box 2960
Austin, TX 78769
(512) 463-2005

Utah

Office of Recovery Services
Department of Social Services
P.O. Box 15400
3195 South Main Street
Salt Lake City, UT 84115
(801) 486-1812

Vermont

Child Support Division
Department of Social Welfare
103 South Main Street
Waterbury, VT 05676
(802) 241-2868

Virgin Islands

Paternity and Child Support Program
Department of Law
P.O. Box 1074
Christiansted
St. Croix, VI 00820
(809) 773-8240

Virginia

Division of Support Enforcement Program
Department of Social Services
8004 Franklin Farm Drive
Richmond, VA 23288
(804) 662-9108

Washington

Office of Support Enforcement
Department of Social and Health Services
P.O. Box 9162-MS PI-11
Olympia, WA 98504
(206) 459-6481

West Virginia

Office of Child Support Enforcement
Department of Human Services
1900 Washington Street, East
Charleston, WV 25305
(304) 348-3780

Wisconsin

State of Wisconsin Department of Health and Human
  Services
Division of Community Services
1 West Wilson Street
P.O. Box 7851
Madison, WI 53707
(608) 266-9909

Wyoming

Child Support Enforcement Section
Division of Public Assistance and Social Services
State Department of Health and Social Services
Hathaway Building
Cheyenne, WY 82002
(307) 777-6083

SELF-HELP GROUPS

American Divorce Association for Men (ADAM)
1008 White Oak
Arlington Heights, IL 60005
(312) 870-1040

America's Society of Separated and Divorced Men
  (ASDM)
575 Keep Street
Elgin, IL 60120
(312) 695-2200

Displaced Homemakers Network
Suite 930
1411 K Street, NW
Washington, DC 20005
(202) 628-6767

Divorce After 60
University of Michigan Medical Center
1010 Wall Street
Ann Arbor, MI 48109
(313) 764-2556

Divorce Anonymous (DA)
P.O. Box 5313
Chicago, IL 60680
(312) 589-2420

Expartners of Servicemen (Women) for Equality
  (EXPOSE)
P.O. Box 11191
Alexandria, VA 22312
(703) 941-5844

Judean Society (JS)
Suite 336
1075 Space Parkway
Mountain View, CA 94043
(415) 964-8936

LADIES (Life After Divorce is Eventually Sane)
P.O. Box 2974
Beverly Hills, CA 90213

Legal Awareness of Westchester, Inc. (LAW)
P.O. Box 35-H
Scarsdale, NY 10583
(914) 472-2371

Men's Rights Association (MRA)
17854 Lyons
Forest Lake, MN 55025
(612) 464-7887

National Action for Former Military Wives (NAFMW)
1700 Legion Drive
Winter Park, FL 32789
(407) 628-2801

National Congress for Men (NCM)
3623 Douglas Avenue
Des Moines, IA 50310
(515) FATHERS (328-4377)

National Health Information Clearinghouse Hotline
(800) 336-4797

National Organization for Men (NOM)
381 Park Avenue, South
New York, NY 10016
(212) 686-MALE

National Self-Help Clearinghouse
Graduate School and University Center
City University of New York
33 West 42d Street
New York, NY 10036
(212) 840-7606

North American Conference of Separated and
  Divorced Catholics (NACSDC)
1100 South Goodman Street
Rochester, NY 14620
(716) 271-1320

PACE (Parent's and Children's Equality)
1816 Florida Avenue
Palm Harbor, FL 34683
(813) 787-3875

Spouses of Gays Association (Gay/Lesbian) (SOGA)
1329 Levick Street
Philadelphia, PA 19111
(215) 288-6959

Women Helping Women (WHW)
525 North VanBuren Avenue
Stoughton, WI 53589
(608) 873-3747

SUBSTANCE ABUSE

Al-Anon Family Group Headquarters
1372 Broadway
New York, NY 10018
(212) 302-7240

Alcoholics Anonymous World Services
Grand Central Station
P.O. Box 459
New York, NY 10164
(212) 686-1100

Narcotics Anonymous
P.O. Box 9999
Van Nuys, CA 91409
(818) 780-3951

National Clearinghouse for Alcohol Information
(Office of Substance Abuse Prevention;
National Institute of Drug Abuse; and
National Institute on Alcohol Abuse and Alcoholism)
Box 2345
Rockville, MD 20852
(301) 468-2600

National Council on Alcoholism
8th Floor
12 W. 21st Street
New York, NY 10010
(212) 206-6770

National Parents' Resource Institute for Drug
  Education
Suite 1002
100 Edgewood Avenue
Atlanta, GA 30303
(404) 651-2548

Women for Sobriety
P.O. Box 618
Quakertown, PA 18951
(215) 536-8026

For a list of additional resources please write to:

Margorie L. Engel, President
Hamilton-Forbes Associates
Exchange Place, 33rd Floor
Boston, MA 02109

Appendix D
FORM-ulas

1: FORM-ula™ for MARRIAGE ASSESSMENT

Begin to acknowledge what has happened to your marriage. Check relevant items. This information will be useful to you later on in the divorce proceedings.

HEALTHY RELATIONSHIPS
Genuine Friendship
- [ ] You like and respect one another.
- [ ] You have fun with each other (take time to laugh and play).
- [ ] You both keep sex in perspective (use your physical contact as an expression of affection and love, and not as an excuse to gloss over conflicts or to get back at each other).

Two Individuals Choosing to Function as a Couple
- [ ] You do things alone as well as together.
- [ ] You are important to each other (good helpmates).
- [ ] You respect each other's privacy.
- [ ] You respect each other's time.
- [ ] You trust each other.
- [ ] You take each other for granted.
- [ ] You are tolerant of each other's idiosyncracies.

Open Communication
- [ ] You are open and honest with each other.
- [ ] You are "tuned in" to your partner (know when to speak and when to remain silent).
- [ ] Your partner does the same for you.
- [ ] You share a positive outlook.

COMMON CAUSES OF MARITAL BREAKDOWNS
Generally Applying to Shorter Marriages:
- [ ] Adultery
- [ ] Mental Cruelty
- [ ] Spouse/child abuse (physical/verbal)
- [ ] Substance abuse (drugs & alcohol)
- [ ] Conflicts over in-laws
- [ ] Financial pressures from how money should be earned and spent

More Apt to Be the Cause of Disenchantment in Longer Marriages:
- [ ] Sexual dysfunction, incompatibility, or infidelity
- [ ] Conflicting value systems and lifestyle preferences
- [ ] Need for greater freedom and independence
- [ ] Personal growth in different directions
- [ ] Boredom or drifting apart (general unhappiness)
- [ ] Obsessive/compulsive behavior (gambling, workaholism, eating disorders, substance abuse, severe phobias)

"SNEAKY" REASONS FOR STAYING MARRIED
- [ ] You don't have to face the unknown . . . yet.
- [ ] You don't have to feel guilty about ending it.
- [ ] You are doing your duty, no matter what the cost.
- [ ] You don't have to reconcile feelings with your religious beliefs.
- [ ] You don't have to confront loneliness.
- [ ] You can play martyr if that's your game.
- [ ] You don't have to assume total responsibility for yourself.
- [ ] You have time to make an even bigger list of "owe me's."
- [ ] You don't have to raise the children all alone.
- [ ] You can keep on pretending to be "happily married."

2: FORM-ula™ for OBSERVING CHILDREN'S DIVORCE BEHAVIOR

Use a separate column for each child to check behavior patterns. We want to warn you about the tendency of adults to attribute all difficult behavior exhibited by offspring to the trials and tribulations of divorce and to ignore other relevant factors. It is wise to consult a professional if you feel that these behaviors apply to your children.

Names:

Unexplained changes in physical appearance	☐	☐	☐	☐
Secretiveness	☐	☐	☐	☐
Withdrawal from usual activities	☐	☐	☐	☐
Rapid mood swings	☐	☐	☐	☐
Excessive preoccupation with another person or a pet	☐	☐	☐	☐
Prolonged model behavior (denial of true feelings)	☐	☐	☐	☐
Regression to earlier stage of development	☐	☐	☐	☐
Defiance of authority	☐	☐	☐	☐
Assumption of too much authority	☐	☐	☐	☐
Avoidance of responsibility	☐	☐	☐	☐
Increased dependency on one or both parents	☐	☐	☐	☐
Preoccupation with idea of parent reconciliation	☐	☐	☐	☐
Refusal to visit with parent who has left the home	☐	☐	☐	☐
Estrangement from parent in the home	☐	☐	☐	☐
Running away	☐	☐	☐	☐
Excessive crying	☐	☐	☐	☐
Headaches or stomachaches	☐	☐	☐	☐
Refusal to sleep in own bed	☐	☐	☐	☐
Refusal to eat or sleep	☐	☐	☐	☐
Prone towards accidents (more than usual)	☐	☐	☐	☐
Lowered school grades	☐	☐	☐	☐
Truancy	☐	☐	☐	☐
Shoplifting or petty thievery	☐	☐	☐	☐

3: FORM-ula™ for DIVORCE BUSINESS SUPPLIES

Gather together or purchase the following items. They will make your divorce work more organized and less frustrating.

BASIC OFFICE SUPPLIES

- ☐ Portable file box (paper, plastic, or metal)
- ☐ Pencils and pencil sharpener
- ☐ File step rack
- ☐ Rolodex and cards in 5 colors
- ☐ Calculator (easiest to use with eraser end of a pencil instead of fingers)
- ☐ Stapler and remover
- ☐ Scissors
- ☐ Ruler
- ☐ Rubber bands
- ☐ Paper clips
- ☐ Cellophane tape
- ☐ Several pastel highlighting markers
- ☐ White-out

PAPER PRODUCTS

- ☐ Complete Form-ula™ set
- ☐ Calendars—wall and pocket-size
- ☐ File folders and file labels
- ☐ Box of Pendaflex® file folders (including labels)
- ☐ Ruled note pads, 8-1/2 x 11-inch
- ☐ Accordion file
- ☐ Post-its™
- ☐ Scratch paper for worksheets

Since notebooks are the easiest way to keep track of thoughts and conversations and for planning lists, keep separate ones for the following:

(small) ☐ Car mileage (keep in car along with pencil)
       ☐ Inside jacket pocket or handbag
       ☐ Bedside (for recording middle-of-the-night thoughts)
(spiral) ☐ Attorney (dates, times, topics)
       ☐ Accountant (dates, times, topics)
       ☐ Discussions with spouse
       ☐ Strategic planning (money, housing, friends, career)

Purchase a good dictionary of words and phrases that are used in family law. We recommend *Family Law Dictionary,* by Robin D. Leonard and Stephen R. Elias, for $13.95. Call Nolo Press (800) 992-6656.

4: FORM-ula™ to PROFILE SELF AND SPOUSE

Fill out one copy of this form for yourself and another copy for your spouse. Some of this information will come right off the top of your head or be readily available. Other facts will have to be researched and developed as you progress through this book. All of the material is relevant to your separation agreement.

SELF/SPOUSE

Name _____ Date of Birth _____

Social Security No. _____ Place of Birth _____

Passport No. _____ Issued At _____ Religious Affiliation _____

Mailing Address _____ Minister/Rabbi/Priest _____

Home Address _____

Former Address _____

Telephone Home (____) _____ Work (____) _____ Other (____) _____

Are there any telephone or mail restrictions? Explain. _____

PARENTS

Father

Name _____

Address _____

Telephone (____) _____

Date of Birth _____ Place of Birth _____

Mother

Name _____

Address _____

Telephone (____) _____ Maiden Name _____

Date of Birth _____ Place of Birth _____

Siblings

Name 1 _____ Name 3 _____

Address _____ Address _____

Telephone (____) _____ Telephone (____) _____

Date of Birth _____ Place of Birth _____ Date of Birth _____ Place of Birth _____

Name 2 _____ Name 4 _____

Address _____ Address _____

Telephone (____) _____ Telephone (____) _____

Date of Birth _____ Place of Birth _____ Date of Birth _____ Place of Birth _____

In the event that there are no parents or siblings, please list

Next of Kin

Name _____

Address _____

Telephone (____) _____

MARRIAGE

City and State _____ Date _____

SEPARATION

Separation Date _____
(This refers to the date on which you or your spouse began to live in different rooms or residences or when one of you definitively communicated to the other that the marriage was over.)

I have resided in _____ County for _____ years.

My spouse has resided in _____ County for _____ years.

Attorney Name _____

Address _____ Phone ( ) _____

☐ I was served with divorce-related papers on (date) _____

☐ I know my spouse's attorney is preparing such papers.

☐ I do not know whether my spouse's attorney is preparing such papers.

Which partner wishes dissolution of the marriage? _____

☐ We have had prior marital separations. How many? _____

☐ I would like a reconciliation.

☐ My spouse is also receiving marital counseling.

☐ My spouse refuses to participate in marital counseling.

☐ I have received marital counseling in the past.

☐ I am presently receiving marital counseling.

☐ I am not, but would be interested in receiving marital counseling in the future.

Alternatives considered other than divorce _____
_____

Reasons for separation:

☐ irretrievable breakdown   ☐ incompatibility

☐ mental/physical cruelty   ☐ marital misconduct

☐ outside pressures

☐ I have had discussions with my spouse about separation or divorce.

What was concluded? _____
_____

Has there been a recent significant change in your sexual relationship with your spouse? Explain.
_____
_____

Have there been any occurrences of violence between you and your spouse? Explain.
_____
_____

Will your spouse allege any occurrences of violence? Explain.
_____
_____

FORM-ula™ 4. *(Continued)*

CHILDREN BORN OR ADOPTED INTO THIS MARRIAGE

Name	Address	Age	Birth Date	Soc. Sec. No.

Is the wife currently pregnant? _____

Has either spouse ever expressed doubts as to the paternity of any of the above children? Please explain.

_____

PREVIOUS MARRIAGES

How many times previously married? _____

Former Spouses

Name of Former Spouse	Termination Date	How (death, divorce)?

Children Born or Adopted Into Previous Marriage(s)

Name	Age	Birth Date	Soc. Sec. No.	Residing With

FORM-ula™ 4. *(Continued)*

Children From a Nonmarital Relationship

Name	Age	Birth Date	Soc. Sec. No.	Residing With

Other Dependents

Name	Age	Birth Date	Soc. Sec. No.	Relationship

Support Paid or Received by Me or by the Above Children *(include overdue amounts in red)*

Support Paid To	Support Received From	Amount	Frequency

For children of this marriage, I want:
☐ Sole legal custody   ☐ Shared legal custody
☐ Sole physical custody   ☐ Shared physical custody   ☐ Visitation rights

FORM-ula™ 4. *(Continued)*

RECORDS AND CERTIFICATES

Birth certificates filed in (location and address): _____

_____

☐ Certified copies?

Citizenship certificates filed in (location and address): _____

_____

☐ Certified copies?

Marriage certificate filed in (location and address): _____

_____

☐ Certified copy?

Note: At some point in your divorce proceedings you will need these papers. If you do not presently have certified *copies, this would be the time to acquire them. There is usually a charge made, so you may wish to phone or write first for the details. Obtaining certified copies may take from two to ten weeks.*

Prior divorce papers filed in (location and address) _____

_____

☐ Certified copy?

Death certificates filed in (location and address) _____

_____

☐ Certified copies?

Date of latest will and codicil _____

Location of will _____

Executor's name _____

Address _____

_____

☐ Cemetery plot   ☐ Mausoleum space

Location _____

Deed of ownership location _____

AUTOMOBILE

Make _____ Model _____ Year _____ Plate No. _____

Motor No. _____ Mileage _____ as of _____ (date).

Condition _____

☐ Purchased   ☐ Leased

Name and address of owner or title holder _____

_____

Driver's license No. _____ Class _____ State _____ Restrictions _____

FORM-ula™ 4. *(Continued)*

PRE-SEPARATION STANDARD OF LIVING

Descriptions

Neighborhood _____

_____

Home and contents _____

_____

Property/yard _____

_____

Automobiles _____

_____

Clothing _____

_____

Social Activities

Memberships	In Whose Name?

Recent Travels and Vacations

Travel To:	Accommodations	Dates

Family Pets

Name of Pet	Type/Breed	Whose?	Age of Pet	Veterinarian

Most Important Aspects of Your Standard of Living

Desirable	Undesirable
_____	_____
_____	_____
_____	_____
_____	_____

FORM-ula™ 4. *(Continued)*

FRIENDS AND NEIGHBORS

Nearest Neighbor

Name _____

Address _____

Telephone ( ) _____

Best Friend

Name _____

Address _____

Telephone ( ) _____

Friends and Neighbors With Special Knowledge and Skills

	Name	Address	Phone
Car pool			
Emergency child care			
Repairs			
General maintenance			
Potential witness			
Listener			
Hugs			
Companion (no strings)			

PERSONAL CONTRIBUTIONS TO MARITAL ASSETS

Describe the acquisition, preservation, and appreciation of current assets. (Include time, skills, and other personal as well as financial contributions.)

_____

_____

_____

_____

Have you foregone any earning capacity because of business association, education, or responsibilities of the marriage, including children? If so, please list and explain.

_____

_____

_____

_____

Have you given up any benefits for which you were eligible prior to this marriage? (Include pensions, Social Security, lower rates for insurance coverages, etc.)

_____

_____

_____

FORM-ula™ 4. *(Continued)*

SUPPORT ARRANGEMENTS

If you have already separated or discussed separation, detail the temporary financial arrangements that have been made:

☐ Periodic payments   How much? $ _____   How often? _____   Have any payments been late? _____   Explain _____

Direct payment of living expenses, monthly and other

Directly Paid Item	Paid by Whom?	Amount Paid	Date Paid

Is there an agreement in writing to cover support arrangements? _____

Where is it located? _____

LEGAL ENTANGLEMENTS

If you check any of the boxes below, please attach a separate sheet with details.

☐ Jailed for _____
☐ Imprisoned for _____
☐ Judgments against _____
☐ Driving offenses _____
☐ Larceny _____
☐ Felony _____
☐ Misdemeanor _____
☐ Disbarred _____
☐ Professional licenses suspended or revoked _____
☐ Driver's license suspended or revoked _____
☐ Court injunction _____
☐ Personal injury cases _____

    Pending:

        ☐ Suits   ☐ Judgments   ☐ Claims   ☐ Causes of action

FORM-ula™ 4. *(Continued)*

PROFESSIONAL RESOURCE LIST (Transcribe information to Rolodex)

Profession	Name	Address	Phone No.
Accountant			
Attorney			
Banker			
Insurance Agent, Auto			
Insurance Agent, Medical			
Insurance Agent, Life			
Insurance Agent, Disab.			
Librarian			
Mechanic			
General Handyman			

5: FORM-ula™ for MYSELF
"The Me Nobody Knows"

Based upon your values and attitudes, you, consciously or unconsciously, have certain priorities and goals to tap into. What is most important to you? Write your answers below. Keep this FORM-ula™ in mind as you continue with the business of divorce. You will refer to it often as you clarify your goals and objectives and prepare material for your attorney. It will be most useful in Section VI, "Big Picture Planning" and Chapter 22, "Your Personal Objectives."

WHAT MOTIVATES ME

Prioritize the following list. Use "1" to indicate your strongest motivation and "10" to indicate your weakest.

____ Interesting activity
____ Type of task
____ Excellence of achievement
____ Opportunity and ambition
____ Negative consequences if I don't do what I should
____ Financial, social, or emotional reward
____ Teamwork and communication with others
____ Responsibility
____ Personal growth and development
____ Sociability (being a "people person")

MY COMFORT ZONES

Kind of people I like:

Kind of ideas I like:

Type of work I prefer:

Environment I prefer (city or country, busy or relaxed, etc.):

WHO AM I?

What makes my life worthwhile?

How do I relate to other people?

What do I do very well (assets)?

What is "special" about me?

What needs to be dropped from my life or personality (liabilities)?

What makes me really angry?

How do I learn what I need to know? (reading, classes or workshops, experience, etc.)

What lessons have I learned already?

What do I need to learn?

What good might come out of this divorce?

What additional problems do I anticipate as a result of this divorce?

6: FORM-ula™ to PROFILE CHILDREN

Be sure to complete a copy of FORM-ula 6 for each child in your household. You will want this information readily available for negotiations about custody and financial arrangements.

Name _____ Social Security No. _____

Relationship to you _____ Birth order _____ Passport No. _____

Legal residence _____ How long? _____

Current address _____ How long? _____

Who is most responsible for this child on a day-to-day basis? _____

Who is financially responsible for this child? _____

Are there any persons, other than the parents, who could claim a custodial right to this child? _____

List names and addresses:

_____

_____

_____

_____

_____

PERSONAL

Does this child have a single or shared room? _____

How is it furnished? _____

Are these furnishings adequate? _____ If not, explain _____

_____

What equipment does this child have? (e.g., TV, stereo, computer, etc.) _____

_____

What kind of clothing does this child have? (seasonal, adequate, frequently changing because of growth, etc.)

_____

EDUCATION

☐ Primary school and location _____

☐ Junior high school and location _____

☐ High school and location _____

☐ College and location _____

☐ Other school and location _____

Special Skills _____

Training and Lessons, etc. _____

_____

ACTIVITIES

Sports _____

Hobbies _____

Memberships _____

Camp _____

BEST FRIENDS

Name	Address	Phone	Parents' Names
_____	_____	_____	_____
_____	_____	_____	_____
_____	_____	_____	_____
_____	_____	_____	_____

DATING EXPERIENCE

Current girlfriend or boyfriend _____

Address and phone number _____

NEAREST RELATIVES

	Name	Address	Phone	Degree of Closeness
Maternal grandparents	_____	_____	_____	_____
	_____	_____	_____	_____
Paternal grandparents	_____	_____	_____	_____
	_____	_____	_____	_____
Aunts	_____	_____	_____	_____
	_____	_____	_____	_____
	_____	_____	_____	_____
Uncles	_____	_____	_____	_____
	_____	_____	_____	_____
	_____	_____	_____	_____

FORM-ula™ 6. *(Continued)*

PERSONAL HEALTH

	Name	Address	Phone	How long has child been a patient?
Pediatrician	_____	_____	_____	_____
Dentist	_____	_____	_____	_____
Orthodontist	_____	_____	_____	_____
Optician	_____	_____	_____	_____
Specialist	_____	_____	_____	_____
Other	_____	_____	_____	_____

Are there any special medical needs? _____

Are there any disabilities? _____

WORK HISTORY

Household chores and responsibilities. _____

_____

Does she/he carry them out dependably? _____

_____

Volunteer or community time _____

FINANCES

Job (for wages)	Location	Phone	Wages Earned
_____	_____	_____	_____
_____	_____	_____	_____
_____	_____	_____	_____
_____	_____	_____	_____

Separate tax return? _____ For how long? _____

Allowance $ _____ Total Wages $ _____ Chores $ _____

Savings $ _____ Unearned income $ _____

What does personal money (earned or unearned) pay for? _____

_____

Bank name and address _____

Checking account No. _____ Savings account No. _____

Bank name and address _____

_____

Bank name and address _____

Checking account No. _____ Savings account No. _____

Bank name and address _____

_____

Special Accounts

Is this child a beneficiary of a trust? _____

Name and address of trust _____

_____

Name and address of trustee _____

_____

Total amount $ _____ Amount per year $ _____

Amount per month $ _____

Is this child the beneficiary of a will? _____

Name and address of executor _____

_____

Total amount $ _____ Amount per year $ _____

Amount per month $ _____

Is this child the beneficiary of a life insurance policy? _____

Name and address of insured _____

_____

Total amount $ _____ Amount per year $ _____

Amount per month $ _____

AUTOMOBILE INFORMATION

Training? _____ License No. _____ State _____

Who owns the car? _____ Make _____ Model _____ Year ____ Mileage _____

Plate No. _____ Insurance Company _____ Policy No. _____

Cost of insurance $ _____ per _____Who pays insurance? _____

Any accidents? _____ Explain _____

Points? _____ Explain _____

Is there a repair record? _____ Who pays for repairs? _____

Who pays for gas and oil? _____

DEVELOPMENTAL MILESTONES

Birth

Was this child's birth normal? _____ Explain _____

Did the infant's growth proceed in a normal way? _____ Explain _____

_____

FORM-ula™ 6. *(Continued)*

Academic and Technical

Comment on child's school experiences related to academic and technical learning.

Nursery school _____

Kindergarten _____

Elementary school _____

Junior High School _____

Senior High School _____

College _____

Other _____

Present class placement _____

Did this child ever have to repeat a grade? _____ What was the reason? _____

Is there currently, or has there been, any requirement for special therapy, tutoring, or remedial work for

this child? _____ Explain _____

School Behavior

Comment on child's school experience related to behavior.

Nursery school _____

Kindergarten _____

Elementary school _____

Junior High School _____

Senior High School _____

College _____

Other _____

Are there any current school behavioral problems that you should make note of? _____

_____

Home Behavior

How does the child behave at home? _____

_____

PEER RELATIONSHIPS

Does this child seek out peer relationships? _____

Do peers seek out this child's friendship? _____

If not, explain problems with peers, as you see them _____

_____

_____

If not, what kind of friends does the child prefer? _____

_____

_____

FORM-ula™ 6. *(Continued)*

INTERESTS AND ACCOMPLISHMENTS

What are the child's main interests? _____

_____

_____

What are the child's main accomplishments? _____

_____

_____

What does the child enjoy doing the most? _____

_____

_____

What does the child dislike doing the most? _____

_____

_____

RELIGION

Denomination _____ Is child involved in any religious training? _____

Religion teacher _____ Phone _____

Minister/Rabbi/Priest _____ Phone _____

SPECIAL ADVISORY RESOURCES

Guidance counselor _____ Phone _____

Teacher or confidante _____ Phone _____

Neighbor or adult friend _____ Phone _____

Therapist or counselor _____ Phone _____

FUTURE

What are this child's educational goals? _____

_____

What are this child's career goals? _____

SUMMARY

Try to describe how you think your divorce might affect this child? _____

_____

_____

Try to describe how you think a divorce will affect your relationship with this child.

_____

_____

_____

7: FORM-ula™ for CHILD IDENTIFICATION

It is important for each child to be readily identified. Keep the original in your Personal file.

Attach the following items to this FORM-ula:

- ☐ current photo of the child
- ☐ copy of child's signature
- ☐ thumb print
- ☐ finger prints

Name _____   Formula Date _____

Address _____   Birth Date _____

Social Security No. _____

Blood Type _____

IDENTIFYING BIRTH MARKS

Signature   **Photo**

Thumb Print   **Finger Prints (Right Hand)**

Finger Prints (Left Hand)   **Thumb Print**

8: FORM-ula™ for EXTENDED FAMILY

If you have one or more extended family members living in the home with you or who are closely involved in family activities, fill out a copy of FORM-ula 8 for each one of them. This is especially important if you are financially interdependent.

Name _____

Address _____

Phone _____

Relationship _____

Financial relationship.

_____

_____

_____

Describe involvement in family activities.

_____

_____

_____

_____

How will a divorce affect this person?

_____

_____

_____

_____

How will a divorce affect you with regard to this person?

_____

_____

_____

_____

What would you like to see happen where this person is concerned?

_____

_____

_____

_____

9: FORM-ula™ for CHRONOLOGICAL MARITAL HISTORY

Use these headings to record the history of your marriage. Make your notes for each heading on a separate sheet of paper. Then, list basic points on this FORM-ula. Stay with the facts and include as many dates as possible.

COURTSHIP, DREAMS AND PLANS

WEDDING, HONEYMOON, EARLY YEARS

LIFE CHANGES (moves, jobs, becoming parents, health problems, unforeseen difficulties)

EXTENDED FAMILY

LIFESTYLE AND DIVISION OF LABOR

FINANCIAL ACTIVITY

COUNSELING

10: FORM-ula™ for CHILD CARE

Decisions will have to be made for support and custody of the children. FORM-ula 10 will indicate who has been responsible for the needs of the children, past and present: mother, father, sibling, relative, neighbor, friend or paid caretaker. This information will be used to formulate the divorce agreement.

	Who? Pre-separation	Who? Post-separation
PHYSICAL CARE		
Change diapers/dress	_____	_____
Bathe/wash hair	_____	_____
Arrange for doctor and dentist	_____	_____
Transport to doctor and dentist	_____	_____
Care for when sick	_____	_____
Keep medical records	_____	_____
Arrange for sitters	_____	_____
Put to bed	_____	_____
Arrange for haircuts, etc.	_____	_____
	_____	_____
NUTRITION		
Plan nutrition	_____	_____
Make meals	_____	_____
Budgeting and shopping	_____	_____
	_____	_____
HOUSEHOLD		
Make beds	_____	_____
Clean and straighten up	_____	_____
Laundry/ironing	_____	_____
	_____	_____
DISCIPLINE		
Set rules	_____	_____
Set limits and penalties	_____	_____
Teach manners	_____	_____
	_____	_____
PERSONAL ATTENTION		
Teach problem solving	_____	_____
Read and play together	_____	_____
Share special activities	_____	_____

	Who? Pre-separation	Who? Post-separation
EDUCATION		
Choose best school and class	_____	_____
Consult with teachers	_____	_____
Attend PTA	_____	_____
Arrange for outside lessons	_____	_____
Transport to outside lessons	_____	_____
Help with homework	_____	_____
Give support and guidance to set objectives and goals	_____	_____
	_____	_____
	_____	_____
SOCIAL		
Arrange birthdays and other festivities	_____	_____
Help to choose and buy gifts	_____	_____
Take trick or treating	_____	_____
Arrange and pack for trips	_____	_____
Help to see friends	_____	_____
Arrange for sports activities	_____	_____
Take to sports activities	_____	_____
	_____	_____
FINANCIAL		
Allowance	_____	_____
Special activities	_____	_____
Special clothing	_____	_____
Transportation to and from jobs	_____	_____
Gifts	_____	_____
Basic clothing	_____	_____
	_____	_____

11: FORM-ula™ for EMOTIONAL ABUSE

There is a wide range of behavior that can be considered emotionally abusive. Remember that each spouse will discuss these issues with an attorney. Check those items that relate to your situation.

You	Your Spouse	
		PLAY PSYCHOLOGICAL GAMES?
☐	☐	Ignore spouse's feelings
☐	☐	Refer to all family assets as "my . . ."
☐	☐	Ridicule or insult opposite gender (male/female) as a group
☐	☐	Ridicule or insult value systems; e.g., religion, race, heritage, class, etc.
☐	☐	Withhold affection, appreciation, or approval as a punishment
☐	☐	Continually criticize, use name calling, shout
☐	☐	Cause private or public humiliation
☐	☐	Refuse to socialize with spouse
☐	☐	Keep from work
☐	☐	Regularly threaten to leave or to throw spouse out
☐	☐	Purposely make all decisions without prior mutual consultation
☐	☐	Manipulate with lies and contradictions
☐	☐	Nag about habits and physical appearance (e.g., weight)
☐	☐	Express excess jealousy and anger about imagined love affairs
☐	☐	Constantly blame spouse for everything that goes wrong
		MAKE PHYSICAL THREATS?
☐	☐	Threaten to hurt spouse or a family member
☐	☐	Abuse family pets when angry
☐	☐	Destroy furniture or property; break things; kick walls, windows, or doors
☐	☐	Continuously and inconsiderately deprive spouse of sleep
☐	☐	Use sex as a "weapon"
☐	☐	Wield objects or weapons in a threatening manner
		USE MONEY AS A WEAPON?
☐	☐	Use money unwisely or without consultation
☐	☐	Withhold money or credit cards
		VIOLATE YOUR PRIVACY?
☐	☐	Tap phones
☐	☐	Follow or have spouse followed

You   Your
             Spouse

MANIPULATE YOU THROUGH THE CHILDREN?

☐   ☐   Punish the children as spousal retaliation

☐   ☐   Threaten to or actually take the children away

☐   ☐   Consistently use the children to force issues

☐   ☐   Influence or try to influence the children against other parent

☐   ☐   Undermine discipline of the children

CHECK THE BOX IF THE ANSWER IS YES.

☐ Do you feel abused?

☐ Are you emotionally afraid of your partner?

☐ Do you express your opinion less freely because of that fear?

☐ Are you preoccupied with watching for your spouse's good or bad moods before you broach certain subjects?

☐ Are you overly concerned or neglectful about checking with your spouse before you do something alone or for yourself?

☐ Do you constantly feel wrong when with your spouse?

☐ Have you withdrawn from your friends to avoid what you think they might know about you or your marriage?

☐ Have you lost confidence in yourself because of repeated "put-downs"?

☐ Are you feeling increasingly depressed, trapped, and powerless?

☐ Do you often doubt your own judgement or wonder which one of you is crazy?

☐ Have your friends been making subtle or direct suggestions that you seek professional help?

12: FORM-ula™ for CURRENT PERSPECTIVES

There are a number of loose ends to consider in preparing for the business of divorce. Begin thinking about them now because the conclusions you reach will be helpful in making the decisions discussed in Section VI, "'Big Picture' Planning" and Chapter 22, "Your Personal Objectives."

Are either of you afraid of litigation? _____ If so, why?

_____
_____
_____

What problems do you foresee in dealing with your spouse (unwillingness to compromise, mistrust, dishonesty, geographic distance, financial ignorance, etc.)?

_____
_____
_____

Do either of you have plans to relocate or remarry?

_____
_____
_____

Do you have friends and relations from the "other side" that you want to maintain? If so, who?

_____
_____
_____

Do you have a time frame in mind for the completion of this divorce?

_____
_____
_____

Can you and your spouse work comfortably with professionals of both sexes? (This may influence your choice of an attorney.)

_____
_____
_____

Do either of you have immediate needs for housing, financial support, or child care?

_____
_____
_____

Will custody be used as a bargaining issue?

_____
_____
_____

Do either or both of you have a strong need to own one or more of the same items of marital property?

_____
_____
_____

13: FORM-ula™ for GROCERY SHOPPING
Circle Needed Items

PRODUCE
apple
pear
plum
cherry
peach
apricot
nectarine
orange
lemon
lime
grapefruit
tangerine
banana
plaintain
pineapple
raspberry
strawberry
cranberry
blueberry
grapes
raisins
melon
pumpkin
squash
cucumber
potato
tomato
eggplant
peppers (red, green, yellow)
yam/sweet potato
onions
garlic
asparagus
chives
celery
carrot
parsley
lettuce
artichoke
sunflower seeds
peas
beans
beets
spinach
cabbage
broccoli
radish
cauliflower
brussels sprouts
turnip
kale
avocado
mushrooms

BAKING
flour-white/whole wheat/rye
arrowroot
corn starch
sugar-granulated/brown/
  powdered
artificial sweetener
shortening-oil/solid
baking powder/soda
molasses
maple syrup
honey
vanilla/almond extracts
salt
pepper
garlic powder
oregano
cinnamon
nutmeg
basil
chocolate chips
cooking wines
nuts: walnut, pecan, macadamia,
  cashew, pistachio, filbert, Brazil,
  pine nut
coconut
cocoa
dried fruits: dates, prunes, raisins,
  apricots, other
pie filling: pumpkin, fruit
mixes: pie crust, biscuits, cake,
  corn meal

GRAINS
buckwheat (kasha)
barley
popcorn
rice-white, brown, wild, mixed

PASTA
spaghetti
shells
elbow macaroni
lasagna
pastina
linguini

BREADS
white bread
rye bread
whole wheat bread

bagels
muffins
hot dog rolls
hamburger rolls
dinner rolls
other rolls
biscuits

CEREALS
boxed cereals
cooked cereals

HEALTH/BEAUTY/PERSONAL
toothpaste
tooth brushes
mouthwash
dental floss
lotion: hand/body
suntan lotion/oil
sunblock
deodorant, antiperspirant
shampoo, conditioner
razors, shaving cream
cotton: swabs, balls
peroxide, alcohol
bandaids, adhesive tape
first-aid creams, ointments
aspirin, acetaminophen
children's aspirin
cold medications
allergy medications
vitamins
emery boards
nail polish remover
shoe polish
prescriptions

CANNED/BOXED FOODS
fruits
  cherry
  mandarin orange
  peach
  pear
  apple sauce
  maraschino cherry
  juice
  fruit cocktail
vegetables
  sweet potato
  tomato-whole, crushed
  tomato sauce/paste

prepared spaghetti sauce
beet
corn
pea
potato
Chinese-(sprouts, shoots,
  water chestnuts)
carrot
string bean
mushroom
sauerkraut
beans-baked
canned pasta
macaroni and cheese
soups (canned or dried)
bouillon, consomme
seafood: fish, oysters, clams,
  shrimp
sauces: spaghetti, gravy
corned beef, hash
dried beef
tuna fish
gefilte fish
powdered milk
canned milk

CONDIMENTS
mayonnaise
mustard
catsup
relish: red, green
olives: black, green
pickles
vinegar: wine, cider, white
horse radish
sauce: cocktail, chili, seafood,
  soy, steak, poultry, hot
bar-b-que sauces
worcestershire sauce
powdered soup and dip mix
powdered mixes
pimiento
jam and jelly
peanut butter
bread crumbs

PAPER ITEMS
napkins
towels
toilet paper
facial tissues
plates
cups
mats
lunch bags
aluminum foil
waxed paper
plastic wrap
microwave wrap
plastic bags: sandwich, food,
  storage, compactor, garbage
vacuum cleaner bags

HOUSEHOLD
light bulbs
bath soap
laundry detergent
fabric softener
starch
bleach
prewash stain treatment
dishwashing liquid
cleansing powder
nonabrasive cleanser
aluminum cleanser
scouring pads
waxes: furniture, floor
polish: silver, brass, furniture
oven cleaner
ammonia
wood cleaner
window cleaner
sponges and wipes
broom

DAIRY CASE
milk: regular, low-fat
cream: half&half, whipping
sour cream
butter/margarine
sliced cheese
cream cheese
cottage cheese
brick cheese
cheddar
ricotta
mozzarella
parmesan
specialty cheese
eggs

yogurt: plain and fruit
refrigerator cookies
pizza dough
biscuits
juices

DRINKS
tea bags
instant tea
specialty tea
ground coffee
instant coffee
coffee beans
coffee bags
fruit juices
vegetable juices
soft drinks: diet and regular
club soda, tonic
cocktail mixers
powdered drink mixes
other

PETS
canned, dried cat food
canned, dried dog food
fish food
bird food
other animal food
cat litter
dog bedding
other animal bedding and litter
aquarium filters
grooming supplies

INFANTS
formula: soy or regular
fruit
vegetables
disposable diapers

DESSERTS/SNACKS
cakes
cookies
chips: corn and potato
pretzels
pies
jello
pudding
sherbet
ice cream
toppings
popping corn

peanuts

PEAS/BEANS
black eyed pea
garbonzo
green/yellow–whole/split
kidney
lima
lentil: green and red
navy pea
pinto
soy beans
string beans

POULTRY
chicken: whole, pieces, boneless,
  sliced
chicken or turkey hot dogs
duck
turkey: whole, pieces, ground,
  sliced
hot dogs
eggs

BEEF
hamburg
brisket
roast
steak
hot dogs
tongue
liver
veal chops
veal cutlets
stew

LAMB
chops
ground
leg
rack
breast

PORK
bacon
chops
ham-fresh
ham-cured
ham-canned
ribs
roast
sausage (sweet or hot)

SHELLFOOD
crab
lobster
shrimp
abalone
clam
mussels
oyster
scallops
squid

FISH
bass
blue
herring
perch
salmon
white fish
flounder
mackeral
sea bass
herring
trout
sole
swordfish
tuna

14: FORM-ula™ for HOUSEHOLD CHORES

Mon.	Tues.	Wed.	Thurs.	Fri.	Sat.	Sun.

COMMENTS

Week 1 _____

Week 2 _____

Week 3 _____

Week 4 _____

Week 5 _____

HOUSECLEANING
dust/polish
vacuum/sweep
wastebaskets
bathrooms
kitchen

CLOTHING
wash/dry
fold/put away
iron/mend
dry clean

OUTDOORS
sweep
water
mow/clip
shovel
garden/weed

MEALS
plan menu
shop for food
meal preparation
clean up/dishes

PLANT CARE
water
feed

CAR CARE
check oil/gas/
    water/fluids
maintenance
inspection
wash/wax
rotate tires

PET CARE
feed
groom
walk
clean up
vet

OCCASIONAL
windows
screens
A/C filters
mirrors
silverware
closets
cabinets
garage
basement
carpets
oven/frig

15: FORM-ula™ for EMERGENCY TELEPHONE NUMBERS

Type or print carefully and post a copy of this list next to each telephone in the house. Make sure all information is filled in. In an emergency, a babysitter or other person needs to be able to give address, phone number, and coherent directions to the house.

THE ADDRESS HERE IS:

THE PHONE NUMBER HERE IS:

DIRECTIONS TO HOUSE:

FIRE:

POLICE:

AMBULANCE:

POISON CONTROL CENTER:

PEDIATRICIAN:

DENTIST:

VETERINARIAN:

ELECTRIC COMPANY:

GAS COMPANY:

OIL COMPANY/FURNACE REPAIR:

PARENT'S WORK TELEPHONE NUMBERS (don't forget to include extension number):

Mother:

Father:

NEIGHBOR (name, phone, address, and description of house—e.g., "red house across the street"):

FRIEND OR RELATIVE (give name, phone, address, and relationship of a responsible person who can and will respond promptly in serious, but nonlifethreatening emergencies.):

16: FORM-ula™ for RESOURCE TELEPHONE NUMBERS

This is your personal *Yellow Pages*. Keep the relevant numbers on your Rolodex and in your address book. This list is a reminder to locate the telephone numbers and record them.

HOME AND AUTOMOBILE

Locksmith:

Handyman:

Garbage service:

Auto club:

Mechanic:

MENTAL/PHYSICAL HEALTH AND SAFETY

Information hotline:

Crisis hotline:

Mental health services:

Family service agency:

Nationwide domestic violence hotline:

Local domestic violence hotline:

Emergency shelter:

Alcoholics Anonymous support line:

Drug information hotline:

Narcotics Anonymous:

FOR AND ABOUT CHILDREN

Parents Without Partners:

Safe Rides:

Child Abuse Hotline:

Al-a-teen:

17: FORM-ula™ for CHILDREN'S WHEREABOUTS

For each of your children, provide information about close friends who live nearby and places they go regularly or periodically. You or a child-care provider may need to call around to locate children if they are not home at scheduled times.

Your Child's Name _____

FRIEND'S NAME Address Phone number Parent's name			
FRIEND'S NAME Address Phone number Parent's name			
FRIEND'S NAME Address Phone number Parent's name			
LIBRARY			
AFTER SCHOOL CLUBS			
COMMUNITY ACTIVITIES			
SPORTS (games, practice)			
LESSONS (academic, religious, creative arts)			
PART-TIME WORK			

18: FORM-ula™ for HOUSEHOLD SUPPLIES

Use this list as a guide when assembling necessary household supplies. You will already have some of the items; you will need to purchase others. By organizing your supplies, you will know where in the house to find them when they are needed. Check off the items you already have.

BASIC TOOL BOX

- ☐ 16 oz. hammer
- ☐ Set of screwdrivers (with cushion grips)
- ☐ 10-in. adjustable wrench (opens to 1 1/8 in.)
- ☐ 20 25-ft. retractable measuring tape
- ☐ Safety glasses/goggles
- ☐ Work gloves

BASIC FIRST-AID KIT

- ☐ Assorted sizes of bandages to dress small cuts
- ☐ Assorted butterfly bandages
- ☐ Sterile gauze pads for larger cuts
- ☐ Roll of adhesive tape
- ☐ Small scissors
- ☐ Sling or triangular cloth
- ☐ Roll of elastic bandage for sprains
- ☐ Tweezers for removing glass, splinters, or bee stings
- ☐ Calamine lotion or baking soda (insect bites or poison ivy)
- ☐ Peroxide or germicide for cleaning cuts
- ☐ Cotton balls
- ☐ Oral fever thermometer
- ☐ Pain killers (e.g., aspirin)
- ☐ Ice pack
- ☐ Small bottle of ipecac syrup to induce vomiting in case of poisoning
- ☐ Tourniquet

SPECIAL EMERGENCY PRECAUTIONS AGAINST STORMS AND NATURAL DISASTERS

- ☐ Extra flashlights, batteries, and bulbs
- ☐ Battery-operated radio
- ☐ Candles and matches in kitchen and next to bed
- ☐ Nonperishable foods
- ☐ Cooking and camping equipment
- ☐ Bottled water
- ☐ Tape

19: FORM-ula™ for FUNCTIONAL AUTOMOBILE

Your automobile may be vital to your independence and livelihood. By doing, or arranging for, the items on this list, you will avoid many problems regarding the safety of your "wheels."

GENERAL PREPARATION

☐ Get proper insurance and be sure you understand your coverage.
☐ Have an extra set of car keys readily available.
☐ Join an official auto club.
☐ Find a reliable mechanic.
☐ Consider taking a basic auto mechanics course (AAA, YMCA, or adult education).
☐ Locate jack and other auto tools.
☐ Practice changing a tire.
☐ Learn how your car should be towed.
☐ Save all warranties, invoices, and repair slips.
☐ Write inspection due-date on your activity calendar.

CARRY IN THE CAR

☐ Insurance card
☐ Accident report forms from your insurance company
☐ Car manual
☐ First-aid kit
☐ Flashlight and spare batteries
☐ Spare fuses
☐ Jumper cables
☐ Flares
☐ White distress signal (handkerchief) and sign that says "HELP"

If You Live in a Cold Climate:

☐ Ice scraper and aerosol defroster
☐ Sand or salt (kitty litter works very well and is prepackaged)
☐ Blanket or sleeping bag

AUTOMOBILE MAINTENANCE

Check at Close Intervals

☐ Fanbelts and hoses
☐ Tires (pressure, wear, alignment)
☐ Fluid levels (engine oil, radiator coolant, transmission and brake fluids)
☐ Exhaust system (connections and supports, muffler and pipes, catalytic converter)

Check Regularly

☐ Engine (ignition wires, carburetor, timing, points and plugs, air filter, gas filter)
☐ Tires (rotate, balance, spare tire pressure)
☐ Brakes (front and rear, emergency brake)
☐ Shock absorbers and springs
☐ Windshield wipers

Seasonal

☐ Twice a year tune-up
☐ Antifreeze and air-conditioner coolant
☐ Battery

20: FORM-ula™ for CHILD CARE OUTSIDE OF THE HOME

Use a separate FORM-ula 20 for each center or individual that you visit.

GENERAL DATA

Name of individual or center _____

Phone _____

Address _____

_____

Recommended by _____

How long has this center been in business? _____

Number of children cared for _____

Age range _____

Hours of operation _____

Size of staff _____

Ratio of caretakers to children _____

What does it cost? _____

FACILITIES AVAILABLE TO CHILDREN

☐ Proper heating and ventilation?

☐ Good indoor and outdoor play areas?

☐ Secure fencing?

☐ Are rooms pleasant and lighted?

☐ Is facility clean and attractive?

☐ Is bathroom safe and clean?

☐ Personal space for each child?

☐ Rest area and cot or pad?

☐ Handrails on stairs?

☐ Educational toys and books?

☐ Are there meals and snacks?

Qualifications, training and licensing _____

_____

_____

Person or center's philosophy concerning child care and discipline _____

_____

_____

_____

_____

<u>REFERENCES</u>

Name _____

Address _____

Phone _____

Notes _____

_____

_____

_____

Name _____

Address _____

Phone _____

Notes _____

_____

_____

_____

Name _____

Address _____

Phone _____

Notes _____

_____

_____

General impressions of the facilities? _____

_____

_____

_____

_____

21: FORM-ula™ for VISITATION SCHEDULE AND RECORDS

Create a monthly record of the plans that you and your children make.

Mon.	*Tues.*	*Wed.*	*Thurs.*	*Fri.*	*Sat.*	*Sun.*

COMMENTS

Week 1 _____

Week 2 _____

Week 3 _____

Week 4 _____

Week 5 _____

Checklist of dates to remember

HOLIDAYS
Memorial Day
July 4th
Labor Day
Thanksgiving
Christmas
Easter
Hannukah
Yom Kippur
Purim
Passover

VACATIONS
Summer
Winter
Spring
Long weekends

SPECIAL OCCASIONS
Mother's Day
Father's Day
Halloween
Graduation(s)
Sports Events
Tryouts
Recitals
Other School and Social
Weddings
Funerals
Death anniversary (Yarzeit)

BIRTHDAYS
Grandparents
Aunts and uncles
Cousins
Mother
Father
Brothers
Sisters
Children
Other relatives
Friends

22: FORM-ula™ for EXPENSES

	Jan.	Feb.	Mar.	Apr.	May	June	July	Aug.	Sept.	Oct.	Nov.	Dec.	TOTAL
Housing													
Mortgage/rent													
Condo/Co-op maintenance chgs.													
Gas/Oil													
Electric													
Water/sewer													
Telephone													
Garbage collection													
Subtotal													
Household Maintenance & Services													
Electrical service/repairs													
Plumbing service/repairs													
Appliance maint./repairs													
Appliance contracts													
Painting (interior/exterior)													
Exterminator													
Lawn & Garden													

FORM-ula™ 22. *(Continued)*

	Jan.	Feb.	Mar.	Apr.	May	June	July	Aug.	Sept.	Oct.	Nov.	Dec.	TOTAL
Snow Removal													
Household help													
Special help (catering, etc.)													
Supplies													
Fireplace wood													
Rug cleaning													
Tips (mailmen, doormen)													
Window washing													
Subtotal													
Major Purchases													
Furniture													
Appliances													
Rugs													
Household items													
Subtotal													
Food													
Groceries													

FORM-ula™ 22. (Continued)

	Jan.	Feb.	Mar.	Apr.	May	June	July	Aug.	Sept.	Oct.	Nov.	Dec.	TOTAL
Meat/fish													
Special diet													
Gourmet													
Liquor													
Lunches (work/school)													
Subtotal													
Clothing for Self (Children's clothes are listed separately)													
Purchase													
Laundry/dry cleaning													
Alterations/tailoring													
Shoes													
Shoe repair													
Furs/storage													
Special (skiing, camping)													
Subtotal													

FORM-ula™ 22. *(Continued)*

	Jan.	Feb.	Mar.	Apr.	May	June	July	Aug.	Sept.	Oct.	Nov.	Dec.	TOTAL
Transportation													
Car loan payment/lease													
Gas/oil													
Tolls/parking													
License/registration													
Emissions/inspection fees													
Maintenance													
Repair													
Towing													
Commutation expenses													
Taxis													
Car rental													
Bus/train tickets													
Carpool contribution/dues													
Automobile Club													
Subtotal													
Entertainment													
Restaurants													
Movies/rentals													
Theater/opera/concert													

FORM-ula™ 22. (Continued)

	Jan.	Feb.	Mar.	Apr.	May	June	July	Aug.	Sept.	Oct.	Nov.	Dec.	TOTAL
Sports events													
Club dues/expenses													
Day trips													
Hobbies													
Boat/plane/RV													
Subtotal													
Vacations													
Lodging													
Food													
Transportation													
Special clothing													
Special equipment													
Day trips													
Tips													
Film													
Subtotal													

FORM-ula™ 22. (Continued)

Children's Expenses	Jan.	Feb.	Mar.	Apr.	May	June	July	Aug.	Sept.	Oct.	Nov.	Dec.	TOTAL
Child care*													
Baby sitters*													
Clothing													
Allowances													
Special events													
Recreation/sports													
Parties (birthday/holiday)													
Costumes (play, special event, holiday, etc.)													
Lunches													
Books/supplies													
Special hobbies/projects													
Lessons (music, etc.)													
Travel													
Summer camp													
Vehicles (bike, boat, auto)													
Vehicle maintenance/fuel													
Vehicle repair													
Dues/fees													
Subtotal													

*Don't forget to get Social Security numbers for baby sitters and child care-giver.

FORM-ula™ 22. (Continued)

	Jan.	Feb.	Mar.	Apr.	May	June	July	Aug.	Sept.	Oct.	Nov.	Dec.	TOTAL
Education*													
Nursery school													
Private school tuition/fees													
Priv. school room & board													
Other school tuition/fees													
Other sch. room & board													
College tuition/fees													
College room & board													
Books/supplies													
Childrens's gifts to others (birthday parties, etc.)													
Travel													
Insurance													
Religious													
Tutoring/special education													
Special clothing (e.g., band or sport uniforms, etc.)													
Subtotal													
Gifts													
Christmas/Chanukkah, etc.													
Birthday													

*If any part of education is for yourself, be sure to check with your accountant for deductibility.

FORM-ula™ 22. (Continued)

	Jan.	Feb.	Mar.	Apr.	May	June	July	Aug.	Sept.	Oct.	Nov.	Dec.	TOTAL
Wedding/anniversary													
Baby/graduation													
Work "Sunshine" funds													
Misc. work donations													
Greeting cards, gift wrap													
Subtotal													
Miscellaneous													
Newspapers/magazines													
Subscriptions													
Stationery supplies													
Stamps/UPS/etc.													
Toys/books/tapes/CDs													
Toiletries													
Hairdresser/barber													
Cable TV													
Tobacco													
Pets													
Pocket money													
Credit card fees													

FORM-ula™ 22. (Continued)

	Jan.	Feb.	Mar.	Apr.	May	June	July	Aug.	Sept.	Oct.	Nov.	Dec.	TOTAL
Emergency fund/cookie jar													
Subtotal													
Special Expenses													
Alimony													
Child support													
Eldercare/nursing home													
Contrib. to parents/ extended family member													
Professional/union dues and memberships													
Professional licenses/fees													
Photocopying													
Misc. office supplies													
Subtotal													
Contributions													
Religious													
Charity (Red Cross, etc.)													
Alumni funds													

FORM-ula™ 22. *(Continued)*

	Jan.	Feb.	Mar.	Apr.	May	June	July	Aug.	Sept.	Oct.	Nov.	Dec.	TOTAL
Community organizations													
Special disaster funds													
Volunteer organizations													
Fraternal organizations													
Subtotal													
Medical/Dental for Self													
Doctors													
Dentists													
Orthodontists													
Allergist													
Psychiatrist/psychologist													
Other specialists													
Unreimbursed expenses													
Prescriptions													
Special nonprescription medications, vitamins, etc.													
Lab fees													
Special tests													
Eye exams/eyeglasses													
First-aid supplies													
Prosthesis													

FORM-ula™ 22. *(Continued)*

	Jan.	Feb.	Mar.	Apr.	May	June	July	Aug.	Sept.	Oct.	Nov.	Dec.	TOTAL
Medical equipment													
Sports-related items													
Contraceptives													
Subtotal													
Medical/Dental for Children													
Doctors													
Dentists													
Orthodontists													
Specialists													
Allergists													
Psychologists/psychiatrists													
Unreimbursed expenses													
Prescriptions													
Special nonprescription medication, vitamins, etc.													
Lab fees													
Special tests													
Eye exams/eyeglasses													
First-aid supplies													
Prosthesis													
Medical equipment													

FORM-ula™ 22. (Continued)

	Jan.	Feb.	Mar.	Apr.	May	June	July	Aug.	Sept.	Oct.	Nov.	Dec.	TOTAL
Sports-related items													
Contraceptives													
Subtotal													
Scheduled Monthly Payments													
Education payments													
Insurance payments													
Personal bank loans													
Home improvement loans													
Credit card payments													
Loan repayments to relatives &/or friends													
Christmas/vacation clubs													
Subtotal													
Insurance													
Life													
Liability													
Fire													
Theft													

FORM-ula™ 22. (Continued)

	Jan.	Feb.	Mar.	Apr.	May	June	July	Aug.	Sept.	Oct.	Nov.	Dec.	TOTAL
Homeowners/tenants													
Automobile													
Medical													
Short-term disability													
Long-term disability													
Excess liability (umbrella)													
Travel													
Subtotal													
Taxes*													
Federal income													
State income													
City income													
Other city													
Personal property													
Real estate													
Improvement bonds													
Assessments (sewer, etc.)													
Social Security													
Motor vehicle													
Sales													

*Please check with your accountant as to what else might be accountable in your particular state and locality.

FORM-ula™ 22. (Continued)

	Jan.	Feb.	Mar.	Apr.	May	June	July	Aug.	Sept.	Oct.	Nov.	Dec.	TOTAL
Other taxes													
Subtotal													
Financial Charges													
Financial counseling													
Accountant													
Bank charges:													
service charges													
overdrafts													
printed checks													
bank card use													
Brokerage fees													
Subtotal													

FORM-ula™ 22. (Continued)

SUMMARY OF EXPENSES

Expense Category	Annual Amount	Monthly Amount	Weekly Amount
Housing			
Household Maintenance & Services			
Major Purchases			
Food			
Clothing for Self			
Transportation			
Entertainment			
Vacations			
Children's Expenses			
Education			
Gifts			
Miscellaneous			
Special Expenses			
Contributions			
Medical/Dental for Self			
Medical/Dental for Children			
Scheduled Monthly Payments			
Insurance			
Taxes			
Financial Charges			
TOTAL			

23: FORM-ula™ for INCOME

Date _____

Source of Income	Jan.	Feb.	Mar.	Apr.	May	June	July	Aug.	Sept.	Oct.	Nov.	Dec.	TOTAL
Salary													
Overtime													
Bonus													
Social Security for self													
Social Security for spouse													
Social Security for children													
Retirement–personal plan													
Retirement–corporate													
Retirement–military													
Workmen's comp., full dis.													
Workmen's comp., partial													
Temporary support													
Trust income													
Interest													

FORM-ula™ 23. (Continued)

Source of Income	Jan.	Feb.	Mar.	Apr.	May	June	July	Aug.	Sept.	Oct.	Nov.	Dec.	TOTAL
Dividends													
Capital gains													
Windfalls													
Loan repayments received													
Other sources													
Other Compensation:													
Food													
Clothing													
Shelter													
Transportation													

24: FORM-ula™ for CREDIT CARD INVENTORY

Information for this FORM-ula is included on credit card monthly billing statements. You may need to call or write to find out if the account is individual or joint. Credit lines have a value. How will they be assigned after the divorce?

Account Name	Company/Location/Phone	Account Name (His/Hers/Joint)	Account Number	Cr. Rpt. Accurate?	Expir. Date	Credit Line
Bank Cards (e.g., Visa)						
Department Stores						
Membership Cards (e.g., Am. Ex.)						
Travel Cards						
Airline						
Rental Car						
Auto Service Cards (e.g., Mobil)						

FORM-ula™ 24. (Continued)

Account Name	Company/Location/Phone	Account Name (His/Hers/Joint)	Account Number	Cr. Rpt. Accurate?	Expir. Date	Credit Line
Telephone Credit Cards						
Important Noncredit Cards						
Library card(s)						
Auto club membership						
Discount/Check-Cashing Cards						
Grocery store check-cashing						
Other check-cashing						
Video-Rental (and similar) **Cards**						

25: FORM-ula™ for REQUESTING AN INDIVIDUAL CREDIT REPORT

Please read Chapter 14, "The Credit in Your Financial System," to understand the purpose and importance of sending this letter to each credit card account that does not report credit information in both names.

Date

Name of Credit grantor (Credit card company, store, etc.)
Address

Dear Madam or Sir:

Under the Equal Credit Opportunity Act, I request that you report all credit information on this account in both names.

Account No. _____

Account Name No. 1 _____
                  (Last)   (First)   (Middle)

Address _____
          (Street)   (Apt. No.)

_____
        (City)   (State)   (ZIP)

Account Name No. 2 _____
                  (Last)   (First)   (Middle)

Address _____
          (Street)   (Apt. No.)

_____
        (City)   (State)   (ZIP)

Sincerely,

_____
   (Signature of either spouse)

26: FORM-ula™ for PERSONAL PAPERS
This "at-a-glance" checklist will tell you which papers you have in the files.

☐ Marriage Certificate

☐ Birth Certificates

   ☐ Self

   ☐ Children

      ☐ _____

      ☐ _____

      ☐ _____

      ☐ _____

☐ Adoption Papers

   ☐ Children

      ☐ _____

      ☐ _____

      ☐ _____

      ☐ _____

☐ Baptism Certificates

   ☐ Self

   ☐ Children

      ☐ _____

      ☐ _____

      ☐ _____

      ☐ _____

☐ Citizenship Papers

   ☐ Self

   ☐ Children

      ☐ _____

      ☐ _____

      ☐ _____

      ☐ _____

☐ Passports

   ☐ Self

   ☐ Children

      ☐ _____

      ☐ _____

      ☐ _____

      ☐ _____

☐ Visas

   ☐ Self

   ☐ Children

      ☐ _____

      ☐ _____

☐ _____

☐ _____

☐ Green Cards

   ☐ Self

   ☐ Children

      ☐ _____

      ☐ _____

      ☐ _____

      ☐ _____

☐ Social Security Cards

   ☐ Self

   ☐ Children

      ☐ _____

      ☐ _____

      ☐ _____

      ☐ _____

☐ Social Security Benefit Records

   ☐ Self

   ☐ Spouse

☐ Power of Attorney

☐ Driver's License (copy)

☐ Name Change Papers

☐ Wills and Codicils

   ☐ Self

   ☐ Spouse

☐ Post Office Box Receipts

☐ Medical Records

   ☐ Self

   ☐ Children

      ☐ _____

      ☐ _____

      ☐ _____

      ☐ _____

☐ Vaccination Records

   ☐ Self

   ☐ Children

      ☐ _____

      ☐ _____

      ☐ _____

      ☐ _____

Date _____

27: FORM-ula™ for HOUSEHOLD INVENTORY AND APPRAISAL

Cross off items that you don't own; add items that are not included. Answer "How Acquired" and "Do You Want It." "Appraisal" is for items that are valuable or in dispute. "Distribution" will be completed as it occurs.

LIVING ROOM	Gift Hers	Gift His	Inherited Hers	Inherited His	Purchased	Yes	No	Value	Date	Hers	His	Received
	How Acquired					Do You Want It?		Appraisal		Distribution		
Carpet/rugs												
Lamps												
Tapestries												
Curtains/drapes												
Shades/blinds												
Window air conditioner												
Desk/secretaries												
Chairs—occasional												
straight												
lounge												
Sofa/love seat												
Sofa bed												
Tables—coffee												
sofa												
Room divider												
Cabinets/etagere												
Clocks												
Mirrors												
Fireplace accessories												
Radio/stereo unit												
Records/tapes												
Television												
Video recorder												
Bar												
Fine arts or collection												
Books												
Pictures												

DINING ROOM												
Carpet/rugs												
Lamps												
Tapestries												
Curtains/drapes												

FORM-ula™ 27. *(Continued)*

DINING ROOM *(continued)*

	How Acquired					Do You Want It?		Appraisal		Distribution		
	Gift		Inherited		Purchased	Yes	No	Value	Date	Hers	His	Received
	Hers	His	Hers	His								
Shades/blinds												
Window air conditioner												
Chairs–straight												
other												
Dining table chairs												
Dining table												
Buffet												
Corner cabinet												
Serving cart												
Clocks												
Mirrors												
Chandelier												
Bar												
China & glassware												
Silverware												
Linens												

LIBRARY/DEN/STUDY

Carpet												
Lamps												
Curtains/drapes												
Shades/blinds												
Window air conditioner												
Chairs												
Portable bar												
Sofa												
Tables												
Desk chair/desk												
Bookcases												
Cabinets												
Etagere												
Clocks												
Mirrors												
Radio/stereo unit												
Television												
Video recorder												
Home computer												
Video games												
Typewriter												
Calculator												

FORM-ula™ 27. *(Continued)*

LIBRARY/DEN/STUDY (continued)

	Gift		Inherited		Purchased	Do You Want It?		Appraisal		Distribution		
	Hers	His	Hers	His		Yes	No	Value	Date	Hers	His	Received
Pictures/paintings												
Books												

RECREATION/FAMILY ROOM

	Gift		Inherited		Purchased	Do You Want It?		Appraisal		Distribution		
	Hers	His	Hers	His		Yes	No	Value	Date	Hers	His	Received
Floor covering												
Lamps												
Curtains/drapes												
Shades/blinds												
Window air conditioner												
Tables												
Chairs												
Ping-pong table												
Radio/stereo unit												
Chest												
Games												
Clocks												
Trophies												
Television												
Video recorder												
Home computer												
Video games												
Fireplace equipment												
Bar												
Card table												
Sofa												
Plants												
Aquarium												
Glassware												
Books												
Photograph albums												
Family												
Vacation												
Children												

BEDROOM 1

	Gift		Inherited		Purchased	Do You Want It?		Appraisal		Distribution		
	Hers	His	Hers	His		Yes	No	Value	Date	Hers	His	Received
Carpets/rugs												
Lamps												
Curtains/drapes												
Shades/blinds												

FORM-ula™ 27. (Continued)

BEDROOM 1 (continued)

	How Acquired					Do You Want It?		Appraisal		Distribution		
	Gift		Inherited		Purchased	Yes	No	Value	Date	Hers	His	Received
	Hers	His	Hers	His								
Window air conditioner												
Bookcase												
Headboards												
Beds/mattresses												
Water bed												
Blankets/sheets												
Night tables												
Dressing table/bench												
Occasional chairs												
Chaise lounge												
Dresser												
Chest												
Wardrobe												
Desk												
Clocks/clock radio												
Stereo unit												
Television												
Mirrors												
Pictures												
Clothing												

BEDROOM 2

	How Acquired					Do You Want It?		Appraisal		Distribution		
	Gift		Inherited		Purchased	Yes	No	Value	Date	Hers	His	Received
	Hers	His	Hers	His								
Carpets/rugs												
Lamps												
Curtains/drapes												
Shades/blinds												
Window air conditioner												
Bookcase												
Headboards												
Beds/mattresses												
Water bed												
Blankets/sheets												
Night tables												
Dressing table/bench												
Occasional chairs												
Chaise lounge												
Dresser												
Chest												
Wardrobe												
Desk												

FORM-ula™ 27. *(Continued)*

BEDROOM 2 *(continued)*

Item	Gift Hers	Gift His	Inherited Hers	Inherited His	Purchased	Do You Want It? Yes	No	Value	Date	Hers	His	Received
			How Acquired					Appraisal		Distribution		
Clocks/clock radio												
Stereo unit												
Television												
Mirrors												
Pictures												
Clothing												

BEDROOM 3

Item
Carpets/rugs
Lamps
Curtains/drapes
Shades/blinds
Window air conditioner
Bookcase
Headboards
Beds/mattresses
Water bed
Blankets/sheets
Night tables
Dressing table/bench
Occasional chairs
Chaise lounge
Dresser
Chest
Wardrobe
Desk
Clocks/clock radio
Stereo unit
Television
Mirrors
Pictures
Clothing

BEDROOM 4

Item
Carpets/rugs
Lamps
Curtains/drapes

FORM-ula™ 27. (Continued)

BEDROOM 4 (continued)

	How Acquired					Do You Want It?		Appraisal		Distribution		
	Gift		Inherited		Purchased	Yes	No	Value	Date	Hers	His	Received
	Hers	His	Hers	His								
Shades/blinds												
Window air conditioner												
Bookcase												
Headboards												
Beds/mattresses												
Water bed												
Blankets/sheets												
Night tables												
Dressing table/bench												
Occasional chairs												
Chaise lounge												
Dresser												
Chest												
Wardrobe												
Desk												
Clocks/clock radio												
Stereo unit												
Television												
Mirrors												
Pictures												
Clothing												

NURSERY

Bassinette												
Youth bed												
Crib												
Chair/table												
High chair												
Chest												
Toy chest												
Playpen												
Rug												

BATHROOM 1

Bath mats												
Towels												
Washcloths												
Shower curtains												

FORM-ula™ 27. (Continued)

BATHROOM 1 (continued)

	How Acquired					Do You Want It?		Appraisal		Distribution		
	Gift		Inherited		Purchased	Yes	No	Value	Date	Hers	His	Received
	Hers	His	Hers	His								
Clothes hamper												
Dressing table												
Chair												
Curtains/drapes												
Medicine chests												
Electrical appliances												
Scales												
Sun lamp												
Decorative accessories												

BATHROOM 2

| Bath mats |
| Towels |
| Washcloths |
| Shower curtains |
| Clothes hamper |
| Dressing table |
| Chair |
| Curtains/drapes |
| Medicine chests |
| Electrical appliances |
| Scales |
| Sun lamp |
| Decorative accessories |

BATHROOM 3

| Bath mats |
| Towels |
| Washcloths |
| Shower curtains |
| Clothes hamper |
| Dressing table |
| Chair |
| Curtains/drapes |
| Medicine chests |
| Electrical appliances |
| Scales |
| Sun lamp |

BATHROOM 3 (continued)

	How Acquired					Do You Want It?		Appraisal		Distribution		
	Gift		Inherited		Purchased	Yes	No	Value	Date	Hers	His	Received
	Hers	His	Hers	His								
Decorative accessories												

LAUNDRY/UTILITY ROOM

Washer												
Dryer												
Iron												
Tables												
Chairs												
Ironing board												
Sewing machine												
Vacuum cleaner												
Floor polisher												
Rug shampooer												

YARD

Outdoor furniture												
Picnic table/benches												
Pool accessories												
Cooking equipment												
Snow plow/blower												
Tiller												
Edge trimmer												
Garden hose												
Sprinkler												
Lawn mower												
Leaf blower												
Spreader												
Garden equipment (rakes, hoes, shovels, etc.)												
Garbage cans												
Croquet set												
Badminton set												
Volleyball set												
Yard sports												
Jungle gym												
Bikes												
Wagons												
Slide												

FORM-ula™ 27. (Continued)

YARD (continued)

	Gift Hers	Gift His	Inherited Hers	Inherited His	Purchased	Yes	No	Value	Date	Hers	His	Received
	Gift		**Inherited**		**Purchased**	**Do You Want It?**		**Appraisal**		**Distribution**		
	Hers	His	Hers	His		Yes	No	Value	Date	Hers	His	Received
Seesaw												
Sleds												
Toys/sports equip.												

MUSICAL/ELECTRONIC INSTRUMENTS AND ACCESSORIES

	Hers	His	Hers	His	Purchased	Yes	No	Value	Date	Hers	His	Received
Piano												
Portable keyboards												
Organ												
Musical instruments												
Televisions												
Video tape recorders												
Video cassette players												
Video cameras												
Photography equipment												
Radios												
Stereo units												
Tape recorders												
Records												
Tapes												
Sheet music												

FINE ARTS/COLLECTIONS

	Hers	His	Hers	His	Purchased	Yes	No	Value	Date	Hers	His	Received
Paintings												
Dolls												
Etchings												
Stamps												
Statuary												
Coins												
Figurines												
China												
Wall hangings												
Glassware												
Mirrors												
Records												
Books												
Rare books												
Liquor/wine												
Precious metals/gems												

HALLS/SUN ROOMS/ PORCHES

	How Acquired						Do You Want It?		Appraisal		Distribution		
	Gift		Inherited		Purchased								
	Hers	His	Hers	His			Yes	No	Value	Date	Hers	His	Received
Floor covering													
Lamps													
Curtains/drapes													
Shades/blinds													
Chairs													
Tables													
Cabinets													
Settees													
Plants													
Mirrors													
Radio													
Clocks													
Television													
Bookcases													
Coat rack													
Etagere													
Books													
Pictures													

KITCHEN

Table/chairs													
Cabinets													
Refrigerator													
Freezer													
Range (electric/gas)													
Microwave oven													
Garbage compactor													
Toaster													
Mixers/processors													
Grills													
Coffee maker													
Rotisserie (electric)													
Skillet (electric)													
Can opener													
Sharpeners													
Floor polisher (electric)													

FORM-ula™ 27. (Continued)

KITCHEN (continued)

	Gift Hers	Gift His	Inherited Hers	Inherited His	Purchased	Do You Want It? Yes	Do You Want It? No	Appraisal Value	Appraisal Date	Distribution Hers	Distribution His	Distribution Received
Disposal unit (portable)												
Automatic dishwasher												
Broom closet contents												
Kitchen utensils												
Kitchen cutlery												
Radio												
Kitchen dishes												
Glassware												
Chinaware												
Silverware												
Spices												
Cookbooks												
Appliances												

ATTIC/BASEMENT/GARAGE

	Gift Hers	Gift His	Inherited Hers	Inherited His	Purchased	Do You Want It? Yes	Do You Want It? No	Appraisal Value	Appraisal Date	Distribution Hers	Distribution His	Distribution Received
Work bench												
Hand tools												
Power tools												
Tool chest												
Metal shelving												
Freezer												
Dehumidifier												
Bicycles												
Lawn mower												
Lawn sweeper												
Garden hose												
Hedge trimmer												
Snow blower												
Barbeque equipment												
Wheelbarrow												
Ladder												
Holiday decorations												
Seasonal decorations												
Luggage												

SPORTS/HOBBY EQUIPMENT

	Gift Hers	Gift His	Inherited Hers	Inherited His	Purchased	Do You Want It? Yes	Do You Want It? No	Appraisal Value	Appraisal Date	Distribution Hers	Distribution His	Distribution Received
Golf clubs												
Fishing tackle												

FORM-ula™ 27. *(Continued)*

SPORTS/HOBBY EQUIPMT (continued)	How Acquired					Do You Want It?		Appraisal		Distribution		
	Gift		Inherited		Purchased	Yes	No	Value	Date	Hers	His	Received
	Hers	His	Hers	His								
Guns/firearms												
Bowling equipment												
Archery sets												
Tennis equipment												
Camera/photography equipment												
Motors												
Camping equipment												
Ice skates												
Ski equipment												
Bicycles												
Billiard table												
Ping-pong table												
Card table/chairs												
Games												
Toys												
Playground equipment												
Coin collections												
Stamp collections												
Art supplies												
Power tools												
Hand tools												
Baseball equipment												
Soccer equipment												
Exercise equipment												

CHINA/GLASSWARE												
Dinnerware–china												
everyday												
Goblets												
Glasses/tumblers												
Sherbet/parfait												
Punch bowl sets												
Cocktail/liqueur glasses												
Glasses												
Pitchers												
Decanters												
Bowls/vases												
Glass dishes												
Centerpieces												

FORM-ula™ 27. *(Continued)*

SILVERWARE

SILVERWARE	How Acquired					Do You Want It?		Appraisal		Distribution		
	Gift		Inherited		Purchased	Yes	No	Value	Date	Hers	His	Received
	Hers	His	Hers	His								
Place settings												
Serving pieces												
Platters/trays												
Dishes/bowls												
Chafing dishes												
Tea service												
Candle holders												

LINENS

LINENS												
Table cloths												
Napkins												
Place mats												
Towels												
Washcloths												
Blankets/spreads												
Quilts												
Pillows												
Sheets												
Pillow cases												
Electric blankets												
Mattress pads												
Comforters												

MISCELLANEOUS

MISCELLANEOUS												
Telephones												
Phone answering machines												
Fans												
Heaters												
Umbrellas												
Home office equipment												

28: FORM-ula™ for MISSING ITEMS

List any items that you have discovered missing from your home. Make notations as to (1) When you noticed them missing; (2) Where you know or suspect they are; (3) How the items were acquired and by whom.

LIVING ROOM

1. _____

2. _____

3. _____

DINING ROOM

1. _____

2. _____

3. _____

LIBRARY/DEN/STUDY

1. _____

2. _____

3. _____

RECREATION/FAMILY ROOM

1. _____

2. _____

3. _____

BEDROOMS

1. _____

2. _____

3. _____

LAUNDRY/UTILITY ROOM

1. _____

2. _____

3. _____

YARD

1. _____

2. _____

3. _____

MUSICAL INSTRUMENTS/ACCESSORIES

1. _____

2. _____

3. _____

FINE ARTS/COLLECTIONS

1. _____

2. _____

3. _____

FORM-ula™ 28. *(Continued)*

HALLS/SUN ROOM/PORCHES

1. _____
2. _____
3. _____

KITCHEN

1. _____
2. _____
3. _____

ATTIC/BASEMENT/GARAGE

1. _____
2. _____
3. _____

SPORTS/HOBBY EQUIPMENT

1. _____
2. _____
3. _____

CHINA/GLASSWARE

1. _____
2. _____
3. _____

SILVERWARE

1. _____
2. _____
3. _____

LINENS

1. _____
2. _____
3. _____

BATHROOMS

1. _____
2. _____
3. _____

MISCELLANEOUS

1. _____
2. _____
3. _____

<u>29: FORM-ula™ for PERSONAL BANKING</u>

The contents and terms of these accounts will be used in negotiating a financial agreement.

BANK ACCOUNTS

Whose Acct. (Hers/His/Both)	Bank	Savings No.	Checking No.	Signee(s)	Distrib.		Balance at Separation
					Hers	His	

TRUST FUNDS

Beneficiary	Title of Trust	Court Jurisdiction	Name of Trustee	Dist. Date	Amount

NOTE: Trust funds often have legal constraints that remove them in part or entirely from negotiations.

CUSTODIAL ACCOUNTS/ CUSTODY MANAGEMENT ACCOUNTS

Custodian	Custodian For	Bank/Location	Account No.	Amount

SAFETY DEPOSIT BOX

Keyholder	Itemized Inventory Made?	Date of Inventory	Value of Contents

SPECIAL ACCOUNTS

Type of Account	Purchase Amount	Purchase Date	Maturity Amount	Maturity Date	Current Value
Certificates of Deposit					
Treasury Bills					
IRA					
Money Market Accounts					

NOTE: What are the minimum balances for your bank accounts to be free of regular service charges?

30: FORM-ula™ for MONEY LOANED TO OTHERS

These assets are frequently overlooked. Repayment or default of the loans could affect current and future income levels.

Type of Loan	Debtor	Date Borrowed	Payment Schedule	Original Amt. Borrowed	Balance Due
Mortgage					
Second mortgage					
Security deposit–rent					
Security deposit–utility					
Promissory note					
Personal loan					
Business loan					
Educational loan					
Auto loan					
Boat loan					
Other loan					

31: FORM-ula™ for MONEY BORROWED FROM OTHERS

All borrowed money is a *liability*. The separation agreement must address repayment responsibilities.

Type of Loan	Borrowed From	Address	Phone	Account No.	Date Acct. Opened	Original Amount	Monthly Payment	Balance Due	Asset Pledged
Mortgage									
Home equity									
Promissory note									
Personal loan									
Business loan									
Educational loan									
Auto loan									
Boat loan									
Other loan									

FORM-ula™ 31. *(Continued)*

Type of Loan	Borrowed From	Address	Phone	Account No.	Date Acct. Opened	Original Amount	Monthly Payment	Balance Due	Asset Pledged
Bank cards (e.g., Visa)									
Department Stores									
Membership Cards (e.g., American Express)									
Travel Cards									
Airline									
Rental car									
Auto Service Cards (e.g., Mobil)									

32: FORM-ula™ for INVESTMENTS

Most of this information can be found on the monthly statements and buy/sell tickets, or from your stockbroker.

Investment Vehicle	Company	Name of Broker	Date Purch.	Purch. Cost	On Margin?	Source of Money to Buy Stock	Owner of Stock	Certif. Location	Annual Income	Current Market Value	Sell Price	Date Sold
Stocks												
Options												
Mutual funds												

FORM-ula™ 32. (Continued)

Investment Vehicle	Issued By	Name of Broker	Date Purch.	Purch. Cost	Face Amount	Source of Money to Buy Item	Owner of Item	Certif. Location	Maturity Date	Current Market Value	Intr. Rate	Sell Price	Date Sold
Bonds													
Corporate													
Municipal													
Tax exempt													
US savings													

ADDITIONAL INVESTMENTS

☐ Agricultural commodities
☐ Precious-metal commodities
☐ Gems
☐ Other commodities/Futures

☐ Oil and mineral leases
☐ Tax-shelter annuities
☐ Tax-shelter investments

☐ Government treasury bills
☐ Government treasury notes
☐ Government treasury bonds
☐ Government savings bonds

☐ Foreign treasury bonds
☐ Foreign treasury notes
☐ Foreign currency
☐ Membership in an investment club

☐ Any offshore (outside the US) bank accounts
☐ Any offshore post office accounts

After compiling this information, you may feel more comfortable seeking professional financial expertise. If your investment information does not fit in the spaces on the grid, or if you have checked any of the boxes above, you *must* seek specialized assistance from financial professionals.

NOTE The market value of securities may not be the same as the actual value because of restrictions or taxes to be paid upon sale.

NOTE If a brokerage house fails, the Securities Investor Protection Corp. (SIPC) is responsible for the transfer of accounts to other houses or reimbursement of equities and cash up to $500,000. Stocks, bonds, notes, and most publicly-offered limited-partnerships are covered. Gold, silver, and commodities are not covered.

33: FORM-ula™ for TITLES AND DEEDS

You should know the current status of real estate and vehicle assets before negotiating a financial settlement. Deeds are registered in the city/town where the property is located. Burial plot records are in the management business offices. Current values of vehicles are in a listing commonly referred to as a "blue book," which is in libraries and at auto dealerships.

	Title Holder	Original Value	Current Value	Assessed Value	Prepayment Penalties (yes/no)	Registry Location	Book	Page	Liens
Vehicles									
Automobile									
Boat									
Recreational vehicle									
Real Estate									
Primary residence									
Vacation home									
Rental property									
Time share									
Vacant land									
Cemetery plot/niche									
Leasehold interests									

NOTE Include copies of appraisals.
1. Are there any title searches or verifications in process? If so, highlight the property in question.
2. Did you provide funds for any marital property for which you are not legally recorded as a co-owner? If so, explain circumstances on this sheet.

34: FORM-ula™ for REAL ESTATE CAPITAL IMPROVEMENTS

Information about capital improvements is used for tax purposes and to help to determine the dollar value of the family home.

Location of Property	Date of Purchase	Orig. Purchase Price	
Capital Improvements	Date	Cost	Copy of Paid Bill Attached?

35: FORM-ula™ for PERSONAL HEALTH

The status of your health is important in negotiating continued medical coverage and the distribution of financial resources.

DO ANY OF THE FOLLOWING APPLY?

☐ Vision problems	☐ Emphysema	☐ Sexual disorders
☐ Moderate	☐ Hernia	☐ Skin disease
☐ Severe	☐ Hemorrhoids	☐ Tuberculosis
☐ Hearing impairment	☐ Insomnia	☐ Varicose veins
☐ Moderate	☐ High blood pressure	☐ Impotence
☐ Severe	☐ Diabetes	☐ Infertility
☐ Arthritis	☐ Heart problems	☐ Sterility
☐ Allergy	☐ High cholesterol	☐ AIDS
☐ Anemia	☐ Epilepsy	☐ Herpes
☐ Asthma	☐ Multiple sclerosis	☐ Genital warts
☐ Cancer	☐ Kidney disease	☐ Other venereal disease
☐ Circulatory problems	☐ Muscular dystrophy	☐ Eating disorders
☐ Ulcers	☐ Parkinson's disease	☐ Hospitalization for psychological illness
☐ Nervous-system disorders	☐ Prostate disorders	☐ Ailments of teeth and gums
☐ Special handicap? _____		

☐ Is there any reason to suspect currently unsymptomatic or potential health problems? (e.g., family history of cancer, stroke, diabetes, or exposure to agent orange, asbestos, lead paint, toxic waste, etc.)

Current or potential health problems requiring special attention or care include:

_____

_____

CURRENT HEALTH RESOURCES

	Name	Address	Phone	Date Last Visit
Physician				
Dentist				
Optometrist				
Specialist				
Therapist				
Pharmacy				

FORM-ula™ 35. *(Continued)*

MEDICATION

Name of Medication	Purpose of Medication	Frequency of Usage	Cost

PERSONAL HABITS

	Frequency	Cost	Comments
Exercise			
Special diet			
Smoking			
Drinking			
Drug addiction			
Gambling			

INSURANCE

Type of Coverage	Name of Company	Address	Policy Number	Amount of Coverage
Medical				
Dental				
Short-term disab.				
Long-term disab.				
Life insurance				
Life insurance				

Which policies will continue after the divorce?

☐ Medical   ☐ Dental   ☐ STD   ☐ LTD   ☐ Life Insurance

36: FORM-ula™ for MEDICAL INSURANCE

What coverage do you have now? What coverage will be needed after the divorce?

Named insured _____ SS/ID No. _____

Policy No. _____ Expiration date _____

Group name and address _____

Insurance co. name and address _____

Premium $ _____ per _____

Is this payment made by:

☐ Payroll deduction? Whose paycheck? _____

☐ Automatic checking-account deduction? Whose account? _____

☐ Paid by third party (trust, other family member, etc.)? Who? _____

☐ Paid by check or money order. Who? _____

Family members covered

_____

_____

_____

_____

_____

_____

Claims procedure _____

_____

_____

COVERAGE

	Payment/per	Limit
☐ Doctor's office visits	_____	_____
☐ Prescriptions	_____	_____
☐ Well-baby care	_____	_____
☐ Routine physicals	_____	_____
☐ Pre-existing conditions	_____	_____
☐ Chronic problems	_____	_____
☐ Immunizations	_____	_____

FORM-ula™ 36. *(Continued)*

COVERAGE

	Payment/per	Limit
☐ Allergy shots	_____	_____
☐ Physical therapy	_____	_____
☐ Chiropractor	_____	_____
☐ Walk-in clinics	_____	_____
☐ Emergency room	_____	_____
☐ Hospital	_____	_____
☐ Dental–cleaning	_____	_____
☐ Dental–restoration	_____	_____
☐ Dental–X-rays	_____	_____
☐ Dental–periodontal	_____	_____
☐ Dental–orthodontic	_____	_____
☐ Psychologist	_____	_____
☐ Psychiatric–outpatient	_____	_____
☐ Psychiatric–inpatient	_____	_____
☐ Drug/Alcohol treatment programs	_____	_____

Are any family members uninsurable or do they require a specialized policy? If so, who? Explain.

_____

_____

_____

37: FORM-ula™ for LIFE INSURANCE

Complete one form for each life insurance policy on any member of the family: husband, wife, and children. Policies can be a negotiable issue regarding ownership, beneficiaries, and support-payment assurance.

Name of insured _____ Owner of policy _____

Company name and address _____

_____

Agent name and address _____

_____ Phone _____

Policy no. _____

Premium $ _____ per _____ paid by _____

Waiver of premium? ☐ Yes   ☐ No

TYPE OF INSURANCE

☐ Term   ☐ Universal   ☐ Whole life

DOLLAR VALUE

Face value _____

Less amount borrowed (–) _____

= Death benefit _____

Avail. cash value _____

Dividends _____ per _____

Primary beneficiary _____

Contingent beneficiary _____

38: FORM-ula™ for DISABILITY INSURANCE

Insurance records are not complete without disability insurance information. Your attorney can tell you if payments under this coverage are relevant to your financial agreement.

Name of insured _____ SS/ID No. _____

How long is the waiting period? _____ How long is the coverage period? _____

Policy No. _____ Expiration date _____

Group name and address (if applicable) _____

_____

_____

Insurance co. name and address _____

Premium $ _____ per _____

Is this payment made by:

☐ Payroll deduction? Whose paycheck? _____

☐ Automatic checking-account deduction? Whose account? _____

☐ Paid by third party (trust, other family member, etc.)? Who? _____

☐ Paid by check or money order. Who? _____

Family members covered

_____ _____ _____

_____ _____ _____

_____ _____ _____

Claims procedure

_____

_____

_____

Terms of coverage

_____

_____

_____

39: FORM-ula™ for HOMEOWNER'S/RENTER'S INSURANCE

This information is written in the individual policies or can be obtained by calling your insurance agent.

	Residence	Second Home
Location address		
Name of insured		
Loss payee (if any)		
Insurance company		
Address		
Agent address/phone		
Policy no.		
Expiration date		
Premium per year		
Amount of Coverage:		
Dwelling		
Contents		

RESIDENCE

Form
☐ Standard
☐ Replacement

Discounts
☐ Burglar alarm
☐ Fire alarm
☐ Major restoration

FEMA Insurance*
☐ Flood
☐ Earthquake

SECOND HOME

Form
☐ Standard
☐ Replacement

Discounts
☐ Burglar alarm
☐ Fire alarm
☐ Major restoration

FEMA Insurance
☐ Flood
☐ Earthquake

*Federal Emergency Management Agency. FEMA policies are separate insurance policies. If you have this type of coverage, copy this form and fill in information for these policies to keep it separate.

RIDERS TO HOMEOWNER'S/TENANT'S INSURANCE POLICIES

Item/Amount	Residence	Second Home

_____
Date

40: FORM-ula™ for AUTOMOBILE INSURANCE

This information appears on individual policies or can be obtained by calling your insurance agent.

Name of insured _____

Insurance co. _____

Policy No. _____ Expiration date _____

Total premium _____ per _____

Agent name and address _____

	Make	Model	Year	ID No.	Plate No.	Mileage	Principal Driver
Vehicle No. 1							
Vehicle No. 2							
Vehicle No. 3							
Vehicle No. 4							

COVERAGE	Vehicle No. 1	Vehicle No. 2	Vehicle No. 3	Vehicle No. 4
Liability				
Bodily injury				
Property damage				
Uninsured motorists				
Collision				
Deductible				
Comprehensive				
Deductible				
Glass				
Rental reimbursement				
Towing and labor				
Discounts:				
Good Student				
Driver's Education				

FORM-ula™ 40. *(Continued)*

COVERAGE	Vehicle No. 1	Vehicle No. 2	Vehicle No. 3	Vehicle No. 4
Distant student				
Antitheft devices				
Older driver				
Loss Payee (if any)				

What coverage, if any, does your insurance provide for rental cars? _____

Are you covered by an umbrella policy? _____

41: FORM-ula™ for RECREATIONAL VEHICLE INSURANCE

This information appears on individual policies or can be obtained by calling your insurance agent.

Name of insured _____

Insurance co. _____

Policy no. _____ Expiration date _____

Total premium _____ per _____

Agent name and address _____

BOAT, RV, etc.	Make	Model	Year	ID No.	Registration Number	Mileage if applicable	Principal Operator
No. 1							
No. 2							
No. 3							
No. 4							

COVERAGE	No. 1	No. 2	No. 3	No. 4
Liability				
Bodily injury				
Property damage				
Uninsured motorists				
Collision				
Deductible				
Comprehensive				
Deductible				
Glass				
Rental reimbursement				
Towing and labor				
Discounts				
Good Student				
Driver's Education				

FORM-ula™ 41. *(Continued)*

COVERAGE	No. 1	No. 2	No. 3	No. 4
Distant student				
Antitheft devices				
Older driver				
Loss Payee **(if any)**				

Special policy provisions

_____

_____

_____

_____

42: FORM-ula™ for TAX RETURNS

If you do not have copies of your prior tax returns, obtain Form 4506, Request for Copy of Tax Form, from a local CPA firm. Copies of jointly-filed tax forms may be furnished to either the wife or husband. Only one signature is required. Allow at least six weeks for processing after the form is filed. Current cost is $4.25 for each tax period requested.

NOTE If you had your tax form filled out by a paid preparer, check first to see if you can get a copy from the preparer.

IRS Form(s) Used

- ☐ 1040A
- ☐ 1040
- ☐ Schedule A
- ☐ Schedule B
- ☐ Schedule C
- ☐ Schedule D
- ☐ Schedule E
- ☐ Schedule SE
- ☐ Form 2106
- ☐ Farm Income
- ☐ Sole Proprietor
- ☐ Partnership
- ☐ Corporation
- ☐ Other IRS schedules and forms _____

_____
(List Numbers)

	Year	Joint	Separate
Federal income tax return (include all schedules filed)			
State income tax return			
City income tax return			
Inheritance/gift tax return			
Other tax records			

FORM-ula™ 42. *(Continued)*

Tax loss carrying forward from current and prior years' tax returns _____

Date of last joint filing with spouse _____

Amount of refund due (if any) _____

Who prepared returns (person/firm)? _____

_____

Location of documentation used to prepare tax returns in prior years? _____

_____

Have plans been made to file jointly or separately for the current tax year? _____

If jointly, who is assuming responsibility for accumulating the necessary information?

_____

_____
Date

43: FORM-ula™ for EMPLOYMENT AND EDUCATION

Complete this form if you do not have a current résumé or curriculum vitae.

CURRENT EMPLOYMENT INFORMATION

Company _____   Title _____

Address _____   Dates of employment _____

Type of company _____

Major responsibilities _____

☐ Full-time   ☐ Part-time   Days _____   Hours _____

Type of business _____

☐ Employee   ☐ Partner   ☐ Associate   ☐ Sole proprietor

(Check all that apply if more than one job or business)

If Not Currently Employed

Why not? _____

Is future employment possible? _____

Is future employment necessary? _____

Does either spouse need further ☐ training or ☐ education? Explain: _____

Is either spouse contemplating an employment change? _____ Which one? _____

How will this affect family income? _____

EMPLOYMENT HISTORY

Company _____   Title _____

Address _____   Dates of employment _____

Type of company _____

Major responsibilities _____

Company _____   Title _____

Address _____   Dates of employment _____

Type of company _____

Major responsibilities _____

Company _____   Title _____

Address _____   Dates of employment _____

Type of company _____

Major responsibilities _____

EDUCATION   Year Graduated   Degree

High school _____

College _____

Graduate school _____

Special training/certification _____

Special licenses/certification _____

MILITARY SERVICE

☐ Currently in service _____

☐ Branch of service _____   Date/location of discharge _____

Rank _____   Service No. _____

44: FORM-ula™ for EMPLOYER POLICIES AND BENEFITS

Many of the following items affect lifestyle, and they all have implications for the future status of your financial security. Use this checklist to make sure that you have documentation for all of the items that apply.

	Does It Exist?		Do You Have It?	
	His	Hers	His	Hers
Employer annual reports (for 2 yrs)				
Employer personnel handbook				
Employer benefit booklets				
medical coverage				
life insurance program				
short- and long-term disability				
unemployment compensation				
employee loan policies				
credit union				
profit sharing				
employee stock option plan				
retirement policies				
401K				
child care facilities				
Travel and expense account				
Agreements				
Employment contracts				
Patents/Copyrights				
Royalties				
Perks (executive compensation)				
Life insurance				
Business and social club memberships				
Credit card(s)				
Automobile(s)				
insurance				
maintenance and repairs				
gas and oil				
Education/training				
Paid vacations				

You may also want to make notes on the company's attitude toward employees' family responsibilities, community involvement, overtime or extended work hours, compensatory time, required travel, and flex time.

45: FORM-ula™ for PROPRIETORSHIPS, PARTNERSHIPS, PROFESSIONAL CORPORATIONS, AND FAMILY-OWNED BUSINESSES

Many of these items affect lifestyle and they all have implications for the future status of your financial security. Use this checklist to make sure that you have documentation for all of the items that apply.

	Does It Exist?		Do You Have It?	
	His	Hers	His	Hers
☐ Financial papers				
☐ Tax returns (last 2-3 years)				
☐ Current profit and loss statements				
☐ Appraisal of nontraded company				
☐ Percentage of ownership				
☐ Personnel handbook				
☐ Benefit booklets				
☐ Medical coverage				
☐ Life insurance program				
☐ Short- and long-term disability				
☐ Unemployment compensation				
☐ Employee loan policies				
☐ Credit union				
☐ Profit sharing				
☐ Employee stock option plan				
☐ Retirement policies				
☐ 401K/Keogh Plan				
☐ Simplified Employee Pensions (SEPs)				
☐ Child care facilities				
☐ Agreements				
☐ Travel and expense account agreements				
☐ Cosigned loans for entrepreneurial ventures				
☐ Buy and sell agreements				
☐ Noncompete clauses				
☐ Employment contracts				
☐ Patents				
☐ Royalties				
☐ Copyrights				
☐ Work-in-progress				
☐ Contracts for personal service				

FORM-ula™ 45. *(Continued)*

	Does It Exist?		Do You Have It?	
	His	Hers	His	Hers
☐ Company-owned personal-use assets				
☐ Vacation home				
☐ Automobile(s)				
☐ Plane				
☐ Boat(s)				
☐ Perks				
☐ Free insurance (fully-paid premiums)				
☐ Business and social club memberships				
☐ Education/training				
☐ Paid vacations				
☐ Automobile expenses				

NOTE All of the above items are useful in negotiating the financial terms of your divorce as well as the child custody and visitation issues. With this in mind, you may want to make additional notes on items such as:

	Does It Exist?		Do You Have It?	
	His	Hers	His	Hers
☐ Unrecorded cash payments				
☐ Barter arrangements/trade-offs				
☐ Flex-time				
☐ Attitude toward family responsibilities and community involvement				
☐ Overtime and extended work hours				
☐ Compensatory time				
☐ Required travel				

46: FORM-ula™ for INCOME RECORDS

Use this checklist to make sure that income records are complete. Make note of any missing items.

	Does It Exist?		Do You Have It?	
	His	Hers	His	Hers

WORK

☐ Wages/salary

   ☐ Paycheck records (stubs, vouchers, etc.)

   ☐ Regular salary

   ☐ Overtime

   ☐ Unused vacation and sick pay

☐ Commission statements

☐ Bonuses

☐ Cash awards and incentives

☐ Salary continuation contract

☐ Service tips

☐ Expense accounts, reimbursed

☐ Tuition refund

☐ Self-employed?

UNEMPLOYMENT/DISABILITY BENEFITS

☐ Unemployment compensation

☐ Workmen's compensation

☐ Full disability

☐ Partial disability

☐ Military disability

INVESTMENTS

   ☐ Dividends

   ☐ Interest

   ☐ Capital gains

   ☐ Rental income

FINANCIAL PLANS

☐ Social Security

   ☐ Self

   ☐ Spouse

   ☐ Children

☐ Retirement

   ☐ Personal plans (IRA, Keogh)

	Does It Exist?		Do You Have It?	
	His	Hers	His	Hers
☐ Corporate (Employer's Pension)				
☐ Annuities				
☐ Military				
OTHER SOURCES				
☐ Gifts				
☐ Inheritances/legacies				
☐ Residual rights				
☐ Royalties				
☐ Trust fund income				
☐ Loan repayments				
☐ Secured				
☐ Unsecured				
☐ Tax refunds				
☐ Fiduciary commissions				
☐ Fraternal/lodge benefits				
☐ Windfall (lottery)				
TEMPORARY				
☐ Child and spousal support				
☐ Contribution to household from other sources				
☐ Public assistance (welfare, AFDC, etc.)				
MISCELLANEOUS				
☐ Unrecorded cash payments				
☐ Value of barter and trade arrangements				
☐ Value of paid vacations				
☐ Deferred income				
☐ Cash value of whole life				
☐ Insurance policies				
☐ Security deposits (rent, utilities, etc.)				

47: FORM-ula™ for RETIREMENT DOLLARS

Use this checklist to make sure that you have documentation for all of the following which apply.

	Does It Exist?		Do You Have It?	
	His	Hers	His	Hers
☐ IRA accounts				
☐ Defined contribution plans				
☐ Profit sharing				
☐ 401K (deferred salary)				
☐ Savings				
☐ Thrift				
☐ ESOP (employee stock ownership)				
☐ Keogh				
☐ Defined benefit plans				
☐ Pension plans				
☐ Excess nonqualified plans				
☐ Simplified Employee Pensions (SEPs)				
☐ Government plans				
☐ US civil service				
☐ State employees				
☐ Military				
☐ Veterans benefits				
☐ Special accounts				
☐ Savings banks				
☐ Credit union				
☐ Other				
☐ Investment accounts				
☐ Insurance plans				
☐ Social Security				

48: FORM-ula™ for ASSETS

INCOME-PRODUCING ASSETS Current Assets	Current Value	Annual Income	How Held			Distribution		
			His	Hers	Joint	His	Hers	Date Rec'd.
Checking accounts–min. bal. kept for no-charge checking								
Savings accounts								
Credit union accounts								
Share draft accounts								
Money market funds								
Certificates of deposit								
Savings bonds								
Promissory notes receivable								
Mortgages receivable								
Rental Income								
Restricted access								
Stock options								
Trust funds								
IRA/Keogh/pension								
401K								
Simplified Employee Pensions (SEPs)								
Legacies								
Residual rights								
Stocks								
Bonds								
Mutual funds								
Syndication interests								

NON-INCOME-PRODUCING ASSETS Current Assets	Current Value	Annual Income	How Held			Distribution		
			His	Hers	Joint	His	Hers	Date Rec'd.
Personal residence								
Recreational property								
Automobiles								
Recreational vehicles/boats								

FORM-ula™ 48. *(Continued)*

NON-INCOME-PRODUCING ASSETS *(continued)* Current Assets	Current Value	Annual Income	How Held			Distribution		
			His	Hers	Joint	His	Hers	Date Rec'd.
Cash value of life insurance								
Business interests								
Home furnishings								
Jewelry/furs								
Antiques/fine arts								
Hobby collection								
Stamp collections								
Foreign currency								

49: FORM-ula™ for LIABILITIES

Liabilities	Who Incurred Debt?	When?	PAYMENTS			
			Monthly Payment	Last Pmt. Made	Final Pmt. Due (date)	Balance Due
Current Bills Outstanding						
Mortgage or rent						
Home-equity balloon loan						
Monthly utilities						
Homeowner's or renter's insurance						
Car insurance						
Life insurance						
Medical insurance						
Charge accounts						
Credit card accounts						
Doctors						
Dentists						
Attorneys						
Accountants						
Subtotal						
Taxes to Date Which Have Not Been Withheld/Paid						
Federal income taxes						
State and city income taxes						
Social Security tax						
Real estate taxes						
Personal property taxes						
Assessments (sewer, etc.)						
Unpaid income taxes for prior years						
Income tax interest or penalties						

FORM-ula™ 49. (Continued)

Liabilities	Who Incurred Debt?	When?	PAYMENTS			
			Monthly Payment	Last Pmt. Made	Final Pmt. Due (date)	Balance Due
Capital-gains tax						
Subtotal						
Loans to be Repaid						
Mortgage(s) on home(s)						
Mortgage(s) on other property(ies)						
Car payment						
Car payment (2d car)						
Recreational vehicle pmt.						
Furniture installment						
Appliance installment						
Home improvement						
Education and training						
Life insurance						
Stock purchase on margin						
Other bank loans						
Debts to friends						
Debts to business assoc.						
Debts due to gambling, drug, or alcohol abuse						
Loans from family living expenses for personal expenditures						
Subtotal						
Contractual Obligations						
Any financial obligations to spouse of former marriage						

FORM-ula™ 49. *(Continued)*

Liabilities	Who Incurred Debt?	When?	PAYMENTS Monthly Payment	Last Pmt. Made	Final Pmt. Due (date)	Balance Due
Lease commitments (cars, buildings, office equipment, etc.)						
Medical/dental						
Sales contracts (encyclopedia companies, dinnerware, record and book clubs, enrichment programs, etc.)						
Union and other dues						
Liens payable						
Cosigned loans						
Subtotal						
Contingent Liabilities						
(Money you may have to pay if you lose a lawsuit or purchase property that you have already agreed to buy, etc.)						

50: FORM-ula™ for GENERIC FINANCIAL STATEMENT

ASSETS	Indiv.	Joint	If joint w/whom	LIABILITIES	Indiv.	Joint	If joint w/whom
Cash on hand and in banks				Notes payable to banks–secured			
US government securities				–unsecured			
Listed securities				Notes payable to relatives			
Unlisted securities				Notes payable to others			
Mortgages owned				Accounts and bills due			
Accounts and notes receivable				Accrued interest, etc.			
due from relatives and friends				Taxes unpaid or accrued			
Accounts and notes receivable				Mortgages payable on real estate			
due from others –good				Chattel mortgages and other liens			
–doubtful				payable			
Real estate owned				Other debts–itemize			
Cash value life insurance							
Automobiles							
Personal property							
Other assets–itemize				TOTAL LIABILITIES			
				NET WORTH			
				TOTAL LIABILITIES			
TOTAL ASSETS				AND NET WORTH			

SOURCE OF INCOME				PERSONAL INFORMATION			

Alimony, child support, or maintenance income need not be revealed if you do not wish it to be considered as a basis for repaying this obligation.

If you are applying for individual credit, information about your spouse or ex-spouse need not be revealed unless you are relying on income from alimony, child support, or maintenance or on the income or assets of another person as a basis for repaying this obligation.

	Indiv.	Joint	If joint w/whom
Salary			
Bonds and commissions			
Dividends and bond interest			
Real estate income			
Other income–itemize			
TOTAL			

Business or occupation:

Partner or officer in other venture:

MARITAL STATUS (Do not complete if this is submitted for individual unsecured credit.)

No. of Dependents

☐ Married
☐ Separated
☐ Unmarried (including single, divorced, or widowed)

CONTINGENT LIABILITIES				GENERAL INFORMATION			

	Indiv.	Joint	If joint w/whom
As endorser or co-maker			
On leases or contracts			
Legal claims			
Taxes not shown above:			
Income taxes			
Delinquent or contested taxes			
OTHER SPECIAL DEBTS			

Are any assets pledged? _____

Are you a defendant in any suit or legal action?
_____

Personal bank accounts carried at:

Individual _____

Joint _____

If joint, with whom? _____

Have you ever taken bankruptcy? If yes, explain _____
_____

LIST OF BANKS AND FINANCE COMPANIES WHERE CREDIT HAS BEEN OBTAINED				
NAME(S) IN WHICH OBTAINED	NAME OF BANK OR COMPANY	HIGH CREDIT	PRESENT BALANCE	TYPE OF LOAN

FORM-ula™ 50. *(Continued)*

REMARKS
_____
_____
_____

US GOVERNMENT AND LISTED STOCKS AND BONDS			
HELD IN NAME(S) OF	DESCRIPTION	COST	MARKET VALUE

MORTGAGES, UNLISTED SECURITIES, AND OTHER INVESTMENTS			
HELD IN NAME(S) OF	DESCRIPTION, INCLUDING MATURITIES	COST	MARKET VALUE

REAL ESTATE OWNED				
DESCRIPTION AND LOCATION	TITLE IN NAME(S) OF	MARKET VALUE	MORTGAGES	TAXES PAID TO

LIFE INSURANCE					
OWNER	NAME OF COMPANY	BENEFICIARY	AMOUNT	CASH VALUE	LOANS

ACCOUNTS AND NOTES RECEIVABLES		
OWNER(S)	DEBTOR AND ADDRESS	PRESENT BALANCE DUE

PERSONAL PROPERTY AND VEHICLES			
DESCRIPTION AND LOCATION	OWNER(S)		MORTGAGES

The foregoing financial statement and explanations have been fairly and correctly presented according to the best of my knowledge and belief.

Date signed _____ , 19 ____   Signature _____

Date signed _____ , 19 ____   Signature _____

51: FORM-ula™ for MEDICAL PERMISSION TO TREAT MINOR CHILD

To Whom it May Concern:

Regarding _____
(Give full name of child, address, date of birth, and Social Security number.)

_____

    As the parents of the above-named child, you have our permission to provide emergency medical treatment to this child.

Known allergies are _____
(List any known allergies to food, medication, etc. or write NONE.)

The child's regular doctor is _____
(Give name, complete address, and telephone number.)

_____

The child is insured under medical policy _____
(Give company, policy number, listed insured's name and ID, if required.)

_____

_____
(Signature)

_____
(Parent name)

_____
(Parent address)

_____

Work phone _____

Home phone _____

_____
(Notary Public)

_____
(Date)

_____
(My commission expires)

_____
(Signature)

_____
(Parent name)

_____
(Parent address)

_____

Work phone _____

Home phone _____

_____
(Notary Public)

_____
(Date)

_____
(My commission expires)

NOTE This letter *must* be notarized.

52: FORM-ula™ for DUPLICATE INFORMATION REQUEST

Date _____

To _____
       (Name)

_____
       (Address)

_____

Regarding _____ and _____.
                              (Names of children)

     There is frequent communication between the parents regarding the health, education, and general welfare of their children.

     This is to advise you that it is agreed between _____ and _____, the parents of the children named above, that all records, verbal information, and written correspondence regarding their children, _____ and _____, is to be equally available to both parents.

Sincerely,

_____   _____
(Signature)   (Signature)

_____   _____
(Parent name)   (Parent name)

_____   _____
(Parent address)   (Parent address)

_____   _____

Work phone _____   Work phone _____

Home phone _____   Home phone _____

_____ **Date**

53: FORM-ula™ for CONSENT TO TRAVEL

Date _____

To Whom It May Concern:

_____ and _____ ,
(Names of parents)

are the parents of _____ and _____ .
(Names of children)

_____ and _____ are
(Names of children)

planning a trip with their (mother) (father) to _____ . The departure date is

_____ , with a scheduled return on _____ . They will be

traveling by _____ .
(If other than by car, give schedules, flight numbers, etc.)

I have knowledge of these trip plans and give my consent for _____

and _____ to travel with _____ .

_____
(Signature of nonaccompanying parent)

_____
(Parent name)

_____
(Parent address)

_____

Work phone _____

Home phone _____

NOTE You may want to have the signature notarized.

54: FORM-ula™ for ATTORNEY SELECTION

Use a separate FORM-ula 54 for each attorney that you interview. These completed pages will give you a basis for comparison and help you to make your final selection. Divorce procedures and regulations vary from state to state. In order to understand your legal, financial, and personal rights, discuss the following questions.

ATTORNEY _____

Firm name _____

Address _____

Phone No. _____ Secretary's name _____

Directions to office _____

_____

Is there a fee for the initial consultation? If so, amount _____

Is a retainer fee required? _____ How much? _____ When? _____

What is the hourly fee? _____

What is the attorney's best estimate of the total cost of the divorce? _____

PROFESSIONAL CREDENTIALS AND BACKGROUND

☐ Member, Academy of Matrimonial Lawyers.

☐ Bar-certified family law specialist.

☐ Active on family law committees.

☐ All or majority of practice in family law.

Years of experience _____

Does attorney have experience in local courts and have familiarity with local court biases regarding:

☐ Child custody and support.

☐ Alimony and property division.

FORM-ula™ 54. *(Continued)*

QUESTIONS TO ASK THE ATTORNEY

LEGAL

For first meeting discussion:

What rights do I have in this jurisdiction? _____

_____

What kind of residency requirements are there? _____

_____

What are the current state laws on marriage dissolution? _____

_____

How do the laws in my state deal with distribution of property?_____

_____

What are my options? (divorce, legal separation, annulment) _____

_____

Which spouse should begin the legal action of filing for divorce? _____

_____

What is the procedure for handling physical, emotional, or child abuse? (documented or suspected) ___

_____

How will we work together to develop the case strategy? _____

_____

For second meeting discussion:

What happens to an existing power of attorney? _____

_____

Do I need witnesses for contested or uncontested action? _____

_____

Will there be legal counsel for our children? _____

_____

What happens to minor children if the custodial parent is incapacitated or dies? _____

_____

Which divorce records are public? _____

_____

FORM-ula™ 54. *(Continued)*

FINANCIAL

For first meeting discussion:

Who is responsible for what debts? (household, credit, loans, medical, insurance, food, clothing, personal, and children) _____

_____

What precedence is set by interim voluntary-support payments? _____

_____

For second meeting discussion:

When do we terminate joint accounts and credit cards? _____

_____

What are the advantages and disadvantages of filing a joint tax return? _____

_____

PERSONAL

For first meeting discussion:

Who is to leave the marital home and when? _____

_____

Is dating permissible during the divorce process? What are the legal and practical implications? _____

_____

Does sex with my spouse affect divorce procedures or agreements? _____

_____

When both spouses are still in the same household during the divorce period, what are their caretaking obligations to each other? _____

_____

What legal information about the divorce should be given to children, family and friends? When? ____

_____

How? _____

_____

For second meeting discussion:

What happens if there is a reconciliation after starting the legal process? _____

_____

Are there special procedures for changing or keeping my last name as part of the divorce agreement?

_____

FORM-ula™ 54. *(Continued)*

WILLINGNESS TO COMMUNICATE ANALYSIS, EVALUATION, AND STRATEGY

- ☐ Explains rules of power and leverage.
- ☐ Explains approach to be taken and advantage over other possible approaches.
- ☐ Explains the order in which events will occur.
- ☐ Explains priorities of the issues.
- ☐ Gives estimates of timing—before agreement.
- ☐ Gives estimates of timing—after agreement.

DOES ATTORNEY UNDERSTAND AND EXPLAIN TAX IMPLICATIONS OF:

- ☐ Divorce proceedings.
- ☐ Divorce settlement.
- ☐ Marital property.
- ☐ Alimony.
- ☐ Child support.

PERSONALITY FIT

- ☐ Empathetic (and on your side).
- ☐ Chemistry seems to work.
- ☐ Compatible ideas and principles.
- ☐ Doesn't overwhelm or intimidate you.
- ☐ Listens for questions you haven't asked.
- ☐ Potentially comfortable working together.
- ☐ Will be well-balanced to spouse's personality.
- ☐ Doesn't overwhelm you with professional jargon.
- ☐ Honest and frank in opinions, analyses, and judgements.
- ☐ Suitable attitudes towards sole or joint custody of children.
- ☐ Will see that you are kept well-informed on a reasonable basis.
- ☐ Is available for emergency calls at home (not just office hours).
- ☐ Seems to have enough interest in you as a person not just as a case.

GENERAL IMPRESSIONS

Do you feel that the attorney has skills as a mediator, arbitrator, negotiator, and litigator to bring about a fair and successful settlement of your divorce?

_____

_____

_____

_____

_____

55: FORM-ula™ for DIVORCE SETTLEMENTS: LIFE INSURANCE CHECKLIST
(Information supplied by Northwestern Mutual Life Insurance Company)

All life insurance policies owned by either spouse should be specifically identified. Policy numbers should be shown along with the name of the insured and the issuing company. The disposition of each policy should be clearly set out in the agreement or judgement.

I.   Ownership

A.   Is the policy ownership to remain as it is?

B.   Is there to be a transfer of policy ownership? If so, who is to be the new owner?

    (1)   Unrestricted transfer?
    (2)   Restricted transfer? What are the restrictions?
    (3)   Is ownership to revert to the original owner at some future date or upon some future occurrence (e.g., death, remarriage, or termination of spousal maintenance)?

C.   If transfer of ownership is subject to existing policy indebtedness, this should be expressly recognized in the agreement or judgement; if repayment of indebtedness is required, that should be clearly specified.

II.   Beneficiaries

A.   Is the policyowner to have the right to designate the beneficiaries on a revocable basis?

B.   Is the policyowner required to designate a certain beneficiary or beneficiaries on a restricted basis? (CAUTION: re use of word "Irrevocable") If so:

    (1)   Is this restriction subject to a contingency for each beneficiary (e.g., restriction ends on remarriage of beneficiary)?

    (2)   If children are to be named, is this requirement for each child to continue only until the child reaches majority or is otherwise emancipated?

C.   If the policy is of a type that matures for payment of proceeds during the insured's lifetime (e.g., endowment, deferred annuity, etc.), who is to receive the maturity proceeds? (Note: Policies of this type typically provide separate beneficial interests for the death proceeds and the maturity proceeds.)

III.   Exercise of the Other Policy Rights

   A.   If restricted policy ownership or restricted beneficiary interests are involved, how are the following policy rights affected?

   (1)   Surrender of policy for cash
   (2)   Policy loans
   (3)   Election of settlement options for payment of proceeds
   (4)   Renewal of a term policy
   (5)   Conversion of a term policy to a permanent policy
   (6)   Disposition of annual dividends
   (7)   Guaranteed right, if any, to purchase additional insurance

IV.   Premiums

   A.   Who will pay the premiums and for what period of time?

   B.   Where the premium payer is required to notify another party each time that a premium has been paid, consideration should be given to an arrangement made between the parties themselves to have evidence of payment furnished at least ten days before the end of the policy's grace period. The insurer cannot furnish this information, since it would not know of any default in premium payment until after the policy grace period has expired.

   C.   Is the appropriate nonforfeiture provision in effect in the event a premium is not paid?

   (1)   Automatic premium loan
   (2)   Paid-up insurance
   (3)   Extended term insurance

V.   Further Considerations

   A.   Are the rights of the parties under the property settlement agreement consistent with the provisions of the judgement?

   B.   If the agreement or judgement provides for a change in the terms of a life insurance policy, it should be drafted so as to order the proper party to make the desired change and to execute the necessary forms required by the insurer to complete the change. The agreement or judgement should also provide that in the event the proper party does not comply with the order by a given date, an officer of the court will be authorized to execute the necessary forms on behalf of the proper party.

   C.   Each insurance company whose policies are referred to in the property settlement agreement or judgement should be notified promptly. Forms, as needed, can then be prepared for signing by the appropriate parties and, in any event, the company's records for each policy can be updated to show the effect on that policy.

INDEX